ℬ

FLOUR

WATER

SALT

YEAST

FLOUR
WATER
SALT
YEAST

The Fundamentals of Artisan Bread and Pizza

KEN FORKISH
PHOTOGRAPHY BY ALAN WEINER

TEN SPEED PRESS
Berkeley

CONTENTS

INTRODUCTION — 1

PART 1: THE PRINCIPLES OF ARTISAN BREAD

1: THE BACKSTORY — 11

2: EIGHT DETAILS FOR GREAT BREAD AND PIZZA — 25

3: EQUIPMENT AND INGREDIENTS — 45

Essay: Where Does Our Flour Come From? — 54

PART 2: BASIC BREAD RECIPES

4: BASIC BREAD METHOD — 61

5: STRAIGHT DOUGHS — 79

6: DOUGHS MADE WITH PRE-FERMENTS — 97

Essay: The Early Morning Bread Baker's Routine — 112

PART 3: LEVAIN BREAD RECIPES

7: UNDERSTANDING LEVAIN — 121

8: LEVAIN METHOD — 129

9: HYBRID LEAVENING DOUGHS — 139

Essay: The 3-Kilo Boule — 162

10: PURE LEVAIN DOUGHS — 167

11: ADVANCED LEVAIN DOUGHS — 181

Essay: Making a Bread (or Pizza) Dough You Can Call Your Own — 190

PART 4: PIZZA RECIPES

12: PIZZA AND FOCACCIA METHOD — 201

13: PIZZA DOUGHS — 217

14: PIZZA AND FOCACCIA — 229

LAGNIAPPE — 258

METRIC CONVERSION CHARTS — 259

ACKNOWLEDGMENTS — 260

INDEX — 261

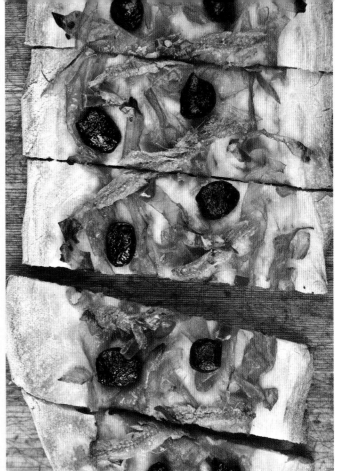

INTRODUCTION

t's been five hundred years since I opened Ken's Artisan Bakery in Portland, Oregon. That's in bakery years, of course. My bakery actually opened in 2001. I had recently left a nearly twenty-year corporate career for the freedom of running my own venture and doing something I loved. In the time leading up to this risky transition, before I knew what that venture would be, I yearned for a craft and wanted to make a living doing something I could truly call my own. But I was itchy and I didn't know where to scratch! For many years, I waited for that lightbulb moment of awareness that would signal an open path worth taking. Then, in the mid-1990s, my best friend gave me a magazine featuring the famed Parisian baker Lionel Poilâne. That article gave me the inspiration I was looking for. Not long after that, I began making frequent trips to Paris, and I was deeply inspired by the authentic, tradition-bound *boulangeries* I visited there. After a few years and a series of evolving ideas, I ended up with a perhaps naive plan to open a French bakery somewhere in the United States. My hope was to re-create the style and quality of the best breads, brioches, croissants, *cannelés*, and other specialties found at *boulangeries* and patisseries all over France.

My ensuing career transition was more Mr. Toad's Wild Ride than simple job change. You could say I answered the call of that ancient Chinese curse: "May you live in *interesting* times." But I came out on the other side with a firm love of the baker's craft, acknowledging it as much more hard work than romance. The daily rhythms of life as a professional baker, once nearly overwhelming, now provide comfort. The aromas, the tactile nature of the work, and the way the finished products look takes me to a faraway place that is still present, and to have that be the way I spend my days continues to thrill me.

ABOUT THIS BOOK

I was fortunate to train with many excellent bakers in the United States plus two in France during the two-year between-careers period before I opened my own bakeshop in Portland. What struck me during my professional baking training was that the most important lessons I was learning—how to use long fermentation, pre-ferments, autolyse, and temperature management, for example—were not discussed in any of the bread books I had read. I later encountered books that did detail these things (like those by Raymond Calvel and Michel Suas), but they were targeted to the professional. I was sure that the techniques I had learned could apply to the home baker too.

In the years that followed the opening of Ken's Artisan Bakery, several notable baking books were published. But I still saw an opportunity to address the techniques used in a good artisan bakery and how they could be adopted for the home kitchen. I wanted to write a book

that didn't totally dumb down these techniques, since the concepts really aren't that difficult for the nonprofessional baker to apply. And I wanted to break from the mold prevalent in almost every bread book out there (at least until very recently): that every recipe had to use a rise time of just one to two hours. Further, I was completely motivated to demonstrate how good bread can be when it's made from just the four principle ingredients: flour, water, salt, and yeast.

I also saw the opportunity to address how to make great bread at home with each of the three principle techniques of dough fermentation: straight doughs, doughs made with pre-ferments, and levain doughs, including an easy, unintimidating method for making a levain culture from scratch in just five days using only whole grain flour and water.

In order to accurately use this book's recipes and follow its logic, I ask you to use an inexpensive digital kitchen scale to execute the recipes and to help you understand baking. One of the fundamentals of artisan baking is using weight measurements instead of cups and tablespoons and being guided by the ratios of ingredients. (Don't worry, I do all the simple math for you.) While the ingredients tables in each recipe do include volume conversions, these measurements are by their nature imprecise (for reasons explained in chapter 2) and they are included only to allow you to bake from this book while you are contemplating which digital kitchen scale to buy.

My purpose in writing this book is twofold: First, I want to entice novices to bake, so it is written for a broad audience. Total beginners can dive right in with one of the entry-level recipes, the Saturday Breads (pages 81 and 85), for example, right after reading chapter 4, Basic Bread Method. Once you feel comfortable with the timing and techniques involved in those breads, try recipes that involve an extra step, like mixing a poolish the night before. Once you have mastered the poolish and biga recipes, try making a levain from scratch and enjoy the particular pleasures of bread or pizza dough made with this culture. By the time you work your way through this book, you will be baking bread in your home kitchen that has a quality level approaching that of the best bakeries anywhere, along with Neapolitan-style pizza that would make your *nonna* smile.

Second, this book is also written for more experienced bakers who are looking for another approach to making dough—one that treats time and temperature as ingredients—and who are perhaps looking for an accessible (or just different) method for making great-tasting levain breads. Mixing dough by hand, a process used in all this book's recipes, may also be new. To me, one of the most unique and important aspects of bread baking is its tactile nature. In asking you to mix the dough by hand, I am also asking you to think of your hand as an implement. Mixing by hand is easier than using a mixer, is fully effective, and teaches you the feel of the dough. People have been mixing dough by hand for thousands of years. If our ancestors did it, we can. And if you haven't done it before, I hope you get great satisfaction from the process and feel a connection to the past and the history of baking, like I do.

FUNDAMENTALS AND METHODS

When you read the recipes in this book, you'll see that they tend to be quite similar in many regards. All of the breads and pizza doughs call for 1,000 grams of flour and often have only slightly differing quantities of water and salt. Although they do vary in types of flour used, in some cases the main differences are in type of leavening and the timeline for development of the dough. Altering these variables can produce a wide variety of breads from very similar formulas. The format of the ingredients lists is designed to help you see these relationships. Basically, they are baker's percentage tables. As you'll notice, the ingredients aren't always listed in the order in which they're used; rather, flour, water, salt, and yeast are always listed in that order, descending by weight. This allows you to compare recipes at a glance.

Each recipe in this book uses the same techniques for mixing, folding the dough, shaping loaves, and baking, so it should be pretty easy to move from one fermentation method in this book to another. As I committed to designing every bread recipe to make round loaves baked in a Dutch oven, I realized that once readers become familiar with my techniques, all of the recipes in this book become accessible, without the need to learn new techniques for each recipe.

Whether you're a first-time baker or someone who already has two dozen bread books on your shelf, this book explains how to use the same methods we use at Ken's Artisan Bakery to make great bread at home. If you're a beginner and feel intimidated by some of the tools or techniques used in my bread recipes, don't be! With a little bit of planning (and maybe a few new pieces equipment, which I promise you'll use again and again), you are well on your way to professional-quality bread.

Your Choice of Baking Schedules

The best breads are those with methods that allow plenty of time for flavor to develop. Time does most of the work for you. Good flavors build while you sleep. Schedule management, a critical aspect of a professional baker's life, applies in the home kitchen too. But offering just a single schedule for making dough (for example, mixing the dough in the evening, letting it develop overnight, shaping it in the morning, and baking a couple hours later) may not work for you. So in this book, I provide recipes that operate on a variety of schedules, each using a long fermentation time, so you can work with the schedule that accommodates your other obligations. You can mix the dough in the morning and bake in time for dinner, mix the dough in the evening and bake in time for the next day's lunch, or mix the dough in the afternoon and bake loaves first thing the next morning. Making these recipes does require a little planning, but each step of any given recipe takes just a modest amount of time. Because of the extended schedules, many of the recipes may only work for you on your weekend, but even if a recipe takes twenty-four hours to prepare, it won't require constant attention.

Dutch Oven Baking

In the past, I struggled to bake bread in my home oven that had the texture, crust color, and oven spring (the initial boost the dough gets in its first ten minutes in the hot oven, caused by the last furious burst of yeast activity) we get at my bakery using the 15,000-pound Italian deck oven, with steam at the push of a button. I owe a particular debt to two recent books that introduced the use of Dutch ovens that fit inside a standard home oven for baking crusty, colorful loaves: Jim Lahey's *My Bread* and Chad Robertson's *Tartine Bread*. Each book recognizes that the previous techniques for home-baked hearth bread, most often baked on a pizza stone with myriad methods for producing steam, were insufficient for recreating the oven steam we enjoy as professional bakers.

The first time I baked in my two Dutch ovens, an Emile Henry enameled model and a Lodge cast-iron model, I immediately decided to approach all the baking for this book in the same way (save for pizza and focaccia, which *are* best on a baking stone—although an iron skillet or sheet pan will also work). Simply placing a loaf in a preheated Dutch oven and baking with the lid on allows the moisture from the dough to steam the loaf as it bakes. The results are decidedly superior to those attained using a baking stone, yielding great oven spring and a dark and beautiful crust with the right texture—thin and crisp. I encourage you to bake until the crust develops dark crimson and ochre colors. Pull a loaf out of the oven too soon and you may be losing out on the best flavors the crust has to give.

Recipe Yields

Each of the bread recipes in this book makes two loaves. As I was testing the recipes in my home kitchen, I often found myself baking one loaf of bread and using the remaining dough to make focaccia or pizza. Some people believe this is how focaccia originated, with bakeries in Liguria using "extra" dough to make flat bread topped with whatever was in season (or with olive oil and salt, or simply left plain). Some bread doughs are more suited to pizza or focaccia than others, so each recipe in this book advises you whether you can make pizza or focaccia with any extra dough, allowing you to get two great things to eat from one dough mix.

Unique Recipes for Pizza and Focaccia

Pizza is a kind of bread too, and pizzas are a natural extension of the product line for many bakers. Bakeries throughout Italy, for example, display pizza or focaccia with their bread, often on a counter, sliced to order. The same principles of dough management that apply to artisan bread baking apply equally to pizza—long, slow dough development for the best flavor, color, and texture.

I love pizza! At my restaurant, Ken's Artisan Pizza, we make our pizza dough with the same care as our bread dough, and in this book I have four pizza dough recipes, again with varying schedules, using both store-bought yeast and a levain culture. The techniques I use for making pizza dough are the same as those for bread dough. Start at either end of the book; once you've learned how to make pizza or bread dough, it will be a straightforward transition to learn the other.

USING THIS BOOK

All of the bread recipes in this book use the same basic techniques, and those are described in detail in chapter 4, Basic Bread Method: weighing the ingredients, autolysing (premixing) the flour and water, mixing the dough, applying folds, shaping loaves, proofing, and baking. Chapter 8, Levain Method, describes how to start a new levain culture and how to feed it, store it in the refrigerator, and restore it for its next use. Chapter 12, Pizza and Focaccia Method, explains the techniques for making pizza from the recipes in this book.

Basically, these three method chapters explain the "how" of the book's recipes. Chapter 2 explains the "what" and "why"—that is to say, the logic behind the methods and the specific details that characterize artisan baking. If you want to cut to the chase and just start baking bread, read chapter 4, Basic Bread Method, and then start with the Saturday White Bread recipe (page 81). If you want to be better informed, spend some time with chapter 2.

The Recipes

The recipes in this book are presented in three parts. Part 2, Basic Bread Recipes, offers recipes for breads made with store-bought instant yeast. In chapter 5, you'll find recipes for long-fermented simple doughs (called straight doughs), which vary in regard to the blend of flours used and the schedule. In chapter 6, you'll find recipes for doughs made with pre-ferments (specifically, biga and poolish), which take just a little more work than straight doughs (five to ten minutes the evening before) but yield breads with more complexity in flavor.

Part 3, Levain Bread Recipes, teaches you how to make a pungent, bubbly, and fully effective levain culture from whole wheat flour and water in five days with little effort. Cre-

ating your own starter culture is a fun science project that makes memorable, crusty, beautiful loaves. Chapter 9 offers recipes for breads with hybrid leavening, which have the unique character of levain breads but also incorporate commercial yeast to give the bread a lighter crumb and a little extra lift. In chapter 10 you'll find recipes for pure levain breads (i.e., breads that have no commercial yeast), and finally, in chapter 11, you'll find two advanced levain recipes. As you work your way through part 3 of the book, you'll learn how to manipulate the variables of a levain to achieve specific qualities in the bread. Ultimately, you can use this information to create a bread that is truly your own and matches your taste preferences, as described in the essay "Making a Bread (or Pizza) Dough You Can Call Your Own" (page 190).

Part 4, Pizza Recipes, is all about how to make delicious pizza and focaccia at home using a pizza stone, a skillet, or a sheet pan. As mentioned, chapter 12 provides basic methods for pizza and focaccia. In chapter 13 you'll find four dough recipes, and in chapter 14 you'll find sauces and recipes for pizzas and focaccia with toppings. Use the best ingredients—good flour, good cheese, San

Marzano tomatoes—and follow my instructions, and you'll be able to make excellent pizza at home. (Being spoiled by the wood-fired oven at my restaurant, I high-fived my dog, Gomez, when I saw killer pizza coming out of my standard home kitchen oven.) It's fun, and it really isn't hard to do. As with making bread, making pizza is something you get better at with repeated efforts. It's like a positive habit: do it and you want to do it again and again until you've mastered it.

Fun Bits to Add Flavor

Writing this book inspired me to riff on a few subjects: either experiences that I lived through (like the failed attempt to open my first bakery) or things that fascinate me (like the fact that a loaf of bread weighing over 6 pounds actually improves with age *and* tastes better than smaller loaves made from the same dough).

Chapter 1 tells the tale of my journey from a Silicon Valley career to the hands-on work of crafting rustic French bread as a professional baker. In part 1 of the book, you'll find the essay "Where Does Our Flour Come From?" I take you on a tour of two of the family farms that grow the wheat that gets milled into the flour we use at my bakery and pizzeria. Evocative photography, commentary from the farmers, and a review of how they manage their land brings home how people like Karl Kupers and Fred Fleming, founders of Shepherd's Grain, are rethinking wheat farming to meet the needs of the land, family farms, and bakers. People often want to know what goes on in the dark hours of the early morning at the bakery. To satisfy that curiosity, in part 2 of the book I've given you a detailed account of a morning representative of what's typical in "The Early Morning Bread Baker's Routine." The essay offers a voyeuristic peek into the nonstop synchronized activity of our bakery.

In part 3 of the book I've included the essay "The 3-Kilo Boule," explaining why I love these massive loaves and share some of their interesting history. My hope is that this book will provide you not only with recipes for bread that will truly impress you, but also a clear understanding of the processes we use at Ken's Artisan Bakery and how they apply in the home kitchen. Once you have this foundation of knowledge, you can use the information in the essay "Making a Bread (or Pizza) Dough You Can Call Your Own" (also in part 3) to craft your own unique breads.

Baking is a craft that makes you want to do it again and again, trying various flour blends, improving your shaping technique, or simply following the same procedure but trying to do it better with each repetition to improve the flavor of your bread, the volume of the loaf, or perhaps the color of the crust. Repetition is part of the pleasure. And once you get a rhythm and learn the techniques, the repetition gives a warming satisfaction that comes from the familiar comfort of doing something well. *Bon appétit.*

PART 1
THE PRINCIPLES OF ARTISAN BREAD

CHAPTER 1
THE BACKSTORY

I t was exhilarating when I quit the last job I hated. I was ready to move on and leap into the unknown future of my life as a baker. Unexpectedly, however, the dream took a detour—or maybe just a longer, more scenic route.

THE KERNEL OF THE IDEA

Flash back to 1995: I was wearing a suit every day, trying to meet my sales quota each year, and drinking the company Kool-Aid. One day that year, my buddy Tim Holt gave me a copy of the January issue of *Smithsonian* magazine, which featured a cover article about the famed Lionel Poilâne. Reading the article, I realized I had found my muse. Poilâne was a French baker running his father's bakeshop at 8 rue du Cherche-Midi on Paris's Left Bank. Lionel coined the phrase "retro-innovation" as a measure of progress. He was possessed by the old-world ways of making great bread: using human hands, time, and fire as an artisan's instruments. These techniques required patience, and they had largely been neglected in postwar France as industrialized baking methods were widely adopted and the quality of French bread, long an icon, declined.

With his genius for promotion and his passionate embrace of bread made in the old way (*pain d'autrefois*), Lionel Poilâne helped repopularize rustic country breads, naturally leavened, made by hand, and baked in wood-fired ovens by men who worked hard in hot, steamy basements at a physically demanding job. (Ask these guys about the romance of baking!) His was the craft of an artisan. Poilâne's ingredients were stone-milled wheat flour, water, and sea salt. A 1.9-kilo *miche* could last an entire week.

His earthy breads were described as having a winelike complexity, and people lined up on the sidewalk to buy them from the iconic *boulangerie*. A charismatic and knowledgeable promoter, Lionel replicated the wood-fired oven routines of his family's *boulangerie* on a large scale outside of Paris during the 1980s and began shipping his big round loaves around the world, baking about fifteen thousand loaves a day in twenty-four wood-fired ovens. Lionel's brother, Max Poilâne, went on to open his own wonderful *boulangerie* in Paris' 15th arrondissement. The two brothers made near-identical loaves the way their father had taught them to: in big rounds weighing almost 2 kilos (4.4 pounds) apiece. (Sadly, Lionel, his wife, Irena, and their dog died in 2002 when the helicopter Lionel was piloting crashed during a fierce storm in high winds off the coast of Brittany.) Both brothers—along with many other Parisian bakers, I later discovered—were fueled by traditionalist convictions about bread baking that inspired me. And even though I'd never worked as a craftsman or had any kind of job related to food, as I held the magazine in my hands I knew instantly, at a very deep level, that being this kind of baker was right for me. It was a certainty like none I had ever experienced.

> **Miche** A large, rustic *boule*, or round loaf of bread, which can weigh 3 kilograms (6.6 pounds) or more.

Prior to reading the Poilâne piece in *Smithsonian*, my personal experience with baking bread was a recipe for an herb bread with dill, anise deeds, parsley, and a lot of sugar. The method involved using a whisk—a *whisk!* I made that bread often, and at the time, I liked it. But I had no reference point for bread at its best, and it was unlikely to be found in the United States anyway. When I lived in London in 1989 and often traveled in Europe for my job at IBM, I loved looking in the windows of pastry shops, butchers, and cheese shops and eating foods specific to the place I was in. I found these markets inspiring and could tell they had been making the same great food in the same way for generations. I asked myself why we didn't have places like these at home and whether I could perhaps someday bring some of the transcendent goodness, quality, and timeless character of these shops back home in a venture of my own. But I had only strands of ideas—nothing concrete that rang true.

I remember sitting in my backyard in Virginia under a cherry tree in full bloom on a warm, sunny spring afternoon, reading my first issue of the quarterly newsletter of the Bread Bakers Guild of America. Cue the chirping bluebirds. The Poilâne piece in *Smithsonian* had inspired me to join the guild as an entry point into the world of good bakers. Reading about serious professionals baking good bread spoke to my soul—and fueled fantasies of rising at 3 a.m. to bake bread. *(What are you, nuts?!)* This issue of the newsletter had a feature on Lionel Poilâne's visit to the guild's annual dinner, another on the U.S. baking team winning the bread category for the first time at the Coupe du Monde de la Boulangerie, and an excellent piece by the original seer of the Guild, Tom McMahon, about the importance

of connection between bakers and the farmers who grow their wheat (a connection I finally achieved ten years later when I switched to Shepherd's Grain flours). Tom had a clear, high-level vision that promoted his ideals of advancing both the quality of bread and environmental responsibility. Throughout the newsletter—my first glimpse into the minds of the bakers and owners of good artisan bakeries—I detected a sense of mission and passion. It helped water the seed of my desire first sown by the *Smithsonian* article about Poilâne. I finished reading the newsletter, and I still remember how, at that very time, it seemed right that I should become one of them.

Until I escaped the corporate womb and became a baker in earnest, I did what I could to learn about the world of artisan baking from the outside looking in. I visited many bakeries in Paris during trips there, two or three times each year. (I had a Parisian girlfriend—how convenient!) I bought baking books. My heroes were French bread bakers: Moisan, Poujauran, Kamir, Ganachaud, Kayser, Gosselin, Saibron, and others.

In the late 1990s I read about a couple of bakeries in northern California: Della Fattoria and Bay Village Bakery. They baked the kind of bread I wanted to bake, in wood-fired ovens (I was absolutely certain that I was going to be a wood-fired oven baker like Poilâne—a certainty later changed by a firmer grip on reality) and their bake houses were in their backyards. I thought that sounded perfect! After two decades of big city commuting on jammed freeways, the thought of walking across my backyard to get to work was alluring to say the least. These bakeries were also idealistic, as mine would be, using organic flour and employing the best-quality methods to make the finest bread they knew how to bake. And they were successful. Della Fattoria was selling bread to the French Laundry in Napa (this was before Thomas Keller opened Bouchon Bakery). Bay Village was developing a reputation for having the best rustic breads in the country, and Chad Robertson was mobbed every time he went to the farmers' market in Berkeley to sell his bread.

I knew that I needed to learn how to bake bread at this level, and my Bread Bakers Guild newsletters made it clear that the best options were at the San Francisco Baking Institute and the newly opened (and now closed) National Baking Center in Minneapolis. I wanted to learn from multiple people and then adapt the collage of lessons into my own baking style. In August of 1999, soon after chucking my last job, I was off to the San Francisco Baking Institute to take Artisan Breads I and II, two weeks of hands-on instruction. I'd finally made the break from my corporate career and I was a free man about to learn a new trade. A free man. Maybe a little crazy.

LEARNING THE CRAFT

I'll never forget my first day at the institute. Ian Duffy, our instructor, had us each mix a small amount of dough by hand—wet, sticky dough. I was trying to work the dough the way Ian did: his hands developed it, turned it, and folded it, and before long it was a smooth ball with an outside skin soft and smooth as a baby's bottom. Then I'd try, and I'd have dough sticking everywhere. No soft, baby's-butt dough skin, just a red face and an oh-shit-what-was-I-thinking exclamation point in my head. That night I went to my hotel more than a little worried that maybe this wasn't the career for me. But by the end of two weeks I could handle the dough okay, and with all of the great instruction I'd received, I thought that with a lot of practice at home maybe I could start to get the feel for this stuff.

While I was in northern California, I met Chad Robertson and Elisabeth Prueitt (now quite famous for their work at Tartine in San Francisco) at Bay Village Bakery in Point Reyes, and Chad and I began a conversation that lasted for years about levains, milling, French versus American flour, and the fermentation needed to bake the kind of old-school French country bread I was after. Chad's bread was the best I'd ever had in the United States. It was baked to a dark chestnut brown and had gentle flavors of wheat and fermentation, and the character of the crust seeped into the soft, light interior. It tasted fantastic, and it was beautiful too. I thought his bread was in league with that of the best *boulangeries* I had visited in Paris.

Chad did all of his bread baking as a solo act. After a ten-second commute through his yard, he mixed the levain and the doughs, chopped wood, built the fire for the oven, and, many hours later, swept out the oven to prepare it for baking. In the filtered sunlight of a Marin afternoon, Chad divided and shaped his dough by hand. The next morning he would bake magnificent bread in the intense radiant heat of his oven, loading loaves in and out on a peel by hand. I left that first visit with Chad nodding my head up and down and thinking, "Yeah, this is it for me."

Next I stopped to visit Della Fattoria in Petaluma, California, where they were baking dramatic round loaves decorated with grape leaves, destined for the annual Sonoma Valley Harvest Wine Auction. I stood out of their way as they baked these loaves in side-by-side wood-fired ovens built and designed by Alan Scott—the same kind Chad had at Bay Village. I was taking pictures, and if there was something I could do to help them out, I did it. The bakery, run by Ed and Kathleen Weber and their son Aaron, is in the most idyllic setting. The bake house is attached to their home on fifteen acres of Petaluma farmland, with beautifully tended gardens and a lot of small, life-is-good details that showed me they were living a great life on their own terms, and it was paid for by baking good bread. Again, I thought, "Yeah, this is it for me." I rode with Ed as he delivered the loaves to the auction, and when I came back Aaron asked if I wanted to come bake with them for a week or two. What a great offer! This was my first chance to spend time in a live craft bakery, and the Webers were extremely generous and forthcoming. It's fun to look back on those days—getting up at 5 a.m. and walking toward my future, down the Webers' lawn to the bake house, staring up at a night full of brilliant stars, about to be humbled by more sticky dough.

After my informal "apprenticeship" with the Webers (really, just one week), I was ready to continue my instruction. I knew I was going to need more pastry skills, and the National Baking Center in Minneapolis had two great instructors, Philippe Le Corre teaching pastry, and Didier Rosada teaching advanced bread baking classes. Two weeks there, plus a one-week pastry class with Robert Jorin at the CIA in Napa, rounded out my formal training. Chad and Liz, after they moved Bay Village Bakery to a retail spot in Mill Valley, were also very generous sharing many of their lessons, and they let me observe their bakery's operation during multiple visits. Without their help my first years at my own bakery would have been even more challenging than they ended up being, and their quality was the gold standard that I aspired to. This kind of give-back and sharing, while being pretty common in the food service trade, is totally not what happens in the last industry I worked in. Small business has so much more heart than big business.

It was time for me to set up a wood-fired oven in my own backyard bakery. Not long before, I had moved into the perfect setting to be near the rest of my family, who had all migrated to Eugene, Oregon. I had a cool house on five acres with a 1,200-square-foot outbuilding that I could convert into a bake house. The zoning allowed for a small home business, and the house wasn't part of any homeowners' association that might have rules against this kind of thing. It looked like a great setup. Plus, I had time to learn the craft, convert the outbuilding, and, before too long, begin my career as a baker—or so I thought.

BUT FOR THE SMELL OF BAKING BREAD

When I moved to Eugene, I assumed all I needed to do to start my enterprise was get a business license, build the bakery, and begin to bake bread. To my surprise, a community uprising against my little venture developed, and the intense energy with which my neighbors pursued their goal created a public NIMBY fuss that landed on the front page of the newspaper, on the local TV news, and in a pair of two-hour public hearings where one neighbor after another took the stand to rage against, among other things, having to smell bread baking every single day: "like Sisyphus, pushing the same rock up the hill, every day into eternity," according to their attorney. Smoke from my chimney stack was going to exaggerate respiratory problems for one family, whose house was several hundred yards away. Sparks from the chimney were going to burn down the entire neighborhood. The bakery would turn into a tourist attraction, causing too much traffic in the neighborhood. My driveway was too steep for a fire truck to navigate in the event of a fire. Ashes from my oven were going to change the pH balance of the soil. Trash from the bakery was going to attract rodents. It was an Alice in Wonderland construct where just saying something makes it true; the process seemed to me to be anything but a court of rational appeal.

The residents of eleven out of eighteen homes in the small neighborhood wrote letters protesting the plans for the bakery. Here is a favorite excerpt of mine:

> Flour dust can be very explosive. A dropped bag of raw flour can be ignited in much the same way as volatile fluids. This may be one of the hazards of baking, but it does not belong in a residential area.

In the course of due process, the legal burden was on me to refute any and all claims, no matter how seemingly absurd, like the exploding bags of flour. I produced a certified letter from the State of Oregon's climatologist identifying the direction of prevailing winds by month. (Away from the neighbors 44 percent of the time, but that didn't account for days of air stagnation, it turns out. *Who knew?*) I had certification from an environmental engineering firm stating that the emissions output from the oven would be no greater than that from a standard woodstove. I should have tried tossing a bag of flour in the courtroom to see if it would explode.

After a pair of lengthy public hearings, four months of angst, and county files at least eighteen inches thick, the final ruling was to deny my application for a business license to run my little bakery in a zone that allowed home businesses. It was time to shift mental gears.

"Trust thyself: every heart vibrates to that iron string."
—Ralph Waldo Emerson

Immediately, I was anxious to put Eugene in my rearview mirror. Too bad about the house; I loved that place. But where to? I decided to start with a fresh plan and give up on the idyllic and admittedly safer route of opening a low-expense backyard startup. I embarked on a mission to find a new town in which to open my idealized retail bakery. To finance this ambitious—and expensive—venture, I would sell my house and apply most of my savings, risking everything I had. I wanted to move somewhere I might actually be welcomed, where people would appreciate buttery croissants that shatter when you bite into them, crisp *cannelés* perfumed with vanilla and beeswax, and rustic country breads—a place where nobody would complain about the smell of baking bread. Where would it be?

IN SEARCH OF PORTLAND

I drew up a list of things the town needed to have: good weather (hindsight snicker), an active restaurant scene that wasn't stodgy, and a good farm-to-table sense. After a six-month quest, which included stops in San Luis Obispo, Yountville, Boulder, Denver, Maryland's Eastern Shore, and Monterey, as well as two weeks of training at l'Institut Paul Bocuse in France (yes, I got to meet the man, at his restaurant, and yes, his big beefy hands rested on my shoulders for a photo that I never received—sounds like a fish story, I know), I finally settled on Portland.

I barely knew the place, but it had me hooked for reasons my future self would understand better than I did at the time. Now, I realize that I was drawn to Portland because so many of its craftsmen were (and still are) doing production on a smaller, less industrial scale, with a focus on quality. Our hands are our most important tools. Our customers can associate names and faces with the food they eat and the beverage they drink. These things are characteristic of the word "artisan" and a principal reason why I named my bakery "Ken's Artisan Bakery." In Portland, it is not unusual to know who made the beer or wine we are drinking, the cheese we are eating, or the salami on our pizza—and that's how I knew it was the place for me.

That said, it is difficult enough to open a restaurant or bakery in a town you know and make it work—especially if you have no history in that line of work. Going into a city where nobody knew me was absolutely insane. But I had a bad case of tunnel vision and I could only see the light at the end: my own bakery in a place I was pretty sure I'd love. Over a three month period, with layout and design help from Michel Suas of TMB Baking (a sister company of the San Francisco Baking Institute), I built the bakery in a shell of a space in an old neighborhood in Portland filled with bars and restaurants. My oven, the big mixer, and the other major equipment I'd ordered all arrived together in a single container that entered the United States at the port of Newport News, Virginia, and then came to me on a flatbed truck. The truck arrived at about 8 o'clock on a cold, rainy weekday night in early November. Along with a team of new hires and our superhero installer, Carlos, I met the driver in front of the bakery and unloaded the truck with a rented forklift. The delivery was a day later than expected. I remember the driver calling from outside Boise, Idaho, letting me know he had a bad toothache and needed to see a dentist but was going to drive through the night to get to me. I had images of the Italian oven and French mixer I had been waiting for all those months, which had traveled from Europe by boat, toppling down some mountain pass between toothache and here.

All of the equipment was installed in mid-November 2001, and we opened on November 21. New hires all around me and I was running the place—my first food job. The shock of the previous two years—misfiring in Eugene, figuring out where to open my bakery, selling my house in Eugene, finding a space in Portland, and getting the place up and running—then suddenly being open and selling bread and pastry? Whoa, that's a big one. But in one moment the past was behind me, and all that mattered was getting people in the door. Ken's Artisan Bakery was born.

FIRST IMPRESSIONS

The neighborhood where the bakery was located had the highest population density of any place between Seattle and San Francisco. But the neighborhood was filled with modest rental apartments, and the per capita income data concerned me. I was going to compete on quality, not price. We opened just two months after September 11. During a recession. And the carb-fearing Atkins and South Beach diets were peaking in popularity. Portland set a record for most consecutive days with measurable rain. The unemployment rate was around 12 percent at the time. Today, an ambitious bakery opening would get instant media attention. At that time it barely got a mention. So we had an intermittent trickle of customers, friends, and family coming through the door, along with curious passersby and a few drunks.

Some people appreciated our efforts, recognized our ambitions, and understood the quality of our ingredients and our intention to produce bread and pastry according to my idealized vision. Now, I tend to remember the things that went wrong more than the things that went right. Our first sheeter, used to laminate croissant and puff pastry dough, was too small. Making it work required that we prop boards on overturned trash cans at either end to catch the dough as it ran back and forth between the rollers. The *cannelés* were inconsistent, but when they were on they were fantastic. We were baking all of our pastries in the deck oven, and constantly reaching into the oven's upper decks for sheet pans gave us all a series of nasty accidental sheet pan burns on our forearms.

I arrived at 4 a.m. each morning, mixed the baguette dough, helped with the morning pastry work, and baked levain breads that had been chilled overnight. Then I divided, shaped, and baked baguettes, with the first batch coming out of the oven around 8:30 a.m. People who came in at 8 or 8:15 a.m. were often angry or dismayed that the baguettes weren't ready yet and sometimes taunted us with comments like "You call yourself a French bakery?" I absolutely couldn't arrive at the bakery any earlier than 4 a.m., and although I could have theoretically put the baguettes in the oven before 8 o'clock, they wouldn't have been as good.

Still, the accusatory glares were hard to take. Our French customers were the most aggravated. I needed to know what people thought of our stuff, but these comments kind of pissed me off, too. It was an open bakery. We were vulnerable to impressions of all kinds.

The retarder, a walk-in cooler where all of the shaped levain breads spend the night for a long, slow, cool fermentation, had some idiosyncrasies. Every week, on Monday, it would shut down. Without telling me first. Before Christmas in 2001 we were closed Mondays, so I never noticed. Of course, Christmas Eve and New Year's Eve fell on a Monday that year. On Christmas Eve morning, I arrived at the bakery a little early, just before 4 a.m., looking forward to baking and selling bread that would be on people's holiday tables. Then I opened the door to the retarder and was greeted by a blast of warm, humid, slightly sour air and loaves overflowing their proofing boards, totally overproofed and beyond any hope of being worth baking. Still, I baked a dozen or so just to see what I could get, and what I got was lousy, sour loaves, each about the size and shape of a double-wide size 20 low-top basketball shoe. *Merde!* All I could do was bake the day's baguettes and be sold out of lousy, sour bread by about 10 a.m. Cory Schreiber, chef-owner of nearby Wildwood Restaurant, walked in and kindly bought one of the pathetic, flat levain loaves—and gave me a shoulder to lean on. Thanks, man. Still, I didn't understand the problem. I thought the retarder shut off because of something I'd done wrong. And at that point, six weeks into running the bakery without a day off, working from 4 a.m. to 6 p.m. or later every day, my judgment was a little cloudy. The following Monday, New Year's Eve day, the same thing happened again. *Waaah!* On January 2 I made some calls and learned that I was using the retarder on a seven-day program cycle, which needed to be refreshed each week, otherwise it went into proofing mode and warmed up. (Yeah, I noticed.) Some lessons we learn the hard way.

Whenever I felt like we were starting to find a rhythm in our production, a new problem would jolt me back to reality. Like the fact that I repeatedly had to crawl on top of the 500°F oven whose burner sometimes stopped firing in the middle of my bread bake to replace a

blown fuse (deep breath), only to realize months later that the wrong value fuse was in one of the sockets, and I kept replacing the wrong fuse with another wrong fuse. Sigh. One time, at 5 a.m., I pushed one of the buttons on the bread oven for steam, but instead of steam I saw a river of water flowing from beneath the oven. I quickly popped a lower front panel off the oven and saw a burst rubber hose, and the water wasn't stopping! Throw the shutoff valve. Inspect. Grab a kitchen knife. Cut the hose just before the break. Reattach it to the pipe and secure with a hose clamp. Then run and grab the mop bucket and a pile of towels for cleanup. This happened over and over for several months. Bad hose. Who gets a bad hose? Nobody said this was going to be easy, but jeez.

I baked the levain breads to a dark caramel color on the outside. I was really proud of those loaves, but Portland didn't seem very impressed. So I put together a handout titled "Why We Bake It Dark." I'm not sure it helped much, but I felt the need to explain myself. We used Valrhona chocolate for our chocolate croissants (and still do). I also made a true *pain au chocolat*: a thick slice of freshly baked levain bread covered in butter and shavings of chocolate and sprinkled with a dash of fleur de sel. We sold at least two or three of those each day. I typically let a few loaves of unbaked levain sit out until they were well overproofed and gassy, then compressed the gas out of them, cut them into *fougasse*, and then baked them. We sold some of them plain and others brushed with olive oil and with fleur de sel sprinkled on top, like giant pretzels. My pastry chef, Angie, made beautiful apple tarts, chocolate and coffee éclairs, puff pastry with pears, chocolate tarts, brioche, *financiers*, *macarons*, brownies, profiteroles with different fillings, *gougères*, *gâteaux de riz*, and *galettes des pérouges*. People would walk in and ask if we had any scones. Or they would hear we were making *cannelés*, come in, and ask, "Where are the cannolis?" People pronounced artisan "artesian." I set out to replicate the bread and pastries of a good *boulangerie* in Paris, so I shouldn't have been surprised when people here didn't recognize all the things we made. Today they mostly do. Portland's food scene has changed a lot in the past decade.

We used organic flour, Tahitian vanilla beans, Niman Ranch ham, bags of sea salt from Brittany, aged Gruyère, the best butter I could buy, and, as mentioned, Valrhona chocolate. I imported tea from Mariage Frères in Paris. We made everything from scratch, and there was usually more staff present at any point in time than customers. We charged $2.50 for a chocolate croissant, and people gave me the stink-eye. I found a note in the comments box that said, "$2.50 for an herbal tea and hot water. You have lost this customer for good!" Other people complained that there weren't free coffee refills. Many people let us know that our pastries were too small, appeared to be overbaked, and were too expensive ($3.50 for a 4-inch fruit tart, $2.50 for an apple turnover, $1.75 for a handmade butter croissant). At least nobody was complaining about the smell of bread baking.

Those were the most intense days of my life. By necessity, I'm tempted to say, and I'm not sure why. Maybe the transformation from a desk-job career to this intensely physical, sleep-deprived work required a kind of shock treatment as segue.

At the end of the day, after fourteen hours at the bakery, I remember cleaning out the big mixer, my head in its bowl, and thinking about my heroes—all the great chefs I had read about, who were known for their all-day work ethic. If they could put in those kinds of hours, I thought, I can do it too. I knew I was truly tired when one day I noticed the sound of my feet dragging across the floor. I was past feeling it. I was probably past good judgment too. About three months after the bakery opened, I finally took a day off. I slept for a solid twelve hours, and when I woke up I felt like a zombie with a severe case of jet lag.

PROOF OF CONCEPT

Despite the initial challenges, I remained optimistic about the future, because that was my only option. Positive feedback started coming in to help balance the negative things. We kept a small green suggestion box out by the coffee station, with pieces of paper and pens (people stole the pens!). I got a much-needed boost in confidence from comments like these:

"The bakery is extraordinary. The best I have been to in the United States."

"We just returned from ten days in Paris and visited a number of well-known bakeries— none of the croissants we tried came close to yours."

"We came today for our four o'clock snack with my son, and I wanted to let you know that we loved the *pain au chocolat*, the profiteroles, and the brioche. It felt like home! Thank you for that pleasure."

"Don't change anything. It's superb!"

In addition, a few good restaurants made inquiries about buying our bread, and I knew I needed the money from wholesale accounts if the bakery was going to make it. When I was ready to buy a delivery van and begin that new phase, I was proud that our first three restaurant accounts—Paley's Place, Higgins, and Bluehour—were (and remain) among Portland's best restaurants. That gave me some sorely needed revenue and visibility.

They gave me tremendous support in other ways, as well. Greg Higgins featured my apple bread on a special menu one night, and Vitaly Paley did a tasting menu event featuring my bread in every course. Other chefs also lent a hand. Dan Spitz, at Ripe, did a similar dinner. Some restaurants put my name on their menus when they featured my bread. In one case, the menu read, "Nice buns, Ken!" Many of these chefs also generously offered advice whenever I needed it.

On a more serious note, by the end of the bakery's first year I had lost almost $70,000 and greatly feared I'd have to close down. I didn't have much cash left. Plus, I hadn't received any publicity or reviews other than a Sunday feature by Sara Perry in the *Oregonian*'s Living section. I believed that what we were offering was unique, and we had dialed in our quality and consistency after a lot of refinement during our first five or six months. But it seemed like nobody was paying attention. Ego was part of the media deal, but more than anything else, I needed press to give us credibility with the buying public who maybe didn't know we were worth the trip. (This was before the days of the hyperactive foodie blogosphere.)

So I decided to try to make some waves on my own. Our first event was a special bread tasting. I ordered a couple loaves of *pain Poilâne*, which you can order online for overnight delivery, and had Grand Central Bakery and Pearl Bakery bring some of their breads to my place. The event was friendly, not competitive. I wanted people to taste my bread alongside France's most famous bakery's. This unusual event—a *bread* tasting!—brought in at least 150 people and got them to focus on bread and its flavors—a rare standalone subject (as evidenced by the fact that we really don't have the same breadth of vocabulary to describe the flavor of bread as we do for wine, beer, or select other things). I was pleased with people's reactions to my bread, still a new product on the local scene, especially as it compared favorably with Poilâne's, a benchmark for me.

Cash flow gradually improved, but we weren't out of the woods yet. Then the city informed me that the street at my intersection was soon going to be closed during the daytime hours for the next three months while underground water pipes were replaced. I had a daytime business. I feared this was going to be the final dagger. But as I thought about how the city would be putting the street back together at the end of each workday, I wondered about trying to do some nighttime business while continuing the daytime bakery operation. I hatched an idea that involved getting a liquor license, selling beer and wine, and turning the bakery's cafe into an evening hangout offering simple fare.

Around this time I met Rollie Wesen and Claudine Pépin, who had just moved to Portland from New York. Claudine is Jacques Pépin's daughter, famous in her own right for doing TV shows on PBS with her dad and writing several cookbooks with him, in addition to her own TV appearances and working as brand ambassador for Moët & Chandon. Rollie is a chef who had worked at a number of hot New York restaurants. Both were looking for work, and each appreciated the bakery. I couldn't pay what either was worth, but they joined the team, and with Rollie in the makeshift kitchen (no stove!) and Claudine running the cafe, Ken's Artisan Bakery became a simple bistro five nights each week, offering a weeklong plat du jour of coq au vin, duck confit, or some other classic. This finally got us the media attention I both craved and needed, and the press extended beyond the bistro to my obsessiveness about baking. Eventually, Rollie and Claudine both ended up leaving for jobs that paid closer to what they were worth, and after eight months I closed down the bistro with a cassoulet party that sold out in a day. Turning the bakery into a restaurant was fine as an experiment, and it helped bridge a gap.

In January 2003, Jim Dixon wrote a piece about the bakery for *Willamette Week*, titled "Yeast of Burden" (which was nominated for a James Beard award in journalism). "Slicing into a loaf, you feel the crust crackle, but it's not tough or too chewy. The crumb is soft, moist and riddled with the holes created by expanding fermentation gases. It has that yeasty, nutlike wheat taste typical of good rustic bread, but there's another, deeper level of complex flavor that's hard to pin down. It makes you want to keep eating." He also referred to baking as my obsession, and as I got more press, it seemed "obsessive" was the operative word in pieces about me. Seeing anything written about the bakery was gratifying after the loud boom of media silence during the first thirteen months.

Finally, people started coming—people from all over. We were sort of prepared, and sort of not prepared. Baked goods aren't like restaurant fare; we can't make them on demand. We start almost everything at least the day before, so we have to guess: How many baguettes are we going to sell tomorrow? How many éclairs, croissants, and tarts?

One day André Soltner, the former chef of the famed New York restaurant Lutèce, and his wife, Simone, walked into the bakery. Chef Soltner later told Claudine and Rollie that my croissants were extraordinary. Then Claudine brought her dad into the bakery, and we had dinner together. He was equally complimentary of my croissant, saying it was among the best he'd ever eaten. He was so kind and very gracious. Having dinner in my bakery with Jacques Pépin, I was floating. These visits from some of my heroes and their praise gave me much-needed confidence.

Over time, when I could afford to hire enough staff to create a more sane schedule for myself, we managed to bake baguettes a little earlier in the morning. And comments that we bake our bread and pastries too dark decreased. Maybe I adjusted; maybe my customers did. Maybe we met in the middle. (Maybe they actually read my "Why We Bake It Dark" manifesto?) The greatest reward in those first years was when it became clear that most people really enjoyed the food we were making. We had a growing number of regulars come in day after day, week after week. We watched as their children grew up before our eyes. And now we have been around long enough to have seen customers that we loved pass on. Having a positive impact on the community was never possible in my previous career. Once it became evident that we weren't going to fail, that my landlord wasn't going to get stuck with a bankrupt bakery, I could stop being nervous that someday I might have to go back to my old life. The work really is its own reward.

CHAPTER 2
EIGHT DETAILS FOR GREAT BREAD AND PIZZA

n this chapter, I'll explain some key, fundamental elements of artisan baking that define my breads. If you just want to cut to the chase and start baking, turn to chapter 4, Basic Bread Method, and chapter 5, Straight Doughs, and return to this chapter (and the rest of part 1) when you have time. That said, don't be afraid to read on. The material in this chapter isn't complicated.

If you think of bread baking as a fermentation craft, then you can orient your thinking to consider the fermentation variables that impact taste and texture. Since this concept may be new for many readers, I want to emphasize that the most important ingredient for making good bread is plenty of time. This does, of course, have its limits. If dough ferments for too long, an excess of alcohol and acidity will develop, masking the sweet flavors of the wheat. In addition, the dough's physical ability to hold the gases produced by fermentation will break down and it will slowly collapse. Managing dough fermentation to get the best results means finding the perfect balance of rising time, proofing time, dough temperature, ambient temperature, and amount of leavening in the dough. A major focus of this chapter is explaining how to achieve a harmony of these elements.

DETAIL 1: THINK OF TIME AND TEMPERATURE AS INGREDIENTS

Patience is indeed a virtue when it comes to making good bread. Consider time to be a powerful instrument in the baker's tool kit. Recognizing time as a discrete and crucial element in a recipe is the first detail that sets the best bakers apart. If you manipulate time in proper balance with dough temperature, ambient temperature, and the amount of leavening in the dough, you give yourself a chance to make something special. You need enough time, but not much effort—a little over seven hours for the simplest recipes in this book—to achieve a really good loaf.

In the United States, the traditional approach to baking bread has been to think of the rise as simply a short amount of time—just an hour or two—necessary for gas to build up in the dough to give it structure. I and other good bakers view the rise as an opportunity to build flavor and an appropriate amount of acidity.

Temperature and time have an inverse relationship, and I like the visual image of a seesaw to communicate the need for balance between the two: more of one means you need less of the other. A warm dough develops more quickly, whereas a cooler dough develops more slowly. Specifically, dough temperature affects the metabolic rate of the yeast: warmer yeast replicates more quickly. Once a dough is mixed, the yeast replicates until no oxygen remains in the dough, at which point the yeast cells, as they consume sugars from the flour, begin to produce gases (carbon dioxide and ethanol). Sugar in, gas out. This gas production is what causes the dough to rise.

Extending the bulk fermentation stage is critical to maximum flavor development. Warmer dough encourages more rapid reproduction of the yeast, and thus faster fermentation. On the other hand, using less yeast when mixing the dough means it will take longer for the yeast to replicate and build up its population to its max: the point where the dough is anaerobic, or completely depleted of oxygen. Up to a point, doughs that take longer to develop (whether due to cooler temperatures, using less yeast, or both) yield breads with a more complex flavor. In fact, this is a key principle that guides me in developing all of my bread recipes: Less yeast and more time yields a better bread.

Bulk fermentation The first rise of the dough after all of the ingredients have been mixed together (flour, water, salt, and yeast, plus any levain or pre-fermented doughs).

Another factor in the evolution of dough is bacteria; flour naturally contains both yeast and a wide variety of bacterial spores. As with natural yeast fermentation, it takes time for these naturally occurring bacteria to grow and produce acids and other flavor components. Bacterial growth also contributes to complexity of flavor, by which I mean the way multiple flavor elements in a good bread hit your palate at the same time: flavors from the flour and all of the products the yeast and bacteria produce, including alcohols, acids, and esters (chemical compounds that produce aromas and flavors).

Time is a critical factor in the production of all of these compounds. What we are looking for is the fermentation "sweet spot." Too much time can throw the flavor elements out

WEIGHT VERSUS VOLUME MEASUREMENTS

If you are to get consistent results, compare recipes, and, after a few repetitions be able to essentially memorize recipes, you'll find it extremely beneficial to use measurements by weight, not volume. For starters, 2 cups of my flour won't be precisely the same amount as 2 cups of your flour. Mine might be packed a little tighter, yours might be looser. With water, although a difference of a few tablespoons may hardly be noticeable visually, the weight will be significantly different. Baking is based on specific ratios between ingredients, and these are imprecise when using volume measurements, but predictable when using weight measurements. In professional and high-caliber baking, the standard is to measure all ingredients by weight and express the quantity in relation to the total amount of flour in the recipe. I encourage you to use weight rather than volume measurements for the recipes in this book.

That having been said, many bakers have yet to invest in a kitchen scale. For those bakers, I have included approximate volume conversions for all the ingredients used in this book. Flour is the most difficult ingredient to measure accurately by volume, since so many variables are in play: how coarsely the flour is ground, how tightly the flour is packed into the measuring cups, whether or not the flour is leveled once it has been placed in the measuring cup, and more. These variables do not come into play when flour is measured instead by weight. To ensure some consistency, all of the recipes in this book were tested using King Arthur brand flour—so the volume measurements correspond to the coarseness of that brand's grain. When measuring flour by volume instead of weight, transfer the flour to a large container, fluff it with a fork, and then spoon it into the measuring cup or spoon until full. Then, use the edge of a knife to level the top of the flour. (If this sounds like a pain, good . . . buy a kitchen scale!)

Of course, when you're baking a bread that involves a pre-ferment, volume measurements really go out the window. Many of my recipes call for using 100 grams of levain, which is a bit more than ⅓ cup. The problem is, when you scoop out the levain and transfer it to measuring cups or spoons, you degas the levain (which makes measurements less reliable). So I cannot overemphasize the value of measuring by weight, not volume, especially once you get to part 3 of this book.

MANIPULATING THE FINAL MIX TEMPERATURE

For all of my breads, I've achieved the best flavor when the freshly mixed dough has a temperature between 75°F and 80°F (24°C and 27°C). The subsequent timing in the recipes and quality of the final product depends on achieving this temperature. When you've mixed your final dough and are about to cover it for rising, or bulk fermentation, take a temperature reading with a probe thermometer. If the dough doesn't fall between 75°F and 80°F (24°C and 27°C), you should make adjustments next time.

To control the temperature of the mixed dough, you need to work with four variables: water temperature, flour temperature, room temperature, and the length of the autolyse (pronounced "auto-lease"; see page 33). The easiest variable to manipulate is the water temperature, and I'll give you some guidelines about using warmer or cooler water. If you pay attention to your results (and keep notes), after a couple of attempts you should be able to figure out the ideal water temperature for mixing your dough.

Most of the recipes in this book specify a target temperature of 78°F (26°C) for the final mixed dough. I consider this to be the sweet spot, but I encourage you to experiment with different temperatures between 75°F and 80°F (24°C and 27°C). The only way to find the optimum combination of time and temperature that gives the best flavor and volume in a given recipe is to repeat and adjust based on what you did last time. It's part of the fun of baking. Each time, write down the temperature of the dough as soon as it's mixed and note what time it is. Also record the time when you do each of the remaining steps and, of course, note how your bread turns out. If you keep a log of temperatures and fermentation times for future reference, you can methodically fine-tune your process to achieve perfect bread. You also get the satisfaction that comes with being a baker who is fully tuned in to what you are doing and why you are doing it.

The recipes in this book specify water temperatures to use. I prefer warmer temperatures for water and dough than some bakers do, along with a smaller amount of yeast. Be careful not to use water that is too hot. Commercial yeast dies at temperatures as low as about 114°F (46°C). When I mix flour at room temperature, which is usually about 70°F (21°C) and water at 95°F (35°C) and let the mixture rest for 30 minutes, the dough ends up at about 78°F (26°C) once I'm finished mixing. That's my target temperature. If it's summer and warmer in the room (in which case the flour is probably warmer too), I use water at 90°F (32°C) to hit my target dough temperature of 78°F (26°C). If you keep your flour in the refrigerator or freezer, I recommend that you pull it out a day before mixing dough. All of the recipes in this book assume the flour is at room temperature.

of balance, whereas not enough time diminishes their development in the first place. When a dough is overdeveloped, the alcohol becomes too strong, overpowering the sweetness of the wheat. Longer developing time also causes dough to become more acidic. Up to a point, this is a good thing. More acidity in bread means it stays fresh longer, and lactic and acetic acids add valuable and unique flavors, aromas, and sensations. However, too much acidity creates a cloying aftertaste that many people, including me, find disagreeable. The trick is finding the right balance between time and temperature so the dough develops a desirable complexity of flavors without becoming too acid or dominated by alcohols, while simultaneously getting optimal development of the structure of the dough. The gluten that holds gas bubbles to create rise and air pockets breaks down with time, and therefore overproofed dough will collapse. On top of all this, the timing needs to work for your schedule too!

There are several ways to extend fermentation time: you can reduce the amount of yeast in the dough, you can reduce the temperature of the dough or of the area where it's is fermenting, or you can do both. If I'm working with a levain dough that normally reaches full maturity in an 80°F (27°C) room in three hours, I can put it in the retarder at my bakery at 49°F (about 9°C) and it will instead take

Retarder A cool chamber that literally retards the development of the dough. At my bakery the retarder is a walk-in unit that holds six rolling racks, and we hold the temperature at about 49°F (9°C). You can use your refrigerator to retard loaves at home, as many recipes in this book do.

THREE DEGREES OF SEPARATION

The raisin-pecan bread we make at my bakery tastes so good that sometimes I just keep eating it even when I'm not hungry. I love this bread when it's at its best. But there was a period when that bread tasted just ordinary, and I figured that it probably wasn't getting the full amount of fermentation it needed to completely develop its flavor. I spoke with the morning bakers and found that the bread was getting a complete proof (meaning it was getting the time and rise it needed after shaping). Therefore, the problem was probably that the dough needed to develop more during bulk fermentation. However, I couldn't play with the schedule because the bakers' shifts were already synchronized with other things. Manipulating time wasn't an option, so my choices were to play with one of three other variables: the amount of leavening in the dough, the ambient temperature of the bulk fermentation stage, or the temperature of the dough after its final mix. I decided to experiment with the latter and mixed the dough with water that was 3°F (about 2°C) warmer than what we had been using. Whereas our dough had been coming out of the mixer at 75°F (24°C), with the warmer water the finished dough was at 78°F (26°C). All of the other variables remained the same. The next day the bread was just as it should be: complete, full of flavor, and not sour, with just a gentle background tingle in the mouth.

twelve hours to completely develop. The extended, cold fermentation yields a better bread with a more complex flavor and a rich, well-rounded aftertaste. While we do use cold bulk fermentation for doughs at the bakery, doing so is less practical at home, where it can be difficult to find room in the refrigerator for the 12-quart Cambro tubs that I recommend. For this book, I adjusted recipes so that overnight doughs are bulk fermented with small amounts of yeast at room temperature. You'll notice that some doughs in this book are bulk fermented at room temperature and then proofed overnight in the refrigerator at temperatures of 37°F to 40°F (about 3°C to 5°C)—this is because it's easier to find space in your refrigerator for proofing baskets than a giant dough tub.

As you read this chapter, you might be thinking, "I don't know what to do with this information." Here's the deal: Making good bread is never completely formulaic. No matter how specific I am in writing a recipe, there will be variables that are outside my control or yours. Some flour is more "active" and ferments faster than other flour. Your kitchen may be at 70°F (21°C) and someone else's might be at 80°F (27°C). That's why most recipes in other books simply default to a timeline for bulk dough development followed with "or until doubled in size." The recipes in this book are designed to take the variables into account. Beyond that, in this section I'm trying to help you develop an awareness of how time and temperature affect the taste and development of the dough, and how you can manipulate those variables to produce exceptional bread.

DETAIL 2: USE PRE-FERMENTS WHEN TIME ALLOWS

The recipes in this book use one of two approaches to making bread with a complex flavor profile. The first approach is to make what's called a straight dough with a slow rise, which means using less yeast and allowing much more time for rising than in traditional recipes— at least five hours between mixing and shaping into loaves. The second approach is enhancing fermentation by adding pre-fermented dough or a levain made up many hours before being included in the final dough mix.

Poolish and biga are examples of commonly used pre-ferments. Both are made with a very small amount of commercial yeast. When using a pre-ferment, you mix 30 to 80 percent of the total flour in the recipe with water and a small amount of yeast ahead of time, let it ferment (usually overnight), and then add the resulting bubbly, fragrant pre-fermented mixture to the rest of the ingredients in the final dough. This process lends greater complexity of flavor to the bread, along with more acidity for longer keeping and richer colors and flavors in the crust. In commercial bakeries, the use of pre-ferments allows for a shorter first rise of the final dough without sacrificing quality, which often works better for production schedules.

Why take this extra step in the home kitchen? For better tasting bread, of course! It will have a little more complexity in flavor than bread from a straight dough, typically. A poolish is particularly suited to making bread with a creamy, slightly nutty character and a crisp, thin crust. Baguette dough is often made with a poolish. A biga, on the other hand,

Straight dough A dough that is made up in a single stage, without pre-fermented dough or a levain culture.

Levain The French word for "sourdough," referring to a naturally leavened dough culture made from just flour and water, containing billions of active wild yeast cells and naturally occurring bacteria that ferment bread dough and allow it to rise. For thousands of years (about five thousand, according to most respected sources) humans have made leavened bread from just flour, water, and, usually, salt, leavened only by the natural yeast in the air and flour, which work to create a bubbly, fragrant dough.

Pre-ferment A pre-ferment is a portion of the dough mixed up in advance, usually six to twelve hours before mixing the final dough. The recipes in this book that use pre-ferments use either a poolish, which is wetter and has equal amounts flour and water, or a biga, which has less water and is stiffer. Pre-ferments add flavor, leavening, and keeping qualities to the bread.

Biga The term used in Italian baking for a pre-fermented dough culture. While there is no strict definition, it typically implies a mix of a somewhat stiff dough (60 to 70 percent water) made up of just flour, water, and a very small amount of yeast, which is allowed to ferment for six to twelve hours before being added to the final dough mix. The biga builds up a lot of flavor-producing gas (carbon dioxide and alcohol), acids, and bacteria. When it is added to the final dough mix, the result is bread that captures those flavors in a very good way.

Poolish A word used in French baking, the name referring to techniques of Polish bakers who transported their methods to France. Like the Italian biga, a poolish is a pre-ferment added to the final dough mix to enhance flavor, in this case with buttery and nutty notes, and improve keeping due to the acidity that accumulates as the poolish culture develops, typically for six to twelve hours. A poolish often contains 30 to 50 percent of the total flour in a recipe and generally contains equal amounts by weight of flour and water and a tiny amount of yeast.

can give breads an earthy, musky flavor profile. At my bakery we use a biga to make ciabatta. Other types of pre-ferments not featured in this book include sponges and so-called old dough (*pâte fermentée* in French). Some pre-ferments contain salt and some don't. What all types of pre-ferments have in common, regardless of name and type, is that each allows for the development of alcohol and bacterial fermentation, which add flavor, acidity, and leavening to the dough. There is a sheen to the crumb of breads made with fully developed pre-ferments. This shiny crumb is a visual sign of good bread, and I often look for it before I smell or taste breads.

When using pre-ferments, it's important to allow them to develop fully but not excessively to attain optimum flavor and leavening. Pre-ferments need a minimum of four hours of development if they are to have a beneficial impact on the bread. When at its peak, a biga will be

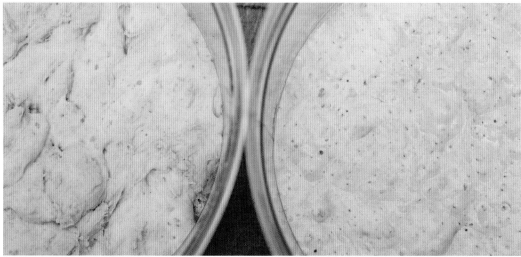

Top: Mature biga (left) and poolish (right). Bottom: Comparing the texture of biga (left) and poolish (right).

bubbly and slightly domed on top and smell strongly of alcohol and yeast. An overdeveloped biga will collapse, which is easy to discern. A properly developed poolish will be very bubbly on top, and if you stare at it you will occasionally see bubbles popping when it is at its best. Like a biga, it too will have an alcohol-yeast smell. An overdeveloped poolish will likewise be visibly collapsed.

If you use an underdeveloped biga or poolish, you miss out on the flavor benefits and also end up with less vigorous fermentation. The result is a denser bread with lower volume and blander taste. On the flip side, overdoing it with fermentation can lead to an excess of alcohol from fermentation, which will mask the sweet wheat flavors.

The first time you mix one of these pre-ferments, you may be skeptical that such a tiny amount of yeast will be enough. Just follow the recipes and prepare to be amazed. Even after all of these years of commercial baking, I still get off on it. My Overnight Pizza Dough with

Poolish (page 225) recipe leavens enough dough for five pizzas with just a scant ⅛ teaspoon of instant yeast. The tiny amounts of yeast used to start a poolish or a biga are just the beginning. The yeast and the enzymes in the flour are activated by water, and all of the yeast cells bud and duplicate quickly and logarithmically until the yeast has fully populated the poolish or biga. That tiny amount of yeast you began with has expanded an untold number of times— about a gazillion. It's so cool.

At my bakery, we have to make seasonal adjustments in the amount of yeast we put in our pre-fermented doughs because the nighttime temperatures are cooler in winter and warmer in summer. We use less yeast when it's warmer, and more yeast when it's cooler. Alternatively, we could use the same amount of yeast and adjust the water temperature up or down for mixing the pre-ferments.

DETAIL 3: USE THE AUTOLYSE METHOD

Every fermented dough in my bakery—be it bread, pizza, croissant, or brioche dough—uses the autolyse method, where the flour and the liquid in the recipe are mixed and left to rest for at least 15 minutes, and preferably 20 to 30 minutes, before adding salt, yeast, levain, or pre-ferments and mixing the final dough. The autolyse allows the flour to more completely absorb the water and also activates enzymes in the flour; for example, amylase enzymes break down the complex carbohydrates in the flour into simple sugars the yeast can feed on, and protease enzymes naturally degrade the gluten forming proteins, in a way that makes the dough more extensible.

The term *autolysis* was first applied to this process in the mid-1970s by French baking icon Professor Raymond Calvel, who developed and promoted the technique. In his book *Le Goût du Pain*, available in English as *The Taste of Bread*, Calvel wrote about being driven to improve on industrial practices that resulted in overmixed and overoxidized dough. Calvel's mission was to educate and to restore the quality of French bread baking, which had been in decline since the 1950s. The autolyse method allowed for proper dough development with a shorter mixing time, thereby reducing oxidation and improving the flavor of the bread. Overmixing and oxidation aren't an issue in home baking, being a by-product of mechanical dough mixers and commercial methods to speed up production. However, the autolyse process is still beneficial for home bakers because it allows for improved gluten development in hand-mixed doughs, resulting in better gas retention and better volume in the finished loaf. When hand mixing, you can feel the difference between a dough that was autolysed and one that wasn't; autolysed dough already has some of the structure that a dough mixed all at once, without the autolyse, doesn't have until later in its development.

Another benefit of the autolyse process is that it increases the extensibility of the dough. *Extensibility* refers to the dough's ability to be stretched and hold its shape without being so elastic that it snaps back. This isn't a big issue for the recipes in this book because all have high hydration (that is, a lot of water), which creates a slack dough that is fully extensible. But this benefit is very useful for bakeries that work with stiffer doughs. Imagine trying to shape a couple hundred baguettes from an elastic dough within a fixed period of time—it's a nightmare! Bread doughs mixed with high-gluten flour tend to be more elastic too, and therefore also benefit from the autolyse.

While I advocate autolysing in the traditional manner described by Calvel, fairly recent developments in the manufacturing of instant dried yeast have led some people to recommend that when instant dried yeast is used in a recipe, it should be included in the autolyse. The benefit is that the yeast will be fully hydrated by the time the final dough mix takes place, resulting in a more vigorous fermentation. If you try this, don't autolyse for more than about 20 minutes. Once activated, yeast in dough that has no salt will reproduce very quickly, and you'll lose the flavor benefits of long, slow fermentation.

DETAIL 4: MIX A WET, SLACK DOUGH

There are opposing points of view on how wet doughs should be. I prefer the flavor and texture of breads and pizza doughs made with more water than is typical. I am by no means alone in this. Many good bakers feel the same, including most of those I learned from. My experience is that including a little more water in the dough, say 75 percent instead of 70 percent hydration, results in more gas production, and if fermentation isn't rushed, those gases provide a lot of flavor. However, these wetter doughs are very slack and need some help building up their physical shape so they don't fall flat. They are also stickier and a little trickier to handle than stiffer doughs.

There is a property of bread dough called *strength* that refers to a dough's ability to hold its form. When dumped onto a baker's bench or kitchen counter, a dough that has sufficient strength will retain its vertical height. It will also have tenacity and some elasticity. On the other hand, a wet, sticky dough with little strength will relax and collapse like a batter, and it won't hold its shape when you try to form it into a loaf. All of this is to say that stiffer doughs hold their shape better than wet doughs.

But there's a catch: wet doughs encourage gas production and flavor development from fermentation more than stiff doughs, which results in more flavorful breads. When properly made, they can also contribute a lighter texture with some big holes. By comparison, dense bread comes from a stiff dough. Therefore, the question is how to develop a wet dough that has enough strength to hold its form and hold on to fermentation gases. While some bakers use ascorbic acid (vitamin C) in very small amounts (measured in parts per million), to add strength to their doughs, I prefer to accomplish this by applying folds (see sidebar, page 35). That way I can give the dough only as much strength as it needs, making a judgment call about how often to fold depending on how loose or tight the dough is as it's fermenting.

One of my favorite parts of the occasional baking class that I teach is hand mixing a super wet dough made with white flour and hydrated to 80 percent. It looks nothing like a bread dough and seems more like a batter. I pass the dough bucket around the room so everyone can see the texture. Invariably, everyone says that if their final mix looked like this, they would assume they had made a mistake and pitch the entire mass or add flour. I then proceed

WHAT IS FOLDING?

One way to strengthen wet, high-hydration doughs is by applying folds. Briefly, folding involves pulling segments of the dough over the dough mass one at a time, stretching each to the point of resistance and no further, then folding it back over the top of the dough. Doing this several times during the bulk fermentation of the dough helps organize the dough's gluten network, which allows it to hold on to gases produced as the dough ferments. (For more on folding, see pages 69–70.) The more complexly knit this network of gluten becomes, the more strength the dough has.

In a commercial bakery, much of this gluten organization occurs in the mixer. Longer mixing at higher speeds develops the dough more intensively. In the process, the proteins that make up gluten are repeatedly stretched and folded over upon themselves to create a three-dimensional fabric that gives the dough tensile strength. These doughs can be fermented faster, which is great for getting more product out the door faster, but not good for flavor and quality. Less intensive mixing organizes the gluten network less aggressively. To compensate, good bakers apply folds to the dough during bulk fermentation.

When do we apply the folds? Because the structure of the gluten network needs to be in place to prevent this gas from escaping, most of the folds should be applied in the early stages of bulk fermentation. Gas buildup in the dough also contributes to its strength, as the gas expands and stretches the web within the gluten network. Folding allows the dough to capture as much of the gas as possible. That said, it isn't unreasonable to give a very slack dough one last fold an hour prior to dividing and shaping. Although the recipes in this book, which have five hours or more of fermentation time, offer a lot of flexibility in when to apply the folds, I recommend applying the first fold 10 minutes or so after the final mix is done. Each successive fold can occur anytime after the dough has completely relaxed from the previous fold.

How many folds does the dough need? This depends on how wet and slack it was when mixed. Wet doughs get very little gluten development during the hand mixing, so they need three or four folds during the first hour or two of fermentation to give the gluten network enough structure to create a light crumb texture in the bread.

The recipes in this book each give guidance on the timing and number of folds recommended, usually specifying a range, such as three to four folds. However, I don't want to be overly hard and fast with rules about this. When working with your dough, you'll be able to see the physical change after you've folded it. If, based on what you observe, you want to give it one more fold, go ahead and do it.

Wet dough The world of American artisan baking lacks specific definitions for many terms. When I think of a wet or high-hydration dough, I think of dough that is naturally slack and needs folds to give it appropriate strength. Wet dough can't be defined by hydration percentage because it depends on the flour or blend of flours in the recipe. If all white flour is used, 75 percent hydration would probably result in a wet, somewhat slack dough, and 80 percent would definitely be considered a high-hydration dough. But if mostly whole wheat flour is used, 75 percent hydration would result in a much stiffer dough, because whole wheat flour absorbs more water than white flour. For a mostly whole wheat dough to be considered wet, it would probably need to have at least 82 percent hydration. Another interesting point is that American wheat flour holds more water and has a different quality of gluten-forming proteins than that used by

Pain de Campagne dough (page 140), 78% hydration, ready for its first fold.

French and Italian bakers. (I haven't worked with German or other European flours, so I can't extrapolate further.) The net result is that a wet dough in France would probably contain about 5 percent less water than an American high-hydration dough.

to demonstrate that with just a few folds over the course of the next 30 minutes, the dough comes together and starts to look like bread dough, albeit a very sticky dough that must be handled at this stage with wet hands.

Of course, using high-hydration, slack dough is only one of the secrets to making good bread with a light crumb and big open holes. You still need to allow the dough to ferment completely, both in bulk and after it is shaped. If you bake it too soon, it will be too dense.

DETAIL 5: ALLOW FOR COMPLETE BULK FERMENTATION

The careful reader may notice that many of the recipes in this book call for the dough to expand beyond the oft-repeated "until doubled in size." Tripled in size is more common here. The amount of expansion depends on the dough. Wet doughs create more gas and therefore expand more than stiff doughs. Maximum flavor development requires allowing enough time for all of the desired biochemical reactions to take place. Every recipe operates on its own ideal timeline. Make sure you give the first rise, or bulk fermentation stage, enough time. Rush it and you lose.

DETAIL 6: HANDLE DOUGH GENTLY

Most home bakers think of kneading dough as a physical act, and the harder you work the dough, the better it is going to be. We don't do that here. Once the final dough is mixed, treat it gently. Being gentle with the dough will help preserve its gluten structure and retain its gas. This applies throughout: when folding, easing the dough out of the tub, dividing it, shaping it, removing it from proofing baskets, and placing the proofed loaf in the Dutch oven for baking.

When folding the dough, extend the sections only until you feel resistance, and never to the point of tearing it. When turning the dough out of the tub and onto a floured work surface for dividing and shaping, toss some flour around the edges of the tub, then work a floured hand beneath the dough and gently ease it out onto the work surface.

At my bakery, we don't punch down the dough before dividing and shaping. I prefer to keep the gas, along with all of its flavor compounds, in the dough. To divide the dough, always flour the surface along the dividing line first, then cut it with a dough knife or other sharp edge—even the end of a wide metal spatula. Tearing it breaks up more of the gluten than necessary. And when shaping, avoid overstretching the dough so you don't run the risk of visibly tearing it. Using sufficient flour to dust the proofing baskets should prevent sticking, but if loaves do stick, be gentle as you ease them out of the baskets. Even when transferring proofed loaves to the preheated Dutch oven, continue to handle them carefully. I use the sides of my hands, rather than my fingertips, to lift the loaves; this spreads the pressure over a broader area.

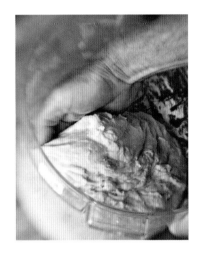

DETAIL 7: PROOF PERFECTLY TO POINT

After the dough has been shaped into loaves, it undergoes one final rise, called proofing. This can take anywhere from one to sixteen hours, depending on the dough and the ambient temperature. Just as you can slow a dough's development during bulk fermentation by putting it in a refrigerator or retarder, you can chill shaped loaves to prolong the proofing process. Slowing the rise during either bulk fermentation or proofing (but not both) is critical to achieving the complexity of flavors we look for in the breads at Ken's Artisan Bakery. It also helps us manage our schedule and bake previously shaped loaves as soon as we get into the bakery in the early morning.

It's usually difficult for home bakers to put bulk dough in the refrigerator overnight because of the size of the 12-quart dough tubs I call for in this book. It's easier to put shaped loaves of bread in the refrigerator, so in this book, doughs are chilled only at the proofing stage. Not only do you get improved flavor and better keeping quality from the acidity that develops, but this overnight proof schedule also gives you the chance to bake bread first thing in the morning. It's a great way to start your day.

The timing works this way: mix the dough in the afternoon, do the bulk fermentation at room temperature following the recipe timing (usually around five hours), and then shape the loaves in the evening. As soon as they're shaped, wrap them to keep them from drying out, then put them the refrigerator. The chilled loaves don't need to be warmed to room temperature before baking then next morning. I bake them straight from the refrigerator.

It's also essential to find the perfect proof point. Don't overproof or underproof your bread. The finger-dent test, described in detail on page 74, is a good indicator here. You'll know the loaves are optimally proofed if you poke them and the indentation springs back very slowly. You can use this test while the loaves are still in their proofing baskets. If the dough collapses as you remove it from the proofing basket, it has gone too far and won't have as much baked volume as it would have if you had removed it earlier. Levain breads have a longer window of time during which they are optimally proofed because their fermentation is less vigorous and they evolve more slowly, and perhaps because they have more acidity. Doughs made with commercial yeast have a shorter window, sometimes as narrow as 10 to 15 minutes.

DETAIL 8: BAKE UNTIL DARK BROWN

The goal in baking any bread is to achieve maximum oven spring, ideal flavor and texture of the crust, and complete baking of the interior. I like the crust to be thin and crisp with some pliability to it. If the oven is too hot, the crust will be completely baked before the middle is done. If the oven is too cool, the crust will be thicker and less delicate. The character of the crust also depends on the type of bread. The crust of a levain bread is naturally toothier than the crust of a baguette. Getting the ideal crust depends on full fermentation, proper oven temperature, the proper amount of steam, and not pulling the bread out of the oven too soon.

Baking bread in Dutch ovens, as recommended here, allows the bread to provide its own steam as it releases moisture into its enclosed chamber during the baking. Learning how

your oven bakes is essential. Most home ovens aren't well calibrated, so the actual temperature is often different from what you set. Use an inexpensive oven thermometer to learn what temperature setting delivers 475°F, for example. Most of the bread recipes in this book direct you to bake for 30 minutes with the Dutch oven's lid on, then another 20 minutes or so with the lid off. If your loaf is done in 30 minutes, your oven is too hot; if it takes an hour, your oven is not hot enough. It's best to bake bread on a rack in the middle of the oven; too low and the bottom of the loaves may scorch, since many home ovens are hottest at the bottom.

In addition to a thin, crisp crust, I like well-baked loaves, well beyond the blond stage throughout the loaf to dark brown and ochre colors throughout the crust. The point of baking until the crust is dark is to get a caramelized complexity of flavor that permeates subtly into the crumb of the bread. Many bakers know the term *Maillard reaction*—the chemical process that results in dark coloration during baking, along with the unique flavors and aromas that arise as a result. The Maillard reaction occurs not just in a well-baked bread crust, but in the crust of browned meats and other foods too.

TROUBLESHOOTING

When a bread at my bakery doesn't come out just right, I ask myself a number of questions to try to understand what went wrong and how to adjust so the problem doesn't recur. This is a normal part of life for every good baker. Over time things change and adjustments need to be made. And no matter how good the bread, I may ask these questions to see if we can improve upon it:

- Dough temperature: What temperature was the dough at the end of the mix? Is that the target mix temperature for that dough?

- Time of bulk fermentation: How long did it take for the dough to expand to the size indicated in the recipe? Was this period too long or too short?

- Folds: Did the dough get enough folding?

- Room temperature: Colder or warmer than usual?

- Condition of the pre-ferment: At the time the dough was mixed, was the pre-ferment (poolish, biga, levain, etc.), underdeveloped, overdeveloped, or just right?

- Dough strength and hydration: Did the dough feel right? Did it have its usual volume and gas? Was it too sticky or too stiff?

- Scaling: Any possibility that a measurement error occurred? For predictable results you need to measure each ingredient accurately, especially salt and yeast. Keep in mind that for home baking, small amounts of yeast (1 to 2 grams, for example) require either a very accurate scale or conversion to a volume measurement (for example, teaspoons), as given in the recipes.

- Complete proof: Was the bread underproofed or overproofed?

GUIDING PRINCIPLES

Here's a summary of guiding principles to help ensure success in creating high-quality artisan breads at home.

- Think of time and temperature as ingredients and keep in mind that they have a reciprocal relationship.
- Use a scale to measure all ingredients by weight (the exception being small quantities of yeast, where teaspoon measures are probably more accurate).
- Use the autolyse process before mixing the final dough.
- Use a thermometer to check the temperature of the dough and learn to hit the ideal temperature consistently at the end of the mix.
- Use more water in the dough than conventional recipes allow.

- Learn to handle sticky dough.
- Apply folds to the dough to give it the strength wet doughs need to hold their form.
- Push the fermentation to just shy of its limits to get the best flavors.
- Bake the bread until it's a deep, dark brown.
- Keep a log of dough temperatures, fermentation times, and other details to help you fine-tune your process.
- Retard levain loaves after shaping for at least twelve hours, or use a very long, overnight bulk dough fermentation.

- Proper baking: Was the oven temperature correct? Was there the right amount of steam? Was the baking time adequate?

- Flour: Was it a new flour? Even the same brand and variety of flour purchased from the same place can vary depending on harvest, weather, milling date, and other factors. Some flours produce slower or faster fermentation, and some flours absorb more or less water, which necessitates slight changes in the amount of water in a recipe.

A NOTE ON BAKER'S PERCENTAGES

When I was studying with Jean-Marc Berthomier at l'Institut Paul Bocuse many years ago, I was impressed by his ability to instantly recite the formulas for many different breads. One of the first basics a French baker learns is baker's percentages, and this knowledge provides a critical foundation for understanding recipes.

All of Jean-Marc's recipes begin with 1 kilogram, or 1,000 grams, of flour, which is the standard recipe basis in French baking. Each of his bread recipes is a variation on a simple formula: 1,000 grams of flour, 680 grams of water, 20 grams of salt, and 20 grams of fresh yeast. In baker's percentages, that can be stated as 100 percent flour, 68 percent water, 2 percent salt,

UNDERSTANDING BAKER'S PERCENTAGES

With baker's percentages, all ingredients in a recipe are stated as percentages of the total flour weight. The total amount of flour is always 100 percent (including a combination of flours). If the amount of flour in a recipe is 1,000 grams and the amount of water is 700 grams, water makes up 70 percent of the flour weight. Likewise, 20 grams of salt in this recipe is 2 percent of the flour weight, and 20 grams of yeast is the same. So this simple recipe could be expressed as 100 percent flour, 70 percent water, 2 percent salt, and 2 percent yeast. This allows recipes to be scaled up or down easily: whatever the flour weight, the other ingredients can simply be measured as the expressed percentage of the flour weight, whether the amount of flour is 500 grams or 5,000 grams. Each bread and pizza dough recipe in this book provides baker's percentages in addition to specific amounts of each ingredient.

You'll note that the volume conversions included in each ingredients table *do not* correspond to the baker's percentage column. This is because the volume conversions are necessarily imprecise (see page 27). If you are interested in scaling these recipes using baker's percentages, you should absolutely measure your ingredients by weight rather than volume. After all, what is 70 percent of 2¾ cups of flour? Wouldn't it be easier to just buy a kitchen scale?

and 2 percent fresh yeast. (Note that 3 grams of fresh yeast equals 1 gram of instant yeast, so this would equate to about 7 grams of instant yeast.) In general, all of these breads autolyse for 20 minutes, have a final mix temperature of 75°F (24°C), are fermented at room temperature for 1½ hours, and are shaped and proofed for 1 hour before baking. What often differentiates the recipes is the type of flour used, slight variations in the amount of water, and the shape of the loaf.

Because larger or smaller batches can be made using the same ratios, Jean-Marc could double, halve, or quintuple a bread formula and expect to get the same results. The ratios of the ingredients as measured by weight thankfully remain the same, regardless of batch size.

Understanding a recipe begins with a grasp of the ratios of the ingredients as measured by weight. This was the point of bringing up Jean-Marc's flour, water, salt, and yeast ratios. If someone describes a dough as being made with solely white flour and 70 percent water, I immediately know from experience what that dough will look like and feel like. The math is easiest when using metric weights. (What's 2 percent of 3 pounds, 5 ounces? *Silence.* What's 2 percent of 1,500 grams? *Thirty grams.*) You can indeed follow the recipes here without doing any math, but having a basic awareness of baker's percentages will allow you to experiment with different flour mixes, knowledgeably adjust water in the dough if your flour is more or less absorbent, and simply understand what you are doing.

COMPARING RECIPES

Manipulating any single detail covered in this chapter can have a significant impact on the final bread, and in fact, many of the differences among breads lie less in ingredients than in these techniques and in whether or how they are applied. This is often reflected in recipes, so knowing how to compare recipes has a very practical use. When I look at a recipe, a number of questions spring to mind: "How is this different from other recipes I already know? What blend of flours is used? What type of leavening and how much? What is the hydration percentage? What temperature of water is used? Is this a novel way to ferment the dough? What temperatures are specified for dough mix, bulk fermentation, and proofing? And how long does the dough develop?"

Two recipes that look alike can in fact be quite different. Always consider the balance between the amount of leavening, dough temperature, and fermentation time when evaluating recipes. Remember the warm-dough-less-yeast/cold-dough-more-yeast seesaw?

To illustrate, consider my recipe for Overnight White Bread (page 89). On the surface, this recipe looks very similar to Jim Lahey's famous no-knead bread recipe. But let's take a deeper look. This comparison isn't about which method or bread is better; it's just interesting because at a quick glance these recipes look very much the same: an easy, no-fuss mix of a soft dough with a small amount of yeast in the evening; shaping into loaves the next morning; and baking in a Dutch oven an hour or two later. However, when you compare our ingredient ratios using baker's percentages, or when you compare the specified water temperatures, it's easy to see the differences. In terms of ingredients, my recipe uses only one-third the amount of yeast; it also has 3 percent more water, and the water temperature is at least 30°F (about 16°C) warmer, resulting in a final mix temperature that's about 18°F (10°C) warmer. As for differences in technique, I call for an autolyse period and I specify applying two folds, preferably in the first hour and a half after mixing the dough. My recipe takes a little bit more work, but not much.

I write this comparison to Mr. Lahey's well-known bread recipe to show that the differences between recipes are easiest to see and understand when you compare recipes' baker's percentages, temperatures, and timelines. Seeing that my bread, which is made on the same schedule, uses one-third the amount of yeast and is mixed with much warmer water is a great illustration of the relationship between the amount of leavening and the temperature of the dough. My dough benefits from a few folds to give it strength. My recipe reflects my personal preference for the flavors developed in warm, wet doughs made with less yeast.

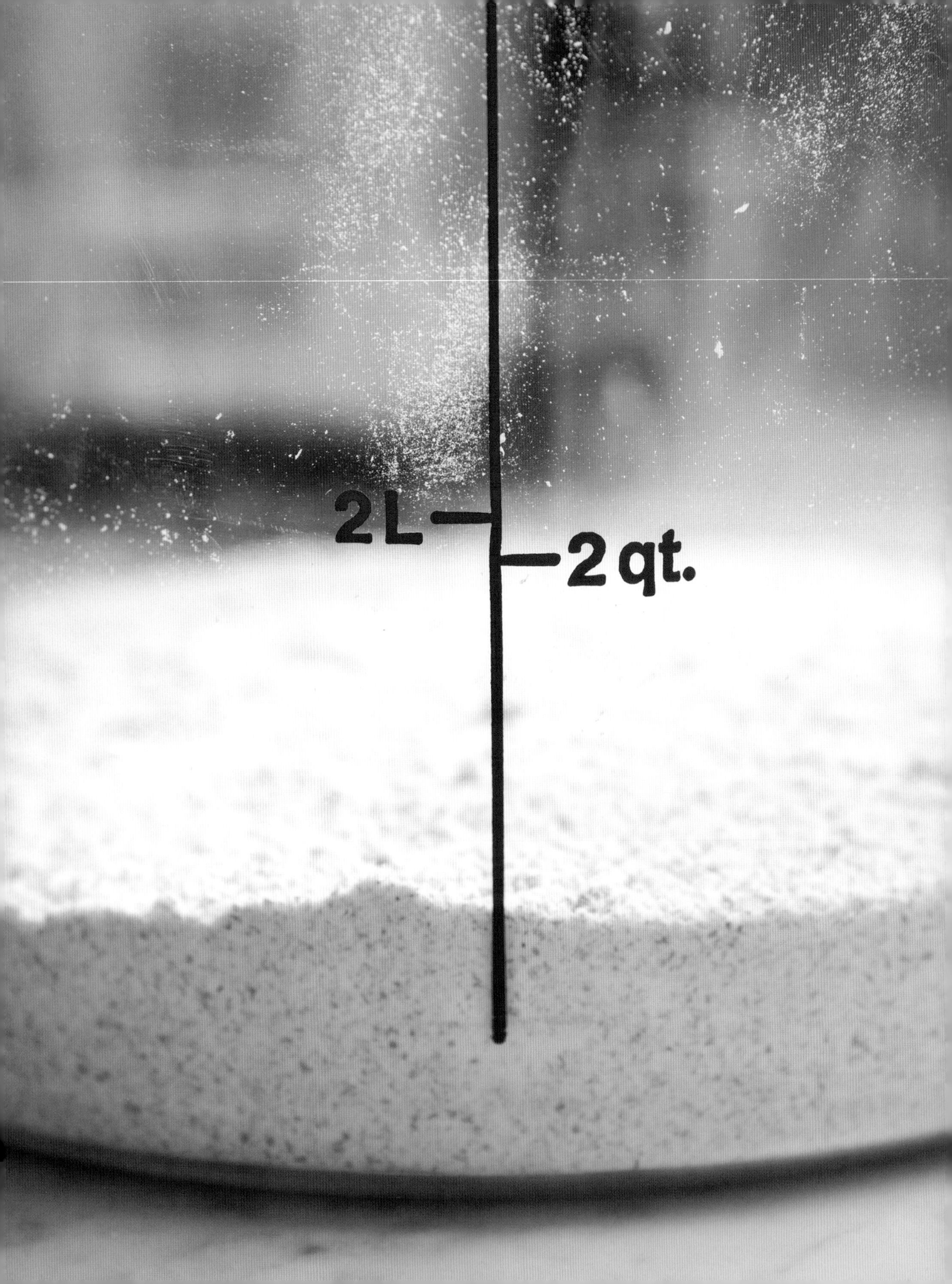
2L
2 qt.

CHAPTER 3
EQUIPMENT AND INGREDIENTS

Both the equipment and the ingredients called for in this book are very straightforward. You probably already have most or all of the ingredients you need, and if you don't, they're easy to obtain. In terms of equipment, I do call for a few things you may not have, so let's take a look at those first. Then, if you need to purchase any equipment, you can go ahead and get started on that.

EQUIPMENT

You'll need just a few special tools or other pieces of kitchen equipment to make the recipes in this book. You may already have some of it on hand. Any you don't have will be readily available online or at a kitchen supply or restaurant supply store. All of the recipes in this book call for mixing the dough by hand, so you don't need a stand mixer.

Dough Tub

You'll need a 12-quart round tub with a lid for mixing your dough by hand and to hold the dough as it rises. I recommend Cambro brand translucent polycarbonate tubs; the model number is RFSCW12. These tubs are available online from Amazon and at most restaurant supply stores that sell to the public.

If you choose another brand, that's fine; just be sure it's a food-grade container. What is important is the size; it needs to be big enough to allow you to mix and fold the dough by hand within the container and to contain the dough as it expands. The round shape makes it easy to incorporate the ingredients, whereas squared edges and corners tend to trap ingredients. A clear container is best because you can see through it to chart the progress of the rise. And of course you need a lid to keep the dough from drying out during its long rise.

The advantage to using a big, 12-quart tub is that you can do everything inside it: weighing, mixing, and folding the dough. There isn't any need to dump the dough onto your countertop until the final stage, when you divide and shape the loaves. Using the tub streamlines the process and makes it easy. I've found that these 12-quart tubs have other uses too. I use mine for brining chicken or turkey, or sometimes as an ice bucket for beer or wine.

If you have something around the house that approximates the same size and shape (round, about 10 inches in diameter, and about 8 inches deep, with a lid), give it a try.

Although smaller tubs are available, it's difficult to mix the dough by hand in them, and impossible to fold the dough without removing it from the tub first.

Smaller Tubs

You'll need one or two 6-quart rounded tubs with lids for holding your levain culture and for making poolish or biga. Again, I recommend the clear Cambro tubs, which are available wherever the 12-quart tubs are sold. You will only need two of these if you plan to make a poolish or biga while you already have a levain culture going. In testing recipes for this book I only ever needed one at a time.

Dutch Oven

All of the breads in this book are baked in a 4-quart Dutch oven with a lid. Baking the bread in a preheated Dutch oven allows you to make fantastic bread at home that looks like it came from a great bakery. While most Dutch ovens are heatproof to 500°F (260°C), some brands, such as Le Creuset, have knobs that may melt at high temperatures. You can replace these knobs with either a metal Le Creuset replacement knob or an inexpensive steel cabinet pull from the hardware store.

Lodge Cast Iron and Emile Henry are two well-known, less expensive, good-quality brands, and that's what I used to test all of the recipes in this book (and both have ovenproof knobs). If you already have a suitable Dutch oven but aren't sure what size it is, just measure water into it in quarts to figure out its capacity. Mine are 10 inches in diameter at the top and 4 inches deep. If you have a 5-quart Dutch oven, it will also work. The dough will spread out more than in a 4-quart Dutch oven, and therefore the loaves will be a bit wider and not quite as tall as those in the photos in this book. Breads baked in a 5-quart Dutch oven may not split open on top in the same way as those baked in a 4-quart model, since there will be less vertical pressure as the loaves get their oven spring. But you'll still get good bread, so why not take advantage of equipment you already have? By the way, all of the recipes in this book make two loaves of bread, so if you have two Dutch ovens you can bake both loaves at once. Otherwise, you'll have to bake your bread in two stages.

Digital Kitchen Scale

I cannot overemphasize the importance of measuring bread ingredients by weight, not volume. (See page 27 for more on the advantages of baking by weight.) Therefore, a digital kitchen scale is essential. It should measure up to 2 kilograms (4.4 pounds) and be accurate to single grams. Also take into account that you need to be able to read the display when a large, 12-quart tub is resting on top of it (this allows you to measure water and flour directly into the tub). If you can't see the display when you put the dough tub on the scale, you can measure out the flour and water into smaller containers and pour them into your 12-quart dough bucket. A scale that measures down to tenths of a gram would be handy for accurately measuring yeast, but that feature isn't essential, as I also provide teaspoon measures for yeast.

One brand I recommend is Oxo. They make a scale with a convenient pull-out display, and that's what I used for testing all the recipes in this book. It is available at Amazon and kitchen supply stores. You can buy a decent scale for under $25.

Instant-Read Probe Thermometer

An instant-read probe thermometer is essential for making sure you're using the right temperature of water and measuring the final mix temperature, and it will come in handy in other ways too. Mine gets repeated use measuring the temperature of meat as it cooks. Taylor and CDN are two brands I can recommend. Both make models that cost less than $20.

Proofing Baskets

Proofing baskets are used to hold shaped loaves as they proof, or undergo their final rise. Because all of the loaves in this book are baked in 4-quart Dutch ovens, you'll only need one size of proofing basket: 9 inches in diameter at the top and 3½ inches deep—or whatever diameter matches the shape of your Dutch oven. If you can afford cane *banneton* baskets, they will last a lifetime. Linen-lined proofing baskets are also a great choice. The recipes in this book were tested with Frieling baskets. Matfer is another respected brand. You can also improvise a proofing basket using a bowl of approximately the same dimensions lined with a flour-dusted, lint-free tea towel.

Odds and Ends

You'll obviously want a pair of oven mitts for dealing with hot Dutch ovens. Make sure the mitts you buy are safe for handling a 500°F (260°C) pot. An oven thermometer also comes in handy, since home ovens rarely deliver the exact temperature you dial in. Mine runs about 25°F cooler, so when I set it to 500°F, I actually get 475°F. Because the quantities of yeast called for in these recipes are typically quite small, it's difficult to measure them accurately with a scale. In a few cases, you'll get the most accurate results if you have a ¹⁄₁₆ teaspoon measure. These are available (including online at Amazon), so I recommend you purchase one. Finally, you'll need something to cover the proofing baskets after you have shaped the loaves. Tea towels work fine for this, although I like to use nonperforated plastic bags, which allow you to proof the loaves overnight in the refrigerator without drying them out. I reuse clean bags I get at the produce section of the market for this purpose.

Pizza Equipment

There are several ways to make great pizza at home, and I describe a few of these methods in chapter 12. A pizza stone works best; they are widely available and usually cost around $30. If you're using a pizza stone, you'll also want a pizza peel to help you scoot the pizza into the hot oven as quickly (and painlessly) as possible. I prefer wood peels; a 14-inch diameter should be the right size for your home oven.

If you don't feel like investing in a pizza stone or peel but do want to try some of the pizza recipes in this book, you *can* make thicker-crust pizzas in a medium-sized oven-proof skillet. I've had great results cooking pizza in my 9-inch cast-iron skillet.

INGREDIENTS

The focus of this book is making great bread and pizza dough from just four ingredients: flour, water, salt, and yeast. There are plenty of wonderful breads that include nuts, whole grains, dried fruits, milk, butter, herbs, or cheese (I have had a great *pain Gruyère* at Boulangerie Onfroy, in Paris). But in my mind, the real craft of artisan bread baking lies in producing something exquisite with only the four principal ingredients. Of course, if you're using only a few ingredients, quality is paramount, so let's take a look at these four basic ingredients and some of the considerations in regard to each.

Flour

First, note that because temperature is such an important element of the equation when making bread, you should use flour at room temperature for all of the recipes in this book. Beyond that, my recommendations on flour come down to this: Use the best-quality flour you can find, assessing its quality by both the appearance and the taste of the bread, and seek out flour with protein in the 11 to 12 percent range. Unfortunately, protein content is rarely detailed on flour packaging, but some brands do put this information on their websites. These lower-protein flours have more in common with the flour used in French and Italian artisan bakeries, and they tolerate a long rise well and produce a crumb that is delicate and easy to digest. They also produce dough that ends up less tight and more pliable, resulting in bread with a nice open crumb and a crust that blooms nicely during baking.

Typically, flours labeled "bread flour" have a high protein content—generally about 14 percent. By contrast, flour labeled "all-purpose," such as King Arthur Organic All-Purpose Flour, with an 11.8 percent protein content, is, in their words, "ideal for European-style hearth

From left: Whole wheat, all-purpose (white), and whole rye flours.

WHEAT FLOUR

Flour is what you get when wheat kernels, also called wheat berries, are ground into a meal. The kernel has three components, which are separated in the modern milling process.

- **Endosperm:** Made up of starch and protein, the endosperm comprises about 84 percent of the wheat berry.
- **Bran:** Making up about 13 percent of the weight of the wheat berry, bran is the outer layer of the kernel; it surrounds and protects the endosperm and germ. Bran contains insoluble fiber and most of the mineral content of the kernel.
- **Germ:** The component of the kernel that contains the wheat's genetic material, the germ makes up about 3 percent of the weight of the kernel. It contains all of the fat and plenty of flavor.

Whole wheat flour is meal made from the entire wheat berry. White flour is just the endosperm. I don't understand why people say "wheat bread" to refer to whole wheat. White bread is made from wheat flour too. To add to the confusion, there is also white whole wheat flour, which is a whole grain flour made from white spring wheat. (Most bread flours are made from red winter wheat.) White whole wheat flour has nutritional benefits similar to those of regular whole wheat flour but a milder flavor.

breads," and I agree. At my bakery and pizzeria, we use Shepherd's Grain Low-Gluten flour as our white flour for breads and pizza dough (see the essay on page 54 for more on Shepherd's Grain). Its protein content is about 11 percent. Try a variety of flours to see which you prefer.

I also recommend using unbleached flour that has a creamy color. Bleaching is a flour treatment that removes carotenoid pigments and literally whitens the flour—removing flavor in the process. This reflects a mass market preference for whiteness over a more natural product with better flavor.

TRADITIONAL FLOUR PRODUCTION

In the old days, meaning the five thousand years preceding the nineteenth century, harvested wheat was manually threshed to separate the wheat berries from the stalks and chaff, then the wheat was ground manually or stone milled. Hard work! Stone milling, whether powered by muscles, wind, or water, produced a whole grain meal. Sometimes bolting screens or sieves were used to sift out some or most of the bran. What remained was flour that had the components of white flour (the endosperm), plus the ground-up germ, and minus some or most of the bran.

I bring this up because one of my original goals as a baker was to produce a country bread that mimicked the best qualities of what Steven Kaplan referred to as *pain d'autrefois*, or bread made the old way, in his book *The Bakers of Paris and the Bread Question, 1700–1775*. This is the kind of bread Poilâne and my other baking heroes were producing in Paris, using flour from artisan mills such as the famed Decollogne-Lecocq mill in Précy-sur-Marne: stone-ground and sifted flour containing the germ in addition to the white endosperm, with a creamy caramel color. Although we don't have mills like that in the United States, I learned from Chad Robertson to approximate the character of the old-school French country bread of my dreams by blending a small amount of whole wheat flour or ground wheat germ in with white flour and using a sweet levain and long, slow fermentation.

THE ROLE OF GLUTEN AND ENZYMES

The main reason wheat flour produces such excellent bread is the presence of proteins that produce gluten. Other members of the wheat family, such as spelt and kamut, also contain gluten, as do rye, barley, and triticale (a hybrid of wheat and rye). Wheat produces a greater amount of gluten than rye and barley, allowing it to hold more gas, and as a result, wheat produces a lighter, airier bread.

Another critical component in both wheat and rye is the enzyme amylase. When water is added to these flours, the amylase is activated and begins its work of breaking down complex sugars in the endosperm into simple sugars that yeast can feed on. The yeast multiply and eventually produce gases, and the gases are contained by the gluten network formed by the proteins, allowing the bread to rise. Without the special proteins that form gluten (glutenin and gliadin) and the enzymes present in wheat and rye, we would all be eating crackers. Although it isn't necessary to have this information in your head when you set out to make bread, it is fascinating to know how the makeup of wheat and rye allows us to have leavened bread.

Gluten A combination of two proteins that occur in flour: glutenin and gliadin. When water and flour are mixed together to make dough, gluten is formed as a web of interlocking strands of these proteins. The water allows the gluten strands to stretch, and mixing and folding the dough allow the strands to elongate and organize in a way that increases their ability to capture the gases produced by fermentation. Gluten expands and holds the gases that contribute flavors to bread and make the dough rise. Increased complexity in the organization of the gluten strands also adds to their resilience, a characteristic bakers call *strength*.

Water

Use water that is good enough to drink. The critical factor here is water temperature, which is covered in detail throughout the book.

Salt

When baking, use either sea salt or mined salt. Kosher salt is fine, but the size of kosher salt flakes means they will take longer to dissolve than fine sea salt. Avoid iodized salt because iodine inhibits fermentation and tastes like . . . iodine. Since the grain size of salt varies from source to source, volume measurements tend to be inconsistent. Therefore it's far better to weigh your salt. I recommend using fine sea salt because it will dissolve quickly in the dough. At home, sometimes I run coarse sea salt through a coffee mill before using it in a hand-mixed bread dough. If you do this, be sure to wipe all of the salt residue out of the grinder so it doesn't corrode.

Salt slows the fermentation of bread dough. The salt-free breads of Italy are famous for their fast rise time (and their bland flavor). The standard amount of salt in recipes for French bread is 2 percent of the weight of the flour. The generally accepted range is between 1.8 and 2.2 percent. I sometimes put 2.2 percent in to get the flavors I like and for the bit of added strength salt can add to high-hydration doughs.

Baker's Yeast

All of the recipes in this book call for instant dried yeast. You're likely to find two or three kinds of yeast at the store: active dry, rapid-rise, and instant yeast. All of these yeasts are the same species: *Saccharomyces cerevisiae*. What differentiates them is their coating, the way the yeast is manufactured, and performance. At my bakery, we use SAF Red Instant Yeast. I recommend that you buy a 16-ounce package of this yeast, which is available from King Arthur Flour's website or Amazon, among other sources. It will keep for six months if stored airtight in the refrigerator. Do not store it in the freezer as freezing will kill off a small percentage of the yeast.

Fresh and Instant Yeast
If you need to convert a recipe that calls for fresh yeast, 3 grams fresh yeast = 1 gram instant dried yeast.

In most of my recipes, it isn't necessary to dissolve the dried yeast first. These doughs have a lot of water in them, so the yeast dissolves rapidly in the dough; just sprinkle it on top of the dough and incorporate it as you mix the dough. There are arguments for dissolving first, but I prefer the effect on flavor produced by dissolving the yeast within the dough. However, be aware that this doesn't work in a stiff dough mixed by hand. My rule of thumb is to predissolve the yeast if the dough has 70 percent or less hydration. This may seem arbitrary, but it takes into account that mixing by hand is gentler and less vigorous than mixing by machine. So, for example, if you're mixing a stiff biga, the dried yeast needs to be dissolved in water before mixing.

Professional bakers use the term *commercial yeast* to refer to what consumers think of as store-bought yeast. Commercial yeast is a monoculture, a single species of yeast (the aforementioned *Saccharomyces cerevisiae*). Levain cultures, on the other hand, are made up of a community of yeasts that occur naturally in the flour and the environment, including the air. These wild yeasts aren't like commercial yeast; they are less vigorous, and they impart their own particular flavors to the bread. Part of the complexity of a levain bread is due to multiple strains of yeast coexisting within the culture that is leavening the dough.

Commercial yeast causes breads to rise faster and provides more lift to the dough, producing bread with a lighter texture and more volume than levain breads. The slower activity of the yeast in levain dough, on the other hand, allows time for naturally occurring bacteria to undergo their own fermentation and impart acidity, which gives the bread more complex flavor, a bit of tang, and a heartier crust. And because of this acidity, levain breads keep longer before going stale.

I often prefer to add small amounts of commercial yeast to my levain bread doughs to get the best of both worlds: bread that has winelike complexity and acidity as well as a light texture in the crumb. Where you do not want the twain to meet is in your levain culture. The more vigorous commercial yeast will ultimately crowd out the wild yeasts and take over in a survival-of-the-fittest scenario.

Where Does Our Flour Come From?

It's mid-August, and my feet crunch and crackle through fragrant, dry wheat stubble. Combines have just passed through here like massive mowers, shearing the stalks and leaving empty rows of stubble extending to the horizon. Behind each combine trails an aromatic dust cloud that smells a little bit like my bakery. Golden wheat fields turn amber as the sun falls. For four weeks in late summer each year, areas of eastern Washington ranging from gentle inclines to the dramatic wavelike hills of the Palouse region are devoted to harvesting wheat, a crop that covers over 2 million acres throughout the state. I arrived bearing one of my bakery's 3-kilo (6.6-pound) *boules* of Country Blonde, my favorite loaf, taking it back to where it was born.

The farmers here depend on these few weeks of harvest to earn their annual wages. This year it's a generous crop, with thick clusters of stalks that mean a high yield. However, a late, wet spring and a cooler-than-usual summer delayed the crop cycle, and harvest began two to three weeks later than normal. The late harvest is putting more time pressure than usual on getting the wheat into the bin. The stress points for these farmers are getting the crop harvested before rain comes and doing it safely, without disabling equipment breakdowns. Many of the farms run their combines every day, nonstop for ten to twelve hours, until sunset, seven days a week; some take Sundays off. Some fields are harvested by a single combine; in others, teams are lined up working in a row; and in yet others, combines are scattered about. Trucks wait to be filled, then head to the grain elevator to be emptied, and then return again, over and over. Or a tractor might be pulling a big hopper, slowly rolling alongside the combine so it can auger its load of wheat into the bankout wagon without stopping the cut. Time is important. Equipment breaks down and sometimes must be repaired in the field in the middle of a hot, occasionally windy August afternoon.

"First thing my father taught me when I was a boy: 'Don't rub your eyes.'" These words of wisdom came from Mike Kunz of Kunz Farms near Davenport, Washington, after I, happily peppered with chaff and clouds of wheat-harvest dust, had been rubbing my eyes for the past hour. Mike is one of a few dozen farmers in the Shepherd's Grain collective of wheat farmers. They are the people who farm the wheat that turns into the flour I bake with.

Mike Kunz is a third-generation farmer living in the house his grandfather built. The schoolhouse down the road is where he, his father, and his grandfather went to school. Mark Richter of R & R Farms in Endicott, Washington, also in the Shepherd's Grain group, is a fourth-generation farmer also working the land of his forebears. Mark's great-grandfather Andrew Richter homesteaded in the 1890s. Mike and Mark see themselves in the context of a multigenerational responsibility; they are caretakers of both their land and a legacy. And they are rewarded by the peace, bounty, and beauty of this magnificent golden terrain they can call their own.

Preserving the land for future generations is responsible stewardship, and these two farmers, along with the others in the Shepherd's Grain network, have converted from traditional till-and-seed farming to no-till direct seeding, a process that prevents erosion, allows organic matter to stay in the soil, and improves efficiency. A plow-pulled drill, looking like a 1950s low-tech sci-fi invader, injects the seeds and fertilizer directly into the soil at each planting. During harvest the combines leave behind the wheat stalks and chaff as a mulch, and after harvest the remaining stubble is slowly consumed by soil microbes. No hay bales in these fields; it all goes back into the soil, increasing its health and its ability to retain moisture. These are dry-farmed wheat fields—without irrigation.

Mike's farm sees about fourteen inches of annual precipitation. Others get as little as twelve inches per year. Moisture retention in the soil and preventing erosion are everything to these guys. Mark says he's amazed at how his fields soak up the rain with no moisture or soil loss, while topsoil on neighboring land that's intensively tilled washes away in the same rain. Crop rotations from spring wheat (planted in March and April), to winter wheat (planted in September and October), to fallow for a season are typical. Other rotation crops include garbanzo beans, peas, and sunflowers.

Mike Kunz shows me his cavernous barn, built in 1915 for horses, cattle, and hay. Before gas-powered combines harvested the crops, teams of up to twenty-five horses pulled combines that did the same thing modern combines do. They were mechanical marvels that cut the wheat stalks and thrashed the wheat, using rotating sieves to separate the wheat from the chaff. The horse-team carriage held a satchel of stones or clumps of dirt at the ready for the driver to toss at the rumps of lagging horses when he needed some extra giddyup.

Today, there is about one farm family for every four that used to populate this land. Farming still appears to be a prosperous business, a fact belied by dying towns, ready for and in need of a new generation of settlers. Streets in towns like Harrington are lined with beautiful, abandoned brick buildings with echoes of faded paint advertisements for feed stores or

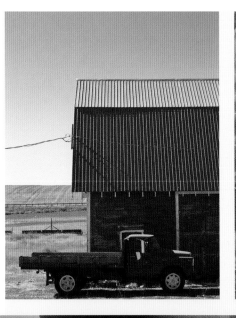

tobacco. No smoking out in the fields, though, as the wheat represents a daily fire hazard—guys carry tins of chew if they need a tobacco fix. A spark from a worn part on the combine can start a fire in a hurry. It is bone dry out here, often with a breeze. These farmers carry both fire and hail insurance. Fire and the dangers inherent in working with heavy equipment are the principal safety hazards. Some of the combines have to negotiate steep hillsides, and experience and caution are important.

Of course, there is the off-season, when equipment is serviced, planting rotations are planned out, and a well-deserved rest is taken. And in June there's the annual Combine Demolition Derby in Lind, Washington. Gotta have some fun!

Protein content has long been a measure of marketability for wheat. The demand from large, industrial bakeries for high-protein flour places a premium on wheat with a higher percentage of protein. Protein content goes up as the plant gets stressed, and stress is higher when the plant has less moisture (to a point—obviously there is a minimum amount of moisture needed for the plant to produce). This year the protein content will be a bit lower because of the late spring and cool summer. The *quality* of protein, however, relates to the gluten's ability to retain fermentation gases and expand without breaking, and this is governed more by the genetics of the variety of wheat and environmental factors like soil health than it is by soil moisture content. So a harvest with lower protein content can have protein of excellent quality. Bakers like me prefer lower-protein flour. I told them not to worry about protein content on my account. Yes, they laughed—I'm not one of their biggest customers.

A bushel of wheat berries weighs 60 pounds. On stalks in the field you can see rows of individual berries that will be ground into flour, surrounded by husks with cat-whisker hairs called awns. The combine cuts the stalks, threshes to separate out the wheat berries from the seed heads, and then uses a blower and a rotary sieve to separate the wheat from the chaff—and all of that happens very quickly. What you get at the end of the process is a bin full of the marketable crop: bushels of wheat. At delivery the wheat is graded for moisture content and cleanliness; farmers pay a price if the grade is reduced, perhaps because their equipment didn't do a good enough job separating the wheat from the chaff. For them, it's not just a saying—a reduction in grade can mean a big loss of money.

Wheat is trucked from the local grain elevators to a mill in Spokane, where it's combined with wheat harvested at other Shepherd's Grain farms and stored in silos. It will be milled throughout the year into whole wheat and white wheat flours, then bagged and shipped to distribution partners for final delivery. The red winter wheat is milled into all-purpose flour with medium protein levels, usually in the 11 percent range, although this season, because the plants weren't stressed as much, the protein content will be around 10.5 percent. This is the white flour I buy. The dark northern spring wheat will be milled to make a sweet, not very bitter whole wheat flour (the wheat variety these farms are planting produces less tannins than many other varieties) and also high-gluten white flour with protein in the 13 percent range. Soft white winter wheat is milled into pastry flour and cake flour.

This is where my flour comes from. And now that I've brought my three-kilo *boule* to these wheat fields, the flour has come full circle.

PART 2
BASIC BREAD RECIPES

CHAPTER 4
BASIC BREAD METHOD

This chapter provides guidelines and instruction in techniques that apply to all of the recipes in this book. The individual recipes differ in schedule, the blend of flours used, the fermentation method, and the complexity of the process. Once you're familiar with the techniques discussed here, including hand mixing the dough, applying folds, shaping round loaves, using refrigeration to retard the loaves, and baking in Dutch ovens, you can successfully make any bread or pizza dough in this book.

Each bread has its own character. The flavor complexity scale that follows indicates the degree to which different processes result in bread with more complexity of taste.

To decide which bread to make, choose a recipe that works with your schedule. If you have some flexibility in your schedule, then you have more freedom to choose a recipe based on the character you want in your bread. For example, if I'm going to be available during the day, I might choose to make the White Bread with Poolish (page 98). If I want to bake first thing in the morning, I'd choose one of the levain breads in part 3 of the book or the Overnight 40% Whole Wheat Bread (page 93) because they proof overnight in the refrigerator. My personal preference, if the timelines work, is almost always to bake one of the levain breads in part 3.

Once you have become familiar with the recipes, the process, and the timing, you can alter the flour blend as you wish. In the essay "Making a Bread (or Pizza) Dough You Can Call Your Own" (page 190), I give specific guidance on how to adjust the types of flour, the

BREAD FLAVOR COMPLEXITY SCALE

LEAST COMPLEX ├──┤ MOST COMPLEX

Same-day breads | Breads with overnight fermentation or overnight proofing | Breads made with pre-ferments | Levain breads

amount of water, or hydration, the timing, and more. That information will allow you to transform any recipe in this book to suit your whim or your pantry.

The recipes in chapter 5, Straight Doughs, are accessible to anyone, regardless of experience. Good first recipes for novice bakers are the two Saturday Breads (pages 81 and 85). They are the simplest, and yield good bread, and both can be made from start to finish in a single day. The Saturday Breads take seven to eight hours of elapsed time, with an initial fermentation of five hours. While eight hours might seem like a long time, the actual time engaged in making them is perhaps forty-five minutes, including cleanup. They are very simple, especially after you have made them a few times.

The remaining recipes in chapter 5 use a little more water in the dough. These softer doughs are actually easier to hand mix but a little more difficult to shape because wetter dough is stickier. They have a little more flavor from fermentation and also offer more schedule options. You can mix the dough in the evening, shape it into loaves the next morning, and bake an hour or two after that; or you can mix the dough in the afternoon, shape it into loaves in the evening, refrigerate the loaves overnight, and bake them first thing the next morning.

The four straight dough recipes are the simplest in the book. The Saturday Breads are great for days when you wake up and decide, "This would be a good day to make some bread." But if you think about it the day or night before, I recommend that you move on to chapter 6, Doughs Made with Pre-Ferments. These recipes are equally approachable; they just take a bit of foresight—and they make tastier bread. See pages 30–33 for more on poolish and biga, the two pre-ferments I use in this book. Once you're familiar with working with pre-ferments, move on to the recipes in part 3 of the book, Levain Bread Recipes.

READING THE RECIPE TABLES

As mentioned, the recipes in this book are a bit atypical in that ingredients aren't necessarily listed in the order in which they're used. Rather, flour is always listed first, followed by water, salt, and yeast, reflecting the relative quantities, or baker's percentage, of these ingredients in the recipe. Here's a quick explanation of the information in the different columns of the recipe tables, followed by an example.

FINAL DOUGH MIX QUANTITY: This column (which is just called "Quantity" in the straight dough recipes) gives the quantities of each ingredient you'll put in your empty 12-quart tub for the final dough mix, to bring the total weight of flour up to 1,000 grams beyond the amount in the poolish, biga, or levain, and add other ingredients as needed. All of the amounts you need to know appear in the various columns and are repeated in the recipe steps for ease of use so you don't have to turn back to the recipe table to recall the amount.

As I'm sure you've figured out by now, I am a strong advocate for measuring ingredients by weight, not volume. However, some home bakers do not own a kitchen scale. For those bakers, I have included approximate volumes of the ingredients you will add to the final dough mix. These volume measurements are not nearly as precise as their corresponding weight measurements; for this reason the volume measurements do not exactly match up to the baker's percentage column on the left. For a more detailed explanation of the issues that arise from baking by volume, see page 27.

QUANTITY IN POOLISH, BIGA, OR LEVAIN: This column shows the amount of flour and water in the poolish, biga, or levain used in the recipe. For the breads in chapter 6, made with pre-ferments, the entire amount of pre-ferment is added to the final dough, and therefore the quantities in this column are the same as those in the poolish and biga ingredients lists, which appear above the baker's percentage table. When making the levain breads in part 3 of the book, you'll only use a portion of your levain culture in the final dough, so the quantities of flour and water in the levain column will be less than the amounts called for in the ingredients lists for feeding the levain—usually far less. The reason for this is you want enough levain left over to keep the culture going.

TOTAL RECIPE QUANTITY: This column lists the total weight of the ingredient in the recipe. If white flour is 90 percent of the 1,000 grams of total flour, then the amount of white flour will be 900 grams. For straight dough breads, the only other column will be the approximate volume measurements for each ingredient.

BAKER'S PERCENTAGE: All ingredient weights are shown as a percentage of the total weight of flour in the recipe. All of the bread and pizza dough recipes in this book use 1,000 grams of flour altogether, making the math easy to follow and the recipes easy to remember. (See pages 41–43 for more information on baker's percentages.)

Final Dough			Baker's Formula		
INGREDIENT	FINAL DOUGH MIX QUANTITY		QUANTITY IN POOLISH	TOTAL RECIPE QUANTITY	BAKER'S PERCENTAGE
White flour	500 g	3¾ cups + 2 tbsp	500 g	1,000 g	100%
Water	250 g, 105°F (41°C)	1⅛ cups	500 g	750 g	75%
Fine sea salt	21 g	1 tbsp + 1 scant tsp	0	21 g	2.1%
Instant dried yeast	3 g	¾ tsp	0.4 g	3.4 g	0.34%
Poolish	1,000 g	All from recipe above			50%

STEP-BY-STEP GUIDE TO BASIC BREAD TECHNIQUES

The recipes throughout this book use the same basic method for all of the stages, from mixing to baking, outlined in the following pages in eight steps. Even the pizza dough recipes in chapter 13 utilize these steps up through the shaping of dough balls. I think it's valuable to review the process steps outside of the recipe format to keep the recipes concise and readable. It encourages a better understanding of the techniques to present them separate from the recipe itself. Since the techniques are the same for all of the recipes, once you get it, you can work with the entire book confidently. I encourage you to sit down and read through this chapter before you begin; it's hard to absorb this information when you are in the middle of making a bread or pizza dough recipe for the first time.

STEP 1: AUTOLYSE THE FLOUR AND WATER

Autolyse is my first step in mixing bread and pizza dough. The flour and water in the recipe are mixed and allowed to rest for a minimum of 15 minutes before the salt and yeast are added. I recommend an autolyse period of 20 to 30 minutes for the recipes in this book. Don't add the salt during the autolyse, as it will inhibit water absorption by the flour, and one of the goals of this step is to allow complete hydration of the flour before mixing the final dough.

Measuring

The autolyse step takes about 5 minutes of hands-on time for measuring the flour and water and mixing them by hand. Place your empty 12-quart dough tub on the scale, zero the scale, then add the weight of flour specified in the recipe's Final Dough Mix column. (Remember, the flour should be at room temperature.)

It's easy to add too much water, so instead of measuring the amount of water directly into the dough tub with the flour in it, I measure it into an empty container, then pour the correct weight of water into the tub with the flour. Also, some scales, like mine, max out on the weight they can measure before all the water has been added to the flour-filled tub. That's another reason to weigh the water separately.

USING YOUR KITCHEN SCALE

Put your empty container on the scale, push the scale's "zero" button (sometimes labeled "tare"), and after the scales zeroes out, carefully pour in the ingredient until you reach the desired weight. When you have multiple ingredients to add to the container, such as two or three different kinds of flour, just press the "zero" button after each addition.

The easiest way to measure out water is to use two containers. Keeping your thermometer handy, put one container under the tap and adjust the hot and cold water mix until the water in the container is at the target temperature, for example, 95°F (35°C). Put the empty container on your scale, zero the scale, and pour in water from the first container until you reach the weight of water called for in the recipe. Be precise with the weighing. Being off by as little as 20 or 30 grams can make a big difference in the consistency of the dough.

Incorporating the Flour and Water

Working directly in the 12-quart dough tub, mix the flour and water with one hand just until incorporated. Your hand will get sticky with dough. Don't worry; you need to get used to using your hand as an implement. Even though dough bits are sticking to you (just like they would stick to a dough hook), keep mixing until the flour and water are integrated. Any dough clumps should be pinched through with your hand. After mixing, use your free hand to squeegee the dough that's stuck to your working hand into the tub. Put a lid on the container and let the dough rest for 20 to 30 minutes. You will know the autolyse mixture is ready when there are no longer any loose bits of dry flour visible in the dough tub.

Working with Water Temperature

In all of the recipes in this book (except the poolish and biga recipes, for reasons explained below), the goal is for the final mixed dough to have a temperature of about 78°F (26°C). As mentioned in chapter 2, this seems to be the ideal temperature for both gas production and flavor development. The dough doesn't need to stay at 78°F (26°C) throughout its development; it just needs to start there. I tested these recipes in my home kitchen, which is usually around 70°F (21°C). Using water at 95°F (35°C), flour at room temperature, and a 20-minute autolyse period, once the dough was completely mixed, it was usually right at 78°F (26°C) during winter. In the summer, I ratchet the water temperature down to 90°F (32°C) to get the same result. All this is to say there's a relationship between the temperature of the water

WHEN NOT TO AUTOLYSE

In this book, the only recipes that don't have an autolyse step are those made with poolish or biga, where half or more of the recipe's total flour is in the pre-ferment. These doughs obtain benefits similar to those produced in the autolyse due to the long, overnight development of the pre-ferment, which includes only a bit of yeast and no salt. Autolysing dough made with poolish is also impractical. For this book's recipes that incorporate a poolish, the additional ingredients for the final dough mix include only 250 grams of water but another 500 grams of flour, which would result in dough clumps that are impossible to work out manually.

you use for the autolyse, the temperature of your kitchen, and the length of time you let the autolyse mixture rest before mixing the final dough.

Although I recommend a 20- to 30-minute autolyse, you can extend it to 40 or even 60 minutes if that's more convenient for you. However, the autolyse mixture will cool down more, so your final mix temperature will be lower and you may need to adjust your water temperature to compensate. Just don't use water above 110°F (43°C). (As you may recall, temperatures much warmer than that can kill the yeast.) If you miss the target final mix temperature of 78°F (26°C), review the temperature of water you used and the timing of the autolyse period, then adjust next time.

Recipes from this book that use a pre-ferment (a poolish or biga) will rarely have a final mix temperature of 78°F (26°C), especially if your house is cool at night. This is because a large proportion of the dough consists of the pre-ferment, which has developed overnight and will therefore be at room temperature—whatever the overnight temperature of your house is. The overnight temperature in my house is about 65°F (18°C), and while I was testing these recipes, the final mix temperature for doughs made with pre-ferments was usually 73°F to 74°F (about 23°C).

WHEN TO HYDRATE THE YEAST

Granular dried yeast takes longer to dissolve in stiffer doughs (in my world, that would be a hydration of 70 percent or less). Store-bought instant yeast is designed to work without being dissolved first, but that's based on the assumption that the dough will be mixed by a machine, which incorporates the ingredients far more aggressively than hand mixing does. We don't hydrate, or proof, instant yeast at my bakery, but that's because we typically use fresh yeast in our stiff doughs.

The first time I hand mixed an overnight biga (at 68 percent hydration) with instant yeast while testing a recipe in this book, I was surprised by the lack of gassiness and rise in the biga the next morning. On my next try, I kept the same mix proportions and water temperature but hydrated the instant yeast for a few minutes first, and—voilà!—my biga looked like a biga in the morning. I did a little research, and one major yeast manufacturer acknowledged that hydrating instant yeast before mixing allows for maximum efficiency of the yeast, even though it's designed for use without proofing. So, based on all of this, I've arrived at recommending the old-school method of proofing instant yeast for this book's stiffer doughs. In these few cases, the recipe specifies proofing the yeast in advance.

All of that said, the majority of the doughs in this book have enough water in them that is isn't necessary to proof instant dried yeast. Even with hand mixing, the high hydration ensures that the yeast granules dissolve completely and become active early in the dough's evolution. The exceptions are for biga (at 68 percent hydration) and pizza doughs (at 70 percent hydration).

STEP 2: MIX THE DOUGH

Hand mixing the final dough should take about 5 minutes. I prefer to mix it by hand in the dough tub, rather than kneading it on the counter or using a mixer. It's simpler, faster, and entails less cleanup, and it's fully effective. The dough stays in the same tub from the autolyse step until it is divided and shaped into loaves about five or six hours later, depending on the recipe. No fuss, no muss!

Incorporating the Salt and Yeast

To mix the dough, first sprinkle the salt and (in most cases) the yeast evenly over the top of the dough. If making a recipe with a pre-ferment, empty the entire amount of poolish or biga, or the specified quantity of levain, into the dough tub on top of the salt and yeast.

Set up a container of warm water next to your dough station. Hold the dough tub by the rim with your weaker hand and wet your stronger hand in the warm water. Begin to mix by reaching underneath the dough and grabbing about one-quarter of the dough. Stretch this section of dough, then fold it over the top to the other side of the dough. When folding

Incorporating the salt and yeast.

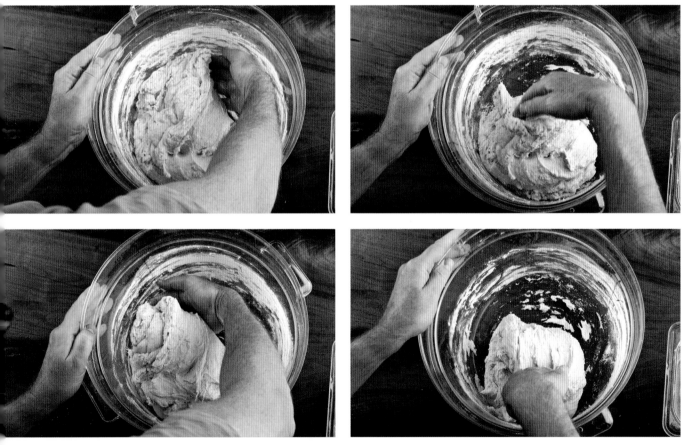

segments of dough, stretch them out to the point of resistance, then fold them back across the entire length of the dough mass. Working your way around the dough, repeat with the remaining quarters of the dough, reaching underneath each time and fully enclosing the salt and yeast inside the folds of dough.

Using the Pincer Method

Once all of the dough has been folded over itself, continue mixing using the pincer method. Using a pincerlike grip with your thumb and forefinger, squeeze big chunks of dough and then tighten your grip to cut through the dough. Do this repeatedly, working through the entire mass of dough. With your other hand, turn the tub while you're mixing to give your active hand a good angle of attack.

Dip your mixing hand back into the container of warm water three or four times throughout this process to rewet it and prevent the dough from sticking to you. If you don't, the dough will be sticky and hard to work. It is normal to feel the granularity of the salt and yeast as you mix; using a moist hand for mixing will help the salt and yeast dissolve.

Cut through the dough five or six times with the pincer method, then fold it over itself a few times, then once again cut through it five or six times and fold over itself a few more times. Repeat this process, alternating between cutting and folding, until you feel and see that all of the ingredients are fully integrated and the dough has some tension in it. For me, this takes 2 or 3 minutes. When you're new at this, it could take 5 or 6 minutes. Let the dough rest for a few minutes, then fold for another 30 seconds or until the dough tightens up. That's it for mixing!

The goal of this step is to thoroughly incorporate all of the ingredients. The pincer method, which I learned at the San Francisco Baking Institute, mimics the dough-cutting action of good mechanical mixers. It effectively incorporates the ingredients and distributes the salt and yeast throughout the mix.

At the end of the mix, measure the temperature of the dough with a probe thermometer. In most of the recipes in this book, the target temperature is 77°F to 78°F (25°C to 26°C). Write down the final mix temperature and the time. If the dough temperature is well below 77°F (25°C), it will take longer to rise, in which case you'll need to follow the recipe instructions regarding how much the dough should expand, rather than the suggested time. Alternatively,

Using the pincer method.

you can compensate by placing the dough tub in a warm spot for the rise—75°F to 80°F (24°C to 27°C) should work.

As mentioned in chapter 2, I recommend keeping a log that records water temperature you used, the time the mix ended and the room temperature, how long it took for the dough to double or triple in volume, at what time you divided and shaped the dough into loaves, and what time you baked it, with some comments on how it all came out. You may make adjustments that better suit your schedule for future mixes—a little more yeast if the dough wasn't ready in five or six hours, or a little less yeast if the dough moved too fast. Use warmer or cooler water next time if your mix temperature was below or well above 78°F (26°C).

Letting the Dough Rise

Cover the tub and let the dough rise. The amount of time this takes depends on many factors, especially the ambient temperature and the final mix temperature. Regard the visual cues in the recipe as your target, keeping in mind that your dough will have a little more volume in warmer months and a little less volume in cooler months.

STEP 3: FOLD THE DOUGH

Folding the dough helps develop the gluten that gives the dough its strength and contributes to good volume in the final loaf. Think of the three-dimensional web of gluten as the frame of the bread "house." For the first recipe, the Saturday White Bread, just two folds are needed. Most of the other bread doughs have higher hydration, and many of these slack doughs benefit from three or four folds to give them the strength they need. Each fold takes about 1 minute. You'll be able to recognize when to apply the next fold based on how relaxed the dough has become: it goes from being a ball with structure to lying flattened out in the tub. With each fold, it firms up a bit. I try to work in all the folds during the first hour or two of the rise.

The action here is just like the folding during mixing in step 2, but after folding, you'll invert the dough to help it hold its tension. For step-by-step photos illustrating the folding process, see page 70. To fold the dough, dip your active hand in the container of warm water to wet it so the dough doesn't stick to you. With your moistened hand, reach underneath the dough and pull about one-quarter of it out and up to stretch it until you feel resistance, then fold it over the top to the other side of the dough. Repeat four or five times, working around the dough until the dough has tightened into a ball. Grab the entire ball and invert it so the seam side, where all of the folds have come together, faces down. This helps the folds hold their position. The top should be smooth.

When the dough relaxes a bit and flattens in the bottom of the tub, repeat the process for the second fold. After each fold, the dough develops more structure, or strength, than it had before and will therefore take longer to completely relax. You can do any subsequent folds called for in the recipe an hour or two later, or you can give the dough all of its folds in the first hour after mixing—whatever is convenient for you. Just don't fold the dough during the last hour of bulk fermentation.

STEP 4: DIVIDE THE DOUGH

When the dough has doubled or tripled (whichever is specified in the recipe), it's time to divide it. One of the reasons clear Cambro tubs are so handy for bread making is that they allow you to quickly determine when bulk fermentation is complete. For example, if a dough should triple in size during bulk fermentation and it starts out at a little more than 1 quart, it should come up to nearly the 4-quart line once tripled. This step will take just a few minutes once you've done it a couple times. At first it may take a little longer.

Lightly flour a work surface; you'll need an area about 2 feet wide. Working next to the floured area, flour your hands and gently loosen the dough all the way around the perimeter of the tub, taking care not to let the gluten strands tear. (At this point the gluten is more delicate than it was when the dough was first mixed.) Then reach to the bottom of the tub and gently loosen the bottom of the dough from the tub. It's helpful to toss some flour along the edges to work underneath the dough and help ease its release. Then turn the tub on its side and use your hands to help gently ease the dough out onto the work surface. Sprinkle flour across the middle of the top of the dough, where you'll cut it, then divide it into two equal-size pieces with a dough knife, plastic dough scraper, or kitchen knife.

STEP 5: SHAPE THE LOAVES

The goal of shaping is to form each piece of dough into a medium-tight round while taking care to preserve the gas that has built up in the dough.

Be aware that when your dough pieces are sitting on the floured work surface, the underside of the dough will become the outside of the loaf; this will help you understand the shaping process. The bottom of each piece of dough is sitting on some flour, so it's not going to be as sticky there. Keeping your hands in contact with that part of the dough is the most important advice I can offer; otherwise the dough will stick to your hands.

Begin by brushing any loose flour off the top of the dough with your hand. Then, using the same technique as in the folding step, stretch and fold one-quarter of the dough at a

This page: Dividing the dough. Opposite page, first and second rows: Folding the relaxed dough. Third row: Dough ready for its first fold, after its first fold, ready for its second fold. Fourth row: Dough after its second fold, ready for its third fold, after its third fold.

time up and over the top to form a round, gently pulling each segment out until you get to its maximum stretch, then folding it over the top to the opposite side. Repeat, working your way around the dough and forming it into a ball, until the interior is fully enclosed and you have a round with a little tension in it. Then flip it over so the seam is on the work surface in an area cleared of flour—at this point you want the friction, or grip, of a clean surface. You are now looking at the smooth surface of the loaf, which will face up in the proofing basket and down while the loaf is baking.

Cup your hands around the back of the dough ball as you face it. Pull the entire dough ball 6 or 8 inches toward you on the dry, unfloured surface, leading with your pinky fingers and applying enough pressure so the dough ball grips your work surface and doesn't just slide across it. As you pull, this will tighten up the ball and add tension to it. You can feel it. It feels good.

Give the loaf a quarter turn and repeat this tightening step. Proceed in this way until you've gone all the way around the dough ball two or three times. The loaf doesn't need to be super tight, but you don't want it to be loose, either. I am looking for enough tension so that the loaf holds its shape and its gases. If the shaped loaves are too soft, without enough tension, there's less physical structure to hold on to the gases. Some gas will escape, resulting in bread that's smaller and a bit heavier than the ideal.

Repeat the shaping process with the second piece of dough and place both shaped loaves seam side down in a proofing container: a flour-dusted wicker proofing basket, a flour-dusted cloth-covered *banneton*, or, in a pinch, large kitchen bowls lined with lint-free tea towels and generously dusted with flour. You need to use enough flour so that the fully proofed loaf can be removed without sticking but not so much that you end up with a lot of excess flour on the loaf.

Lightly flour the top of the shaped loaves and cover with a kitchen towel or put the proofing baskets in nonperforated plastic bags.

STEP 6: PROOF THE SHAPED LOAVES

In the baking industry, the term *proofing* is commonly used to refer to the final rise, after the loaf is shaped. (It is also used to refer to hydrating yeast before the dough mix; see page 66.) To achieve the full potential of your loaves, you need to proof them completely. The loaves must reach their physical limit for holding on to their gases before the gluten network begins to break down as the proteins degrade over time. Bake too soon, and you lose the last smidgen of flavor and volume development the bread was capable of, and the loaves will be too tight and will bloom unevenly. Bake too late (overproof) and the loaves will deflate, collapsing and losing volume. (Me and Goldilocks would have been friends.) The timeline for proofing varies by recipe in this book, from a little over one hour for the Saturday Breads to overnight in the refrigerator for most of the levain recipes and the Overnight 40% Whole Wheat Bread.

Opposite page: Shaping the loaves. First row: Stretching a segment of dough and folding it over itself. Second row: Stretching a second segment of dough and folding it over itself. Third row: Folding the final segment of dough over itself. Fourth row: Cupping hands around the back of the dough ball and pulling it across the unfloured work surface; a finished dough ball.

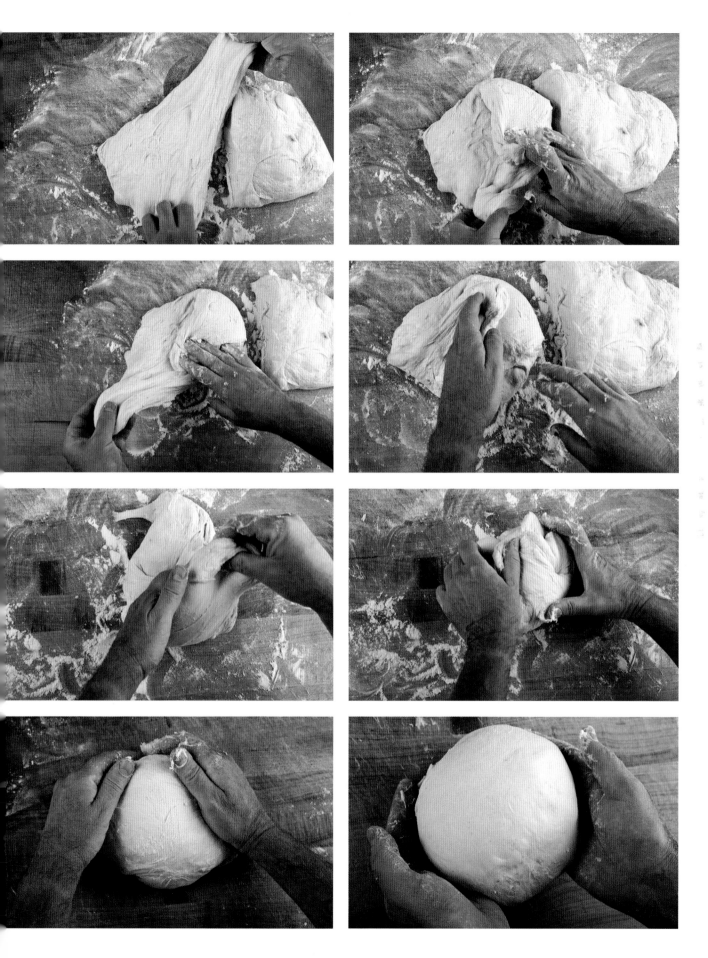

Also keep in mind that a more tightly shaped loaf will hold its proof longer, whereas a loosely shaped loaf will lose its gases more quickly.

One mark of a seasoned baker is the ability to bake the bread at that perfect point of the proof every time, and it remains a frequent topic of conversation at my bakery. It's true not just for breads, but for croissants and brioche, too. We learn by doing, and sometimes the best way to learn is to be willing to have a loaf that's a bit overproofed. This will help you understand what the limits are.

The Finger-Dent Test

In each recipe I mention the finger-dent test for proofing. It remains the most foolproof method I know. To do the test, poke the rising loaf with a floured finger, making an indentation about ½ inch deep. If it springs back immediately, the loaf needs more proofing time. If the indentation springs back slowly and incompletely, the loaf is fully proofed and ready to bake. If the indentation doesn't spring back at all, the loaf is overproofed. You've waited too long, and the loaf may collapse a bit when you remove it from its basket or put it into the Dutch oven for baking. (Still, occasionally I'm surprised to find that a loaf I thought overproofed holds its form and bakes up just fine.)

The straight doughs made with store-bought yeast, in chapter 5, rise faster than levain breads and also have a shorter window of time for being at the perfectly proofed stage— sometimes as short as 10 to 15 minutes. This is when you need to put the loaves in the oven. You can extend that window by proofing these breads overnight in the refrigerator. The cold dough will develop more slowly, giving you a window of ideal proofing up to a couple of hours.

STEP 7: PREHEAT THE OVEN AND DUTCH OVEN

Position a rack in the middle of the oven. If you bake too close to the bottom of the oven, you run the risk of scorching the bottom of the loaves. Put your 4-quart Dutch oven inside with the lid on. There is no need to place the Dutch oven on a pizza stone; the cast-iron mass serves a similar purpose. Preheat the oven to 475°F (245°C) for at least 45 minutes. The goal is for the Dutch oven to be fully saturated with oven heat before you place the loaf inside.

It's important to know your oven. Most home ovens run hotter or cooler than the temperature you set them to. Mine runs about 25°F cooler, so when I set it to 500°F I actually get 475°F. The temperatures given in the recipe are, of course, the actual temperature the bread should be baked at, so I recommend that you use an oven thermometer. They only cost a few dollars, and using one will assure you that you're baking at the proper temperature, allowing you to follow the suggested baking times with confidence.

If you have two Dutch ovens and can fit both of them in the oven at the same time, preheat both of them. If you only have one Dutch oven, each recipe offers specific instructions on how to store the second loaf while the first one bakes. Generally speaking, if your loaves proof at room temperature, you should put the second loaf in the refrigerator somewhere around 15 to 20 minutes before baking the first loaf. If your loaves proof in the refrigerator overnight, keep the second loaf in the refrigerator while the first loaf is baking. Once the first loaf comes out of the oven, reheat the Dutch oven for about 5 minutes before baking the second loaf.

STEP 8: BAKE—VERY CAREFULLY

All of the breads in this book bake in covered preheated Dutch ovens for 30 minutes at 475°F (245°C), then the lid is removed while the bread finishes baking, usually 15 to 20 minutes longer. Each recipe specifies baking times.

When working with Dutch ovens, I heartily recommend using oven mitts rather than kitchen towels or pot holders. Oven mitts go partway up your forearms, providing greater protection from the high heat of the Dutch oven and its lid. I act with greater confidence when wearing oven mitts and encourage you to wear them. Once a Dutch oven is out of the oven, I find it helpful to put the mitts on the hot lid handle so I won't absentmindedly pick it up without first putting a mitt back on. Take every precaution.

To transfer the dough from the proofing basket to the Dutch oven, first carefully invert the proofed loaf from its basket onto a floured countertop, keeping in mind that the top of the baked loaf will be the side that was facing down while it was rising. If the dough sticks to the edges of the proofing basket, use one hand to delicately release the dough—and make a mental note that you need to dust the basket with a bit more flour the next time. Ideally, the weight of the dough should cause it to ease onto the countertop without any assistance. New wicker baskets need a little more flour than seasoned baskets, and they do not need to be cleaned between uses.

Experienced bakers may notice that I don't call for scoring the loaves with a razor before baking. Because the loaves are baked with the seam side up (the side opposite the smooth top of the shaped loaf in the proofing basket) and after a complete proof, fissures will naturally open on the top of the loaf as it expands in the oven. I love the organic look of the natural splits. It's the way ciabatta opens up in the oven at my bakery.

Next, very carefully place the loaf in the hot Dutch oven. It's already resting on the counter right side up, so just carefully drop it into the Dutch oven without flipping it over. Use the sides of your bare hands to pick up the loaf and place it in the pot. Don't pick it up with your fingertips; it's delicate at this stage and it's best to spread the pressure needed to pick it up across the dough. Use mitts to put the lid on the Dutch oven and place it in the preheated oven.

When you remove the lid after 30 minutes of baking, the loaf will be fully risen and you should see one or more attractive splits in the top where the dough expanded. The crust should have a light brown color. Use the time in the recipe as a guideline for how long to bake the loaf uncovered, but be sure to check about 5 minutes before the time has elapsed so you're in tune with the loaf's progress. Bake until dark brown all around the loaf. I like to bake until there are spots of very dark brown for the full flavors those bits of crust have. At least once, you should try baking a loaf just shy of the point of burning it—I'm wowed by the way these dark loaves look and taste.

When the bread is fully baked, remove the Dutch oven from your kitchen oven and tilt it to turn the loaf out. Let it cool on a rack or set on its side so air can circulate around it. Let the loaf rest for at least 20 minutes before slicing. The inside of the loaf continues to bake after it's removed from the oven, and it needs that time to finish. Enjoy the crackling sound of the cooling bread.

MAKING PIZZA OR FOCACCIA WITH HALF THE DOUGH

If you don't want to make two loaves of bread, some of the doughs can be used to make pizza or focaccia, as noted after the yield. I actually believe that any dough, even rye, can be used for focaccia, but in the recipes, I only call out the doughs most conventionally suited for this use. For pizza, divide the remaining dough into 340-gram balls and follow any of the pizza recipes in chapter 14. For focaccia, you'll find guidelines on amounts of dough and preparation methods in the section "Making Focaccia with Bread Dough" (page 215). Shape the dough into balls and let them rest in the refrigerator for several hours or up to a couple of days.

STORING BAKED BREAD

I got over my aversion to storing bread in plastic bags many years ago, after trying all the alternatives and realizing nothing else keeps the bread as well. The crust will soften, but the bread won't dry out. The straight dough breads will keep for two or three days. The breads made with pre-ferments will keep a day longer than that, and the levain breads from this book will keep for five to six days, if you don't eat it all before then!

CHAPTER 5
STRAIGHT DOUGHS

THE SATURDAY WHITE BREAD 81

THE SATURDAY 75% WHOLE WHEAT BREAD 85

OVERNIGHT WHITE BREAD 89

OVERNIGHT 40% WHOLE WHEAT BREAD 93

From left: Field Blend #2 (page 158), The Saturday White
Bread (page 81), Bran-Encrusted Levain Bread (page 147).

THE SATURDAY WHITE BREAD

This recipe is designed for someone who wants to make good, crusty loaves of white bread from start to finish in one day. Mix the dough first thing in the morning, shape it into two loaves about five hours later, and then bake in the late afternoon in time for dinner. It's also a good first recipe to try from this book to help you get familiar with my dough handling techniques, which are the same for all the recipes in this book. Here you get the taste-good benefits of a medium-length fermentation, resulting in a versatile, delicious bread that's great as a dinner bread and also works well for sandwiches and toast.

Sometimes I like to make this bread with 10 percent whole wheat flour for the round, earthy flavors it adds. If you want to do that, simply make this recipe with 900 grams of white flour and 100 grams of whole wheat flour.

You can bake one or two loaves from this recipe. If you bake just one loaf, you can divide the remaining dough into two or three dough balls to make iron-skillet focaccia or pizza; refrigerate the dough balls and use them any time during the next two or three days. I love focaccia with olive oil, salt, pepper, and maybe a sprinkling of herbs, cut into small pieces to share with friends before dinner, or just for snacks. (See chapter 14 for specific focaccia and pizza recipes, and page 215 for pointers on using bread doughs for focaccia.)

THIS RECIPE MAKES 2 LOAVES, EACH ABOUT 1½ POUNDS, AND IS SUITABLE FOR PIZZA OR FOCACCIA.

BULK FERMENTATION: About 5 hours

PROOF TIME: About 1¼ hours

SAMPLE SCHEDULE: Begin at 9:30 a.m., finish mixing at 10 a.m., shape into loaves at 3 p.m., and bake at 4:15 p.m.
    The bread will come out of the oven just after 5 p.m.

INGREDIENT	QUANTITY		BAKER'S PERCENTAGE
White flour	1,000 g	7¾ cups	100%
Water	720 g, 90°F to 95°F (32°C to 35°C)	3⅛ cups	72%
Fine sea salt	21 g	1 tbsp + 1 scant tsp	2.1%
Instant dried yeast	4 g	1 tsp	0.4%

CONTINUED>>

The "Ingredients" section in chapter 3 gives advice on what type of flour to use. I don't recommend high-protein bread flour (sometimes called high-gluten flour). All-purpose flour is ideal for the recipes in this book. Flour should always be at room temperature.

If this is your first time making a recipe from this book, please review chapter 4, Basic Bread Method, for a detailed discussion of techniques for mixing and folding dough, shaping loaves, and baking.

1. Autolyse Combine the 1,000 grams of flour with the 720 grams of 90°F to 95°F (32°C to 35°C) water in a 12-quart round tub or similar container. Mix by hand just until incorporated. Cover and let rest for 20 to 30 minutes.

2. Mix Sprinkle the 21 grams of salt and the 4 grams (1 level teaspoon) of yeast evenly over the top of the dough. Mix by hand, wetting your working hand before mixing so the dough doesn't stick to you. (It's fine to rewet your hand three or four times while you mix.) Reach underneath the dough and grab about one-quarter of it. Gently stretch this section of dough and fold it over the top to the other side of the dough. Repeat three more times with the remaining dough, until the salt and yeast are fully enclosed.

Use the pincer method to fully integrate the ingredients. Make five or six pincer cuts across the entire mass of dough. Then fold the dough over itself a few times. Repeat, alternately cutting and folding until all of the ingredients are fully integrated and the dough has some tension in it. Let the dough rest for a

few minutes, then fold for another 30 seconds or until the dough tightens up. The whole process should take about 5 minutes. The target dough temperature at the end of the mix is 77°F to 78°F (25°C to 26°C). Cover the tub and let the dough rise.

3. Fold This dough needs two folds (see pages 69–70 for instructions). It's easiest to apply the folds during the first 1½ hours after mixing the dough. Apply the first fold about 10 minutes after mixing and the second fold during the next hour (when you see the dough spread out in the tub, it's ready for the second fold). If need be, it's okay to fold later; just be sure to leave it alone for the last hour of rising.

When the dough is triple its original volume, about 5 hours after mixing, it's ready to be divided.

4. Divide Moderately flour a work surface about 2 feet wide. Flour your hands and sprinkle a bit of flour around the edges of the tub. Tip the tub slightly and gently work your floured free hand beneath the dough to loosen it from the bottom of the tub. Gently ease the dough out onto the work surface without pulling or tearing it.

With floured hands, pick up the dough and ease it back down onto the work surface in a somewhat even shape. Dust the area in the middle, where you'll cut the dough, with a bit of flour. Cut the dough into 2 equal-size pieces with a dough knife or plastic dough scraper.

5. Shape Dust 2 proofing baskets with flour. Shape each piece of dough into a

KNOW YOUR OVEN

I recommend using an oven thermometer to confirm that when you set your oven to 475°F, you actually get 475°F. Some ovens run hotter than their setting, and some run cooler. (Mine runs 25°F cooler, so when I want to heat it to 475°F, I set it to 500°F.)

WHAT IF THE DOUGH ISN'T AT THE TARGET TEMPERATURE?

If the final mix temperature is cooler, don't worry, it will just take longer to fully rise (in this case tripling in size). If you have a warm spot where the dough can rise, that will help make up for the cooler dough temperature. If your dough is warmer, the dough will triple in size sooner. (The next time you make the recipe, you can adjust the final mix temperature by using warmer or cooler water.)

medium-tight ball following the instructions on pages 71–73. Place each seam side down in its proofing basket.

6. Proof Lightly flour the tops of the loaves. Set them side by side and cover with a kitchen towel, or place each basket in a nonperforated plastic bag.

Plan on baking the loaves about 1¼ hours after they are shaped, assuming a room temperature of about 70°F (21°C). If your kitchen is warmer, they will be optimally proofed in about 1 hour. Use the finger-dent test (see page 74) to determine when they are perfectly proofed and ready to bake, being sure to check the loaves after 1 hour. With this bread, 15 minutes can make the difference between being perfectly proofed and collapsing a bit.

7. Preheat At least 45 minutes prior to baking, put a rack in the middle of the oven and put 2 Dutch ovens on the rack with their lids on. Preheat the oven to 475°F (245°C).

If you only have 1 Dutch oven, put the second loaf into the refrigerator about 20 minutes before baking the first loaf and bake the loaves sequentially, giving the Dutch oven a 5-minute reheat after removing the first loaf. Alternatively, you can keep the second loaf in the refrigerator overnight, in its proofing basket inside a nonperforated plastic bag, and bake it early the next morning; if you do this, put the second loaf in the refrigerator immediately after shaping.

CONTINUED>>

8. Bake For the next step, please be careful not to let your hands, fingers, or forearms touch the extremely hot Dutch oven.

Invert the proofed loaf onto a lightly floured countertop, keeping in mind that the top of the loaf will be the side that was facing down while it was rising—the seam side. Use oven mitts to remove the preheated Dutch oven from the oven. Remove the lid. Carefully place the loaf in the hot Dutch oven seam side up. Use mitts to replace the lid, then put the Dutch oven in the oven. Maintain the temperature at 475°F (245°C).

Bake for 30 minutes, then carefully remove the lid and bake for about 20 more minutes, until at least medium dark brown all around the loaf. Check after 15 minutes of baking uncovered in case your oven runs hot.

Remove the Dutch oven and carefully tilt it to turn the loaf out. Let cool on a rack or set the loaf on its side so air can circulate around it. Let the loaf rest for at least 20 minutes before slicing.

THE SATURDAY 75% WHOLE WHEAT BREAD

If you want an easy and tasty high-fiber bread that you can make in one day, this is the recipe for you. If you want to work with this schedule and adjust to use your own blend of flours, take a look at the essay "Making a Bread (or Pizza) Dough You Can Call Your Own," starting on page 190. The process and timeline for this bread is the same as the Saturday White Bread (page 81), but there's more water in this dough because whole wheat flour is more absorbent than all-white flour, a little less yeast because whole wheat encourages a more active fermentation than all-white flour, and a fraction more salt for taste.

This bread has much more whole wheat in it than most loaves labeled "whole wheat" at the store. It will also be more pure, having just flour, water, salt, and yeast as ingredients. Happily, even with 75 percent of the flour being whole grain, this recipe makes a loaf with decent volume and a reasonable lightness of texture—don't expect to be baking bricks here! A baker in France might refer to this type of bread as *pain de régime* (*régime* being the French word for "diet") because of its high fiber content. I like it because it tastes great.

THIS RECIPE MAKES 2 LOAVES, EACH ABOUT 1½ POUNDS, AND IS SUITABLE FOR FOCACCIA.

BULK FERMENTATION: About 5 hours

PROOF TIME: About 1¼ hours

SAMPLE SCHEDULE: Begin at 9:30 a.m., finish mixing at 10 a.m., shape into loaves at 3 p.m., and bake at 4:15 p.m. The bread will come out of the oven just after 5 p.m.

INGREDIENT	QUANTITY		BAKER'S PERCENTAGE
Whole wheat flour	750 g	5¾ cups + 1½ tbsp	75%
White flour	250 g	1¾ cups + 3 tbsp	25%
Water	800 g, 90°F to 95°F (32°C to 35°C)	3½ cups	80%
Fine sea salt	22 g	1 tbsp + 1 tsp	2.2%
Instant dried yeast	3 g	¾ tsp	0.3%

CONTINUED>>

1. Autolyse Mix the 750 grams of whole wheat flour and the 250 grams of white flour by hand in a 12-quart round tub or similar container. Add the 800 grams of 90°F to 95°F (32°C to 35°C) water and mix by hand just until incorporated. Cover and let rest for 20 to 30 minutes.

2. Mix Sprinkle the 22 grams of salt and the 3 grams (¾ teaspoon) of yeast evenly over the top of the dough. Mix by hand, wetting your working hand before mixing so the dough doesn't stick to you. (It's fine to rewet your hand three or four times while you mix.) Reach underneath the dough and grab about one-quarter of it. Gently stretch this section of dough and fold it over the top to the other side of the dough. Repeat three more times with the remaining dough, until the salt and yeast are fully enclosed.

Use the pincer method to fully integrate the ingredients. Using your thumb and fore-finger, make five or six pincer cuts across the entire mass of dough. Then fold the dough over itself a few times. Repeat, alternately cutting and folding until all of the ingredients are fully integrated and the dough has some tension in it. Let the dough rest for a few min-utes, then fold for another 30 seconds or until the dough tightens up.

The target dough temperature at the end of the mix is 77°F to 78°F (25°C to 26°C). Cover the tub and let the dough rise.

3. Fold This dough needs three gentle folds (see pages 69–70 for instructions). Whole wheat dough does not stretch as far as white flour dough, so don't be too aggressive with it. It's easiest to apply the folds during the first 1½ hours after mixing the dough. Apply the first fold about 10 minutes after mixing and the remaining folds during the next hour (when you see the dough spread out in the tub, it's ready for the next fold). If need be, it's okay to fold later; just be sure to leave it alone for the last hour of rising.

When the dough is triple its original vol-ume, about 5 hours after mixing, it's ready to be divided.

CONTINUED>>

4. Divide Moderately flour a work surface about 2 feet wide. Flour your hands and sprinkle a bit of flour around the edges of the tub. Tip the tub slightly and gently work your floured free hand beneath the dough to loosen it from the bottom of the tub. Gently ease the dough out onto the work surface without pulling or tearing it.

With floured hands, pick up the dough and ease it back down onto the work surface in a somewhat even shape. Dust the area in the middle, where you'll cut the dough, with a bit of flour. Cut the dough into 2 equal-size pieces with a dough knife or plastic dough scraper.

5. Shape Dust 2 proofing baskets with flour. Shape each piece of dough into a medium-tight ball following the instructions on pages 71–73. Place each seam side down in its proofing basket.

6. Proof Lightly flour the tops of the loaves. Set them side by side and cover with a kitchen towel, or place each basket in a nonperforated plastic bag.

Plan on baking the loaves about 1¼ hours after they are shaped, assuming a room temperature of about 70°F (21°C). If your kitchen is warmer, they will be optimally proofed in about 1 hour. Use the finger-dent test (see page 74) to determine when they are perfectly proofed and ready to bake.

7. Preheat At least 45 minutes prior to baking, put a rack in the middle of the oven and put 2 Dutch ovens on the rack with their lids on. Preheat the oven to 475°F (245°C).

If you only have 1 Dutch oven, put the second loaf into the refrigerator about 20 minutes before baking the first loaf and bake the loaves sequentially, giving the Dutch oven a 5-minute reheat after removing the first loaf. Alternatively, you can keep the second loaf in the refrigerator overnight, in its proofing basket inside a nonperforated plastic bag, and bake it early the next morning; if you do this, put the second loaf in the refrigerator immediately after shaping.

8. Bake For the next step, please be careful not to let your hands, fingers, or forearms touch the extremely hot Dutch oven.

Invert the proofed loaf onto a lightly floured countertop, keeping in mind that the top of the loaf will be the side that was facing down while it was rising—the seam side. Use oven mitts to remove the preheated Dutch oven from the oven. Remove the lid. Carefully place the loaf in the hot Dutch oven seam side up. Use mitts to replace the lid, then put the Dutch oven in the oven. Maintain the temperature at 475°F (245°C).

Bake for 30 minutes, then carefully remove the lid and bake for about 20 more minutes, until at least medium dark brown all around the loaf. Check after 15 minutes of baking uncovered in case your oven runs hot.

Remove the Dutch oven and carefully tilt it to turn the loaf out. Let cool on a rack or set the loaf on its side so air can circulate around it. Let the loaf rest for at least 20 minutes before slicing.

OVERNIGHT WHITE BREAD

This is a great-tasting, crusty white bread with nice big holes. It makes me want to slice a couple of pieces, top them with fresh slices of in-season, ripe tomatoes, cover with good olive oil, and live, for the moment, in happy contentment. For those who have made bread using Jim Lahey's no-knead method, you'll find the timing of this recipe familiar. This is, however, a distinctly different recipe; it calls for water that's about 30°F (17°C) warmer and uses one-third the amount of yeast. This recipe also includes an autolyse period and calls for giving the dough a couple of folds after the mix. The result is two breads with different tastes and textures, and this is a great way to demonstrate that two seemingly similar recipes produce two different breads.

This dough rises overnight, and the extended bulk fermentation gives it more time to develop complexity in its flavors than the two Saturday Breads (pages 81 and 85). The baked loaves should have a nice open interior and a crisp crust—assuming you bake the loaves well beyond the blond stage. This bread has many uses and won't last long.

THIS RECIPE MAKES 2 LOAVES, EACH ABOUT 1½ POUNDS, AND IS SUITABLE FOR FOCACCIA OR IRON-SKILLET PIZZA.

BULK FERMENTATION: 12 to 14 hours

PROOF TIME: About 1¼ hours

SAMPLE SCHEDULE: Mix at 7 p.m., shape into loaves at 8 a.m. the next morning, and bake at 9:15 a.m. The bread will come out of the oven a little after 10 a.m.

INGREDIENT	QUANTITY		BAKER'S PERCENTAGE
White flour	1,000 g	7¾ cups	100%
Water	780 g, 90°F to 95°F (32°C to 35°C)	3⅓ cups	78%
Fine sea salt	22 g	1 tbsp + 1 tsp	2.2%
Instant dried yeast	0.8 g	Scant ¼ tsp	0.08%

CONTINUED>>

1. Autolyse Combine the 1,000 grams of flour with the 780 grams of 90°F to 95°F (32°C to 35°C) water in a 12-quart round tub or similar container. Mix by hand just until incorporated. Cover and let rest for 20 to 30 minutes.

2. Mix Sprinkle the 22 grams of salt and the 0.8 gram (a scant ¼ teaspoon) of yeast evenly over the top of the dough. Mix by hand, wetting your working hand before mixing so the dough doesn't stick to you. (It's fine to rewet your hand three or four times while you mix.) Reach underneath the dough and grab about one-quarter of it. Gently stretch this section of dough and fold it over the top to the other side of the dough. Repeat three more times with the remaining dough, until the salt and yeast are fully enclosed.

Use the pincer method to fully integrate the ingredients. Using your thumb and forefinger, make five or six pincer cuts across the entire mass of dough. Then fold the dough over itself a few times. Repeat, alternately cutting and folding until all of the ingredients are fully integrated and the dough has some tension in it. Let the dough rest for a few minutes, then fold for another 30 seconds or until the dough tightens up. The target dough temperature at the end of the mix is 77°F to 78°F (25°C to 26°C). Cover the tub and let the dough rise.

3. Fold This dough needs two or three folds (see pages 69–70 for instructions). Three would be best for maximum gas retention and volume in the finished loaf, but if you only have time to do two folds it will be fine. It's easiest to apply

the folds during the first 1½ hours after mixing the dough. After doing the last fold, cover the dough and let it continue to rise overnight at room temperature.

When the dough is 2½ to 3 times its original volume, 12 to 14 hours after mixing, it's ready to be divided.

4. Divide Moderately flour a work surface about 2 feet wide. Flour your hands and sprinkle a bit of flour around the edges of the tub. Tip the tub slightly and gently work your floured free hand beneath the dough to loosen it from the bottom of the tub. Gently ease the dough out onto the work surface without pulling or tearing it.

With floured hands, pick up the dough and ease it back down onto the work surface in a somewhat even shape. Dust the area in the middle, where you'll cut the dough, with a bit of flour. Cut the dough into 2 equal-size pieces with a dough knife or plastic dough scraper.

5. Shape Dust 2 proofing baskets with flour. Shape each piece of dough into a medium-tight ball following the instructions on pages 71–73. Place each seam side down in its proofing basket.

6. Proof Lightly flour the tops of the loaves. Set them side by side and cover with a kitchen towel, or place each basket in a nonperforated plastic bag.

Plan on baking the loaves about 1¼ hours after they are shaped, assuming a room temperature of about 70°F (21°C). If your kitchen is warmer, they will be optimally proofed in about 1 hour. Use the finger-dent test (see page 74) to determine when they are perfectly proofed and ready to bake, being sure to check the loaves after 1 hour. With this bread, 15 minutes can make a difference between being perfectly proofed and collapsing a bit.

7. Preheat At least 45 minutes prior to baking, put a rack in the middle of the oven and put 2 Dutch ovens on the rack with their lids on. Preheat the oven to 475°F (245°C).

If you only have 1 Dutch oven, put the second loaf into the refrigerator about 20 minutes before baking the first loaf and bake the loaves sequentially, giving the Dutch oven a 5-minute reheat after removing the first loaf.

8. Bake For the next step, please be careful not to let your hands, fingers, or forearms touch the extremely hot Dutch oven.

Invert the proofed loaf onto a lightly floured countertop, keeping in mind that the top of the loaf will be the side that was facing down while it was rising—the seam side. Use oven mitts to remove the preheated Dutch oven from the oven. Remove the lid. Carefully place the loaf in the hot Dutch oven seam side up. Use mitts to replace the lid, then put the Dutch oven in the oven. Maintain the temperature at 475°F (245°C).

Bake for 30 minutes, then carefully remove the lid and bake for 20 to 30 minutes, until at least medium dark brown all around the loaf. Check after 15 minutes of baking uncovered in case your oven runs hot.

Remove the Dutch oven and carefully tilt it to turn the loaf out. Let cool on a rack or set the loaf on its side so air can circulate around it. Let the loaf rest for at least 20 minutes before slicing.

VARIATION: WEEKNIGHT WHITE BREAD

It's possible to adjust the timing of the Overnight White Bread recipe so it will work for somebody with a day job during the workweek. Follow the recipe for Overnight White Bread through step 3. Then, in the morning before going to work, take 5 to 10 minutes to divide and shape loaves from the dough you mixed the evening before. Put the proofing baskets in plastic bags and let the loaves proof slowly in the refrigerator while you are at work.

When you get home from work, remove the loaves from the refrigerator and let them sit out on the counter to finish proofing while you preheat the Dutch ovens. If you get home at 6 p.m., you will have fresh baked bread by 7:30 p.m. Note that in this variation, the bulk fermentation time is 12 to 14 hours, and the proof time is about 10 hours (depending on when you get home from work).

OVERNIGHT 40% WHOLE WHEAT BREAD

My preferred ratio of whole wheat flour to white flour in a brown bread is 30 to 40 percent whole wheat. Sometimes I bake a 75 percent whole wheat bread for the extra fiber, but from a purely gastronomic point of view, using just 30 to 40 percent gives the flavor and texture I like best. With this ratio, the final bread has good volume and a light, open texture, along with the nuttiness and depth of flavor whole wheat provides.

In this recipe, the shaped loaves spend the night in the refrigerator rising very slowly; this allows the dough to develop more of the complexity of flavors that come from an extended, slow rise. We use this technique for much of the bread we bake at Ken's Artisan Bakery, especially our levain breads, but it works for straight doughs too, as here. The schedule in this recipe makes it possible for you to bake the bread early the next morning. Baking this bread is a very nice way to begin the day, perhaps on a Sunday morning, filling the air with baking aromas (unless you live in Eugene).

I like this bread for pretty much any use: for sandwiches, as croutons, grilled, toasted, or just as table bread. Or try using stale pieces of this bread for savory bread pudding or *panzanella*.

You can use this recipe schedule and yeast quantity as a starting point for variations using different blends of flours. If you decide to experiment with the ratio of whole wheat to white flour, keep in mind that the more whole grain flour you use, the more water you'll need to achieve the same dough consistency.

THIS RECIPE MAKES 2 LOAVES, EACH ABOUT 1½ POUNDS, AND IS SUITABLE FOR FOCACCIA.

BULK FERMENTATION: About 5 hours

PROOF TIME: 12 to 14 hours

SAMPLE SCHEDULE: Mix at 1 p.m., shape into loaves at 6 p.m., proof in the refrigerator overnight, and bake at 8 a.m. the next morning. The bread will come out of the oven a little after 8:45 a.m.

INGREDIENT	QUANTITY		BAKER'S PERCENTAGE
White flour	600 g	4⅔ cups	60%
Whole wheat flour	400 g	3 cups + 2 tbsp	40%
Water	800 g, 90°F to 95°F (32°C to 35°C)	3½ cups	80%
Fine sea salt	22 g	1 tbsp + 1 tsp	2.2%
Instant dried yeast	3 g	¾ tsp	0.3%

CONTINUED>>

1. Autolyse Mix the 600 grams of white flour and the 400 grams of whole wheat flour by hand in a 12-quart round tub or similar container. Add the 800 grams of 90°F to 95°F (32°C to 35°C) water and mix by hand just until incorporated. Cover and let rest for 20 to 30 minutes.

2. Mix Sprinkle the 22 grams of salt and the 3 grams (¾ teaspoon) of yeast evenly over the top of the dough. Mix by hand, wetting your working hand before mixing so the dough doesn't stick to you. (It's fine to rewet your hand three or four times while you mix.) Reach underneath the dough and grab about one-quarter of it. Gently stretch this section of dough and fold it over the top to the other side of the dough. Repeat three more times with the remaining dough, until the salt and yeast are fully enclosed.

Use the pincer method to fully integrate the ingredients. Using your thumb and forefinger, make five or six pincer cuts across the entire mass of dough. Then fold the dough over itself a few times. Repeat, alternately cutting and folding until all of the ingredients are fully integrated and the dough has some tension in it. Let the dough rest for a few minutes, then fold for another 30 seconds or until the dough tightens up. The target dough temperature at the end of the mix is 77°F to 78°F (25°C to 26°C). Cover the tub and let the dough rise.

3. Fold This dough needs three or four folds (see pages 69–70 for instructions). I recommend doing all of the folds in the first 2 hours after mixing the dough.

When the dough is triple its original volume, about 5 hours after mixing, it's ready to be divided.

4. Divide Moderately flour a work surface about 2 feet wide. Flour your hands and sprinkle a bit of flour around the edges of the tub. Tip the tub slightly and gently work your floured free hand beneath the dough to loosen it from the bottom of the tub. Gently ease the dough out onto the work surface without pulling or tearing it.

With floured hands, pick up the dough and ease it back down onto the work surface in a somewhat even shape. Dust the area in the middle, where you'll cut the dough, with a bit of flour. Cut the dough into 2 equal-size pieces with a dough knife or plastic dough scraper.

5. Shape Dust 2 proofing baskets with flour. Shape each piece of dough into a medium-tight ball following the instructions on pages 71–73. Place each seam side down in its proofing basket.

6. Proof Place each basket in a nonperforated plastic bag and refrigerate overnight.

The next morning, 12 to 14 hours after the loaves went into the refrigerator, they should be expanded but not overflowing their proofing baskets. There should be about a 2-hour window when the cold loaves, still in the refrigerator, are optimally proofed. They can go straight from the refrigerator into the oven. There is no need for or benefit in allowing them to come to room temperature first.

7. Preheat At least 45 minutes prior to baking, put a rack in the middle of the oven and put 2 Dutch ovens on the rack with their lids on. Preheat the oven to 475°F (245°C). The bread can go into the oven right out of the refrigerator. There is no need for it to warm up first.

If you only have 1 Dutch oven, put the second loaf into the refrigerator about 20 minutes before baking the first loaf and bake the loaves sequentially, giving the Dutch oven a 5-minute reheat after removing the first loaf.

8. Bake For the next step, please be careful not to let your hands, fingers, or forearms touch the extremely hot Dutch oven.

Invert the proofed loaf onto a lightly floured countertop, keeping in mind that the top of the loaf will be the side that was facing down while it was rising—the seam side. Use oven mitts to remove the preheated Dutch oven from the oven. Remove the lid. Carefully place the loaf in the hot Dutch oven seam side up. Use mitts to replace the lid, then put the Dutch oven in the oven. Maintain the temperature at 475°F (245°C).

Bake for 30 minutes, then carefully remove the lid and bake for 20 to 25 minutes, until at least medium dark brown all around the loaf. Check after 15 minutes of baking uncovered in case your oven runs hot.

Remove the Dutch oven and carefully tilt it to turn the loaf out. Let cool on a rack or set the loaf on its side so air can circulate around it. Let the loaf rest for at least 20 minutes before slicing.

CHAPTER 6
DOUGHS MADE WITH PRE-FERMENTS

WHITE BREAD WITH POOLISH 98

HARVEST BREAD WITH POOLISH 103

WHITE BREAD WITH 80% BIGA 106

50% WHOLE WHEAT BREAD WITH BIGA 109

Left: White Bread with 80% Biga (page 106).
Right: Field Blend #2 (page 158).

WHITE BREAD WITH POOLISH

This recipe makes a palate-sparkling, almost buttery-flavored bread with a thin, crisp crust. Extremely versatile, it can be used for sandwiches, toast, dinner bread, or however you see fit. It also makes excellent baguettes, focaccia, and soft pizza dough. If you have the baking stone and know how to make baguettes in your home kitchen, this is the dough recipe to use.

To make this bread, begin the evening before baking, hand mixing a poolish—a mixture of flour and water with just a tiny bit of yeast. This only takes a few minutes. In the morning the poolish will be bubbly and gassy (I love its goopy texture) and ready to be mixed with the remaining flour, water, salt, and yeast. There is no autolyse stage because after mixing the poolish, there is so little remaining water to mix with the remaining flour that it clumps up and cannot be worked out by hand.

I like shaping this dough into the *fendue* shape, taking the fully proofed loaf and pressing a dowel over the middle of the loaf (which is floured first) all the way to the work surface to create a seam down the middle (see photos on page 99). The lovely result is a kidney shape, with two big lobes of crusty bread joined in the middle.

THIS RECIPE MAKES 2 LOAVES, EACH ABOUT 1½ POUNDS, AND IS SUITABLE FOR PIZZA AND FOCACCIA.

POOLISH FERMENTATION: 12 to 14 hours

BULK FERMENTATION: 2 to 3 hours

PROOF TIME: About 1 hour

SAMPLE SCHEDULE: Mix the poolish at 6 p.m., mix the final dough at 8 a.m. the next morning, shape into loaves at 11 a.m., and bake at noon.

Poolish

INGREDIENT	QUANTITY	
White flour	500 g	3¾ cups + 2 tbsp
Water	500 g, 80°F (27°C)	2¼ cups
Instant dried yeast	0.4 g	Scant ⅛ tsp

Final Dough / Baker's Formula

INGREDIENT	FINAL DOUGH MIX QUANTITY		QUANTITY IN POOLISH	TOTAL RECIPE QUANTITY	BAKER'S PERCENTAGE
White flour	500 g	3¾ cups + 2 tbsp	500 g	1,000 g	100%
Water	250 g, 105°F (41°C)	1⅛ cups	500 g	750 g	75%
Fine sea salt	21 g	1 tbsp + 1 scant tsp	0	21 g	2.1%
Instant dried yeast	3 g	¾ tsp	0.4 g	3.4 g	0.34%
Poolish	1,000 g	All from recipe above			50%*

* The baker's percentage for poolish is the amount of flour in the poolish expressed as a percentage of the total flour in the recipe.

CONTINUED>>

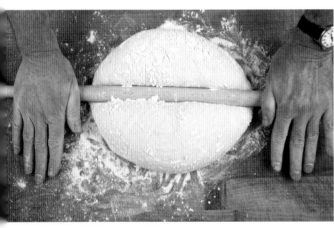

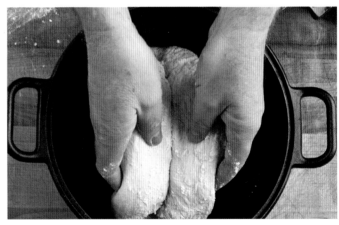

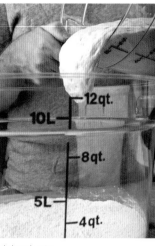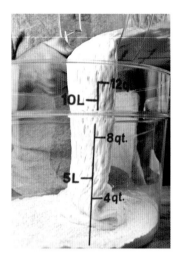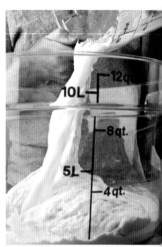

Pouring poolish into the final dough mix.

1. Mix the poolish The evening before you plan to bake, mix 500 grams of flour and 0.4 gram (a scant ⅛ teaspoon) of yeast by hand in a 6-quart round tub. Add 500 grams of water at 80°F (27°C) and mix by hand until completely blended. Cover and leave out overnight at room temperature. The following timeline assumes overnight room temperature is between 65°F and 70°F (18°C and 21°C).

When fully mature, 12 to 14 hours later, the poolish should be bubbly and about tripled in volume, with bubbles popping on the surface at least every few seconds. Poolish will stay at this peak level of maturity for about 2 hours, unless your room temperature is warm—say, above 76°F (24°C)—in which case it will be at its peak for just about 1 hour. At this point you can mix the final dough.

2. Mix the final dough Measure 500 grams of flour into a 12-quart round tub. Add the 21 grams of salt and 3 grams (¾ teaspoon) of yeast and mix by hand.

Pour the 250 grams of 105°F (41°C) water around the perimeter of the poolish, loosening it from its tub. Then pour the water and poolish into the flour mixture in the 12-quart tub.

Mix by hand, wetting your working hand before mixing so the dough doesn't stick to you. (It's fine to rewet your hand three or four times while you mix.) Use the pincer method (see page 67) alternating with folding the dough to fully integrate the ingredients. Most of the ingredients are already in the poolish and the poolish is at room temperature, so the final mix temperature depends on the ambient temperature. For an overnight temperature of about 67°F (19°C), the final mix temperature will probably be 74°F to 75°F (23°C to 24°C).

3. Fold This dough needs two or three folds (see pages 69–70). It's best to apply the folds during the first hour after mixing the dough.

When the dough is about 2½ times its original volume, 2 to 3 hours after mixing, it's ready to be divided.

4. Divide With floured hands, gently ease the dough out of the tub and onto a lightly floured work surface. With your hands still floured, pick up the dough and ease it back down onto the work surface in a somewhat even shape. Use a bit of flour to dust the area in the middle where you'll cut the dough, then cut it into 2 equal-size pieces with a dough knife or plastic dough scraper.

5. Shape Dust 2 proofing baskets with flour. Shape each piece of dough into a medium-tight ball following the instructions on pages 71–73. Place each seam side down in its proofing basket.

6. Proof Lightly flour the tops of the loaves. Set them side by side and cover with a kitchen towel, or place each basket in a nonperforated plastic bag. The proof period for this bread is only about 1 hour, so make sure to preheat the oven in time. Use the finger-dent test (see page 74) to determine when the loaves are fully proofed.

7. Preheat At least 45 minutes prior to baking, put a rack in the middle of the oven and put 2 Dutch ovens on the rack with their lids on. Preheat the oven to 475°F (245°C).

If you only have 1 Dutch oven, put the second loaf into the refrigerator about 20 minutes before baking the first loaf and bake the loaves sequentially, giving the Dutch oven a 5-minute reheat after removing the first loaf.

8. Bake For the next step, please be careful not to let your hands, fingers, or forearms touch the extremely hot Dutch oven.

Invert the proofed loaf onto a lightly floured countertop (moderately floured if making the *fendue* shape). The seam side, now facing up, will be the top of the baked loaf. To make the *fendue* shape (which is optional), sprinkle a moderate amount of flour across the middle of the loaf and use a 1-inch-diameter dowel to press down through the loaf all the way to the work surface. Roll the dowel back and forth just a bit to create about 1 inch of space flattened down the middle of the loaf.

Remove the preheated Dutch oven from your kitchen oven, remove the lid, and carefully place the loaf in the Dutch oven seam side up. Cover and bake for 30 minutes, then uncover and bake for 20 to 30 minutes, until at least medium dark brown all around the loaf. Check after 15 minutes of baking uncovered in case your oven runs hot.

Remove the Dutch oven and carefully tilt it to turn the loaf out. Let cool on a rack or set the loaf on its side so air can circulate around it. Let the loaf rest for at least 20 minutes before slicing.

HARVEST BREAD WITH POOLISH

This recipe has 10 percent whole wheat flour, along with wheat germ and a bit of wheat bran. The resulting bread has aromas that remind me of wheat fields at harvest. If you like, you can coat the proofing baskets with bran before placing the shaped loaves inside. The bran will adhere to the loaves and, when baked, will give the bread an extra degree of crunch. This recipe also works well without any bran in the dough. Either way, the poolish imparts a buttery flavor that marries well with the other ingredients.

THIS RECIPE MAKES 2 LOAVES, EACH ABOUT 1½ POUNDS, AND IS SUITABLE FOR FOCACCIA.

POOLISH FERMENTATION: 12 to 14 hours

BULK FERMENTATION: 2 to 3 hours

PROOF: About 1 hour

SAMPLE SCHEDULE: Mix the poolish at 6 p.m., mix the final dough at 8 a.m. the next morning, shape into loaves at 11 a.m., and bake at noon.

Poolish

INGREDIENT	QUANTITY	
White flour	500 g	3¾ cups + 2 tbsp
Water	500 g, 80°F (27°C)	2¼ cups
Instant dried yeast	0.4 g	Scant ⅛ tsp

Final Dough / Baker's Formula

INGREDIENT	FINAL DOUGH MIX QUANTITY		QUANTITY IN POOLISH	TOTAL RECIPE QUANTITY	BAKER'S PERCENTAGE
White flour	400 g	3 cups + 2 tbsp	500 g	900 g	90%
Whole wheat flour	100 g	¾ cup + ½ tbsp	0	100 g	10%
Water	280 g, 105°F (41°C)	1¼ cups	500 g	780 g	78%
Fine sea salt	21 g	1 tbsp + 1 scant tsp	0	21 g	2.1%
Instant dried yeast	3 g	¾ tsp	0.4 g	3.4 g	0.34%
Wheat germ	50 g	Scant ⅔ cup	0	50 g	5%
Wheat bran	20 g	⅓ cup + 1 tbsp	0	20 g	2%
Poolish	1,000 g	All from recipe above			50%*

The baker's percentage for poolish is the amount of flour in the poolish expressed as a percentage of the total flour in the recipe.

CONTINUED>>

1. Mix the poolish The evening before you plan to bake, mix 500 grams of white flour and 0.4 gram (a scant ⅛ teaspoon) of yeast by hand in a 6-quart round tub. Add 500 grams of water at 80°F (27°C) and mix by hand until completely blended. Cover and leave out overnight at room temperature. The following timeline assumes overnight room temperature is between 65°F and 70°F (18°C and 21°C).

When fully mature, 12 to 14 hours later, the poolish should be bubbly and about tripled in volume, with bubbles popping on the surface at least every few seconds. Poolish will stay at this peak level of maturity for about 2 hours, unless your room temperature is warm—say, above 76°F (24°C)—in which case it will be at its peak for just about 1 hour. At this point you can mix the final dough.

2. Mix the final dough Measure 400 grams of white flour into a 12-quart round tub. Add the 100 grams of whole wheat flour, 50 grams of wheat germ, 20 grams of wheat bran, 21 grams of salt, and 3 grams (¾ teaspoon) of yeast and mix by hand.

Pour the 280 grams of 105°F (41°C) water around the perimeter of the poolish, loosening it from its tub. Then pour the water and poolish into the flour mixture in the 12-quart tub.

Mix by hand, wetting your working hand before mixing so the dough doesn't stick to you too much, but be aware that the germ and bran make this dough stick more than usual. Don't stress; just use your other hand to squeegee any dough off your mixing hand and back into the tub. (It's fine to rewet your hand three or four times while you mix.)

Use the pincer method (see page 67) alternating with folding the dough to fully integrate the ingredients. Most of the ingredients are already in the poolish and the poolish is at room temperature, so the final mix temperature depends on the ambient temperature. For an overnight temperature of about 67°F, the final mix temperature will probably be 74°F to 75°F (23°C to 24°C).

3. Fold This dough needs just two folds (see pages 69–70). It's best to apply the folds during the first hour after mixing the dough. When the dough is about 2½ times its original volume, 2 to 3 hours after mixing, it's ready to be divided.

4. Divide With floured hands, gently ease the dough out of the tub and onto a lightly floured work surface. With your hands still floured, pick up the dough and ease it back down onto the work surface in a somewhat even shape. Use a bit of flour to dust the area in the middle where you'll cut the dough, then cut it into 2 equal-size pieces with a dough knife or plastic dough scraper.

5. Shape Dust 2 proofing baskets with flour. Shape each piece of dough into a medium-tight ball following the instructions on pages 71–73. Place each seam side down in its proofing basket.

If you want to coat the crust of the bread with bran, use about 10 grams of bran per loaf (more than that won't adhere) and sprinkle it evenly in the empty proofing baskets after dusting them with flour. Before placing the loaves in the proofing baskets, roll them seam side up and lightly spritz the top (seam side) with water to help the bran adhere. If you don't have a spray bottle for spritzing, you can use your hand to spread a very thin film of water over the seam side of the loaves. Put the loaves in the baskets, seam side down as usual. The bran will adhere to the loaf while it's proofing.

6. Proof Lightly flour the tops of the loaves. Set them side by side and cover with a kitchen towel, or place each basket in a nonperforated plastic bag. The proof period for this bread is only about 1 hour, so be sure to preheat the oven in time. Use the finger-dent test (see page 74) to determine when the loaves are fully proofed.

7. Preheat At least 45 minutes prior to baking, put a rack in the middle of the oven and put 2 Dutch ovens on the rack with their lids on. Preheat the oven to 475°F (245°C).

If you only have 1 Dutch oven, put the second loaf in the refrigerator about 20 minutes before baking the first loaf and bake the loaves sequentially, giving the Dutch oven a 5-minute reheat after removing the first loaf.

8. Bake For the next step, please be careful not to let your hands, fingers, or forearms touch the extremely hot Dutch oven.

Invert the proofed loaf onto a lightly floured countertop, keeping in mind that the top of the loaf will be the side that was facing down while it was rising—the seam side.

Remove the preheated Dutch oven from your kitchen oven. Remove the lid, carefully place the loaf in the Dutch oven seam side up. Cover and bake for 30 minutes, then uncover and bake for 20 minutes, or until at least medium dark brown all around the loaf. (If you coated the loaves with bran, it's okay for the bran to take on a deep color, and you want to bake the loaves as long as possible to get the crispest crust.) Check after 15 minutes of baking uncovered in case your oven runs hot.

Remove the Dutch oven and carefully tilt it to turn the loaf out. Let cool on a rack or set the loaf on its side so air can circulate around it. Let the loaf rest for at least 20 minutes before slicing.

WHITE BREAD WITH 80% BIGA

Eighty percent of this recipe's total flour is pre-fermented! How cool is that? It is fun when you mix the final dough the next morning, and all you have to use is 200 grams of flour and a little bit of water, salt, and yeast, then dump in the gassy, odorific biga. You may think, "Is this really going to work?" That's natural—and the doorway to a fun experiment in baking bread.

A biga imparts a distinctive kind of earthiness to the flavor of the bread, so what if you want more of that? This recipe is the answer. It provides a tasty example of how you can push the boundaries with pre-fermented doughs in recipes. Note that this biga is a stiff dough, so mixing it is a little more work than usual, but it takes just a few minutes.

I encourage you to bake one loaf from this recipe and use the remaining dough to make pizza or focaccia. Its round flavors are very satisfying in a flat bread with toppings. For pizza, divide the remaining dough and follow any of the pizza recipes in chapter 14; for focaccia, you'll find guidelines on amounts of dough in the section "Making Focaccia with Bread Dough" (page 215). Shape the dough into balls and let them rest in the refrigerator for several hours or up to a couple of days.

THIS RECIPE MAKES 2 LOAVES, EACH ABOUT 1½ POUNDS, AND IS SUITABLE FOR PIZZA OR FOCACCIA.

BIGA FERMENTATION: 12 to 14 hours

BULK FERMENTATION: 2½ to 3½ hours

PROOF TIME: About 1 hour

SAMPLE SCHEDULE: Mix the biga at 6 p.m., mix the final dough at 8 a.m. the next morning, shape into loaves at 11 a.m., and bake at about noon.

Biga

INGREDIENT	QUANTITY	
White flour	800 g	6¼ cups
Water	544 g, 80°F (27°C)	2⅓ cup
Instant dried yeast	0.64 g	³⁄₁₆ tsp

Final Dough

INGREDIENT	FINAL DOUGH MIX QUANTITY		QUANTITY IN BIGA	TOTAL RECIPE QUANTITY	BAKER'S PERCENTAGE
White flour	200 g	1½ cups + 1 tbsp	800 g	1,000 g	100%
Water	206 g, 105°F (41°C)	⅞ cup	544 g	750 g	75%
Fine sea salt	22 g	1 tbsp + 1 tsp	0	22 g	2.2%
Instant dried yeast	2 g	½ tsp	0.64 g	2.64 g	0.26%
Biga	1,345 g	All from recipe above			80%*

Baker's Formula

* The baker's percentage for biga is the amount of flour in the biga expressed as a percentage of the total flour in the recipe.

1. Mix the biga The evening before you plan to bake, put 800 grams of flour in a 6-quart tub. Put 544 grams of water at 80°F (27°C) in a separate container. Put 0.64 grams (³⁄₁₆ teaspoon) of yeast in a separate, small container. Add about 3 tablespoons of the 80°F (27°C) water to the yeast. Let the mixture rest for a few minutes, then stir with your finger; the yeast may not be completely dissolved, but you've given it a good start.

Pour the yeast mixture into the tub with the flour. Pour a few more tablespoons of the 80°F (27°C) water into the yeast container, swirl it around to incorporate any remaining yeast, and dump it into the dough tub, along with the remaining warm water.

Mix by hand, using the pincer method (see page 67) alternating with folding the dough, just until all of the ingredients are incorporated. Cover and leave out overnight at room temperature. The following timeline assumes overnight room temperature is between 65°F and 70°F (18°C and 21°C).

When fully mature, 12 to 14 hours later, the biga should be slightly domed, about tripled in volume, and pocked with gas bubbles and have a strong, ripe smell of alcohol. At this point you can mix the final dough.

2. Mix the final dough Measure 200 grams of flour into a 12-quart round tub, add the 22 grams of salt and 2 grams (½ teaspoon) of yeast, and mix by hand. Pour in the 206 grams of 105°F (41°C) water and mix by hand just until incorporated. Add all of the biga, using your hand to ease it out of its container.

Mix by hand, wetting your working hand before mixing so the dough doesn't stick to you. (It's fine to rewet your hand three or four times while you mix.) Use the pincer method (see page 67) alternating with folding the dough to fully integrate the ingredients. Most of the dough is the biga and the biga is at room temperature, so the final mix temperature depends on the ambient temperature. For an overnight temperature of about 67°F (19°C), the final mix temperature probably won't be much higher than 74°F (23°C). For this bread, that will be fine, although a final mix temperature of 78°F to 80°F (26°C to 27°C) would be ideal. For a final mix temperature of 74°F (23°C), bulk dough fermentation will take about 3½ hours; for a final mix temperature of 78°F to 80°F (26°C to 27°C), it will probably take 2½ to 3 hours.

3. Fold This dough needs two or three folds (see pages 69–70). It's best to apply the folds during the first 1½ hours after mixing the dough. When the dough is about triple its original volume, 2½ to 3 hours after mixing, it's ready to be divided.

4. Divide With floured hands, gently ease the dough out of the tub and onto a lightly floured work surface. With your hands still floured, pick up the dough and ease it back down onto the work surface in a somewhat even shape. Use a bit of flour to dust the area in the middle where you'll cut the dough, then cut it into 2 equal-size pieces with a dough knife or plastic dough scraper.

CONTINUED>>

5. Shape Dust 2 proofing baskets with flour. Shape each piece of dough into a medium-tight ball following the instructions on pages 71–73. Place each seam side down in its proofing basket.

6. Proof Lightly flour the tops of the loaves. Set them side by side and cover with a kitchen towel, or place each basket in a nonperforated plastic bag. The proof period for this bread is only about 1 hour, so make sure to preheat the oven in time. Use the finger-dent test (see page 74) to determine when the loaves are fully proofed.

7. Preheat At least 45 minutes prior to baking, put a rack in the middle of the oven and put 2 Dutch ovens on the rack with their lids on. Preheat the oven to 475°F (245°C).

If you only have 1 Dutch oven, put the second loaf in the refrigerator about 20 minutes before baking the first loaf and bake the loaves sequentially, giving the Dutch oven a 5-minute reheat after removing the first loaf.

8. Bake For the next step, please be careful not to let your hands, fingers, or forearms touch the extremely hot Dutch oven.

Invert the proofed loaf onto a lightly floured countertop, keeping in mind that the top of the loaf will be the side that was facing down while it was rising—the seam side.

Remove the preheated Dutch oven from your kitchen oven, remove the lid, and carefully place the loaf in the Dutch oven seam side up. Cover and bake for 30 minutes, then uncover and bake for 20 to 30 minutes, until at least medium dark brown all around the loaf. Check after 15 minutes of baking uncovered in case your oven runs hot.

Remove the Dutch oven and carefully tilt it to turn the loaf out. Let cool on a rack or set the loaf on its side so air can circulate around it. Let the loaf rest for at least 20 minutes before slicing.

50% WHOLE WHEAT BREAD WITH BIGA

This recipe uses a biga to make whole wheat bread. I like the way the earthiness of the biga complements the flavors of the bran and wheat germ present in whole wheat flour. And there's the fiber benefit, too. This is an excellent sandwich bread. It's great for toast and croutons, and I like whole wheat bread with fresh cheese or with butter and honey. It is excellent with liver mousses or pâtés, and maybe apricot preserves on the side. Toss on some crushed pistachios if you have them. Boy howdy!

THIS RECIPE MAKES 2 LOAVES, EACH ABOUT 1½ POUNDS, AND IS SUITABLE FOR FOCACCIA.

BIGA FERMENTATION: 12 to 14 hours

BULK FERMENTATION: 3 to 4 hours

PROOF TIME: About 1 hour

SAMPLE SCHEDULE: Mix the biga at 6 p.m., mix the final dough at 8 a.m. the next morning, shape into loaves at 11 a.m., and bake at noon.

Biga

INGREDIENT	QUANTITY	
White flour	500 g	3¾ cups + 2 tbsp
Water	340 g, 80°F (27°C)	1½ cups
Instant dried yeast	0.4 g	Scant ⅛ tsp

Final Dough / Baker's Formula

INGREDIENT	FINAL DOUGH MIX QUANTITY		QUANTITY IN BIGA	TOTAL RECIPE QUANTITY	BAKER'S PERCENTAGE
White flour	0	0	500 g	500 g	50%
Whole wheat flour	500 g	3¾ cups + 2 tbsp	0	500 g	50%
Water	460 g, 100°F (38°C)	2 cups	340 g	800 g	80%
Fine sea salt	22 g	1 tbsp + 1 tsp	0	22 g	2.2%
Instant dried yeast	3 g	¾ tsp	0.4 g	3.4 g	0.34%
Biga	840 g	All from recipe above			50%*

The baker's percentage for biga is the amount of flour in the biga expressed as a percentage of the total flour in the recipe.

CONTINUED>>

1. Mix the biga The evening before you plan to bake, put 500 grams of flour in a 6-quart tub. Put 340 grams of water at 80°F (27°C) in a separate container. Put 0.4 grams (a scant ⅛ teaspoon) of yeast in a separate, small container. Add about 3 tablespoons of the 80°F (27°C) water to the yeast. Let the mixture rest for a few minutes, then stir with your finger; the yeast may not be completely dissolved, but you've given it a good start.

Pour the yeast mixture into the tub with the flour. Pour a few more tablespoons of the 80°F (27°C) water into the yeast container, swirl it around to incorporate any remaining yeast, and dump it into the dough tub, along with the remaining warm water.

Mix by hand, using the pincer method (see page 67) alternating with folding the dough, just until all of the ingredients are incorporated. Cover and leave out overnight at room temperature. The following timeline assumes overnight room temperature is between 65°F and 70°F (18°C and 21°C).

When fully mature, 12 to 14 hours later, the biga should be slightly domed, about tripled in volume, and pocked with gas bubbles and have a ripe smell of alcohol. At this point you can mix the final dough.

2. Mix the final dough Measure 500 grams of whole wheat flour into a 12-quart round tub. Add the 22 grams of salt and 3 grams (¾ teaspoon) of yeast and mix by hand. Pour in the 460 grams of 100°F (38°C) water and mix by hand just until incorporated. Add the biga, using your hand to ease it out of its container.

Mix by hand, wetting your working hand before mixing so the dough doesn't stick to you. (It's fine to rewet your hand three or four times while you mix.) Use the pincer method (see page 67) alternating with folding the dough to fully integrate the ingredients. The target dough temperature at the end of the mix is 80°F (27°C).

3. Fold This dough needs three or four folds (see pages 69–70). It's best to apply the folds during the first 1½ hours after mixing the dough.

When the dough is about triple its original volume, 3 to 4 hours after mixing, it's ready to be divided.

4. Divide With floured hands, gently ease the dough out of the tub and onto a lightly floured work surface. With your hands still floured, pick up the dough and ease it back down onto the work surface in a somewhat even shape. Use a bit of flour to dust the area in the middle where you'll cut the dough, then cut it into 2 equal-size pieces with a dough knife or plastic dough scraper.

5. Shape Dust 2 proofing baskets with flour. Shape each piece of dough into a medium-tight ball following the instructions on pages 71–73. Place each seam side down in its flour-dusted proofing basket.

6. Proof Lightly flour the tops of the loaves. Set them side by side and cover with a kitchen towel, or place each basket in a nonperforated plastic bag. The proof period for this bread is only about 1 hour, so make sure to preheat the oven in time. Use the finger-dent test (see page 74) to determine when the loaves are fully proofed.

7. Preheat At least 45 minutes prior to baking, put a rack in the middle of the oven and put 2 Dutch ovens on the rack with their lids on. Preheat the oven to 475°F (245°C).

If you only have 1 Dutch oven, put the second loaf in the refrigerator about 20 minutes before baking the first loaf and bake the loaves sequentially, giving the Dutch oven a 5-minute reheat after removing the first loaf.

8. Bake For the next step, please be careful not to let your hands, fingers, or forearms touch the extremely hot Dutch oven.

Invert the proofed loaf onto a lightly floured countertop, keeping in mind that the top of the loaf will be the side that was facing down while it was rising—the seam side.

Remove the preheated Dutch oven from your kitchen oven, remove the lid, and carefully place the loaf in the Dutch oven seam side up. Cover and bake for 30 minutes, then uncover and bake for 20 to 25 minutes, until at least medium dark brown all around the loaf. Check after 15 minutes of baking uncovered in case your oven runs hot.

Remove the Dutch oven and carefully tilt it to turn the loaf out. Let cool on a rack or set the loaf on its side so air can circulate around it. Let the loaf rest for at least 20 minutes before slicing.

The Early Morning Bread Baker's Routine

For the first several years after opening the bakery, this was me three or four days a week. On the other days I worked the afternoon bread baker's shift, which meant I was responsible for mixing the levain doughs, baking the afternoon batch of baguettes and brioches, dividing and shaping the levain breads for morning baking, mixing the pre-ferments (poolish and biga) for the next morning's baguette and ciabatta mixes, mixing the late afternoon levain, and then sweeping and locking up. On top of working either the morning or afternoon shift, I also did bread deliveries on Sundays and Mondays and was always on call if anything came up. Some days I baked pastries or rolled croissants, and I worked the counter when the line backed up. Meanwhile I had to find time to take care of office tasks: production scheduling, wholesale account management, bookkeeping, and personnel management. Once a month I drove across town to Hair of the Dog brewery to pick up a bucket of spent grains (and to have a quick glass of Fred) from owner and brewer Alan Sprints, to use in the bakery's rye bread. Dough is always moving. Finding the twenty or thirty minutes needed to run any errand was a mad dash. *Where is the pause button?!*

As the bakery grew I could afford to hire more bakers. Gradually I was able to remove myself from many of the day-to-day production tasks, thanks to a staff that can handle the workload and maintain the bakery's high standards for quality. Most of my staff work eight hours straight, without breaks except for the occasional smoke or quick bite to eat.

Here's the schedule of the last early morning bread baking shift I worked. As you'll see from reading through it, the activities are nonstop, and the shifts continue that way to this day.

3:30 A.M.: Arrive at the bakery. Turn the oven up to 500°F. Check the tubs of poolish and biga for the morning mixes to see if they're at their ideal point of maturation and ready to be used in the dough mixes.

Remove sheet pans of croissants and other *viennoiserie* products for the morning's bake from the refrigerator and the retarder. Set up a rack with the croissants for proofing so they'll be ready for the pastry team to begin baking around 6 a.m. If it's chilly in the bakery, put the rack in front of the oven.

Remove 50-pound bags of flour from the retarder, where they were chilled overnight to allow for a proper finished dough temperature in the heat of the bakery (friction from the dough mixer adds heat to the dough too).

4 A.M.: Autolyse the baguette dough. Scale the flour, usually 60 to 80 kilos (depending on what is specified on today's mix sheets) and dump it in the mixer. Carry big buckets of cold water between my legs (it's not graceful) from the refrigerator to the mixer. If it's hot, add some ice to keep the dough mix from warming up too much—break up the ice with a knife steel. Scale the ice and water to the amount on the day's mix sheet and dump it into the mixer. We use dough tubs that hold a little more than 20 kilos of water—the groggy baker will learn to use the same increments each day, so if, for example, 42.4 kilos of water are needed for this baguette mix, then I use an empty tub on the scale filled to 20 kilos twice, then add the final 2.4 kilos. Turn the mixer on to low speed and mix for about 1 minute. Then run the mixer in reverse for 5 or 10 seconds to pick up any dry flour from the bottom of the bowl.

Turn off the mixer. Set a timer for 20 minutes. Go into the office and put on some music. Make a coffee.

4:15 A.M.: Scale out yeast and salt for the baguette mix and the ciabatta mix. Dump the poolish, mixed the previous afternoon, into the bread mixer. Depending on the day and the size of the mix, that's between three and six tubs of poolish, which should be at its optimum point at this time in the morning: with hundreds of small bubbles that give the top surface the appearance of tapioca. If you stare at it, you can see occasional little eruptions as bubbles pop on the surface. The classic French method for removing the poolish is to reserve some of the water for the mix to pour around the edges and loosen the poolish from its container, but I find it slides into the mixing bowl easily enough, especially with a little encouragement from a hand and a plastic dough scraper. Add the fresh yeast and salt.

4:25 A.M.: Begin the baguette mix, on first speed. Set timer for 5 minutes. Take empty poolish tubs to the dish pit and rinse them out. Grab a bunch of empty dough tubs and a bar towel, take them to the baker's bench, and oil the seven or more dough tubs needed for the finished baguette dough.

4:30 A.M.: Timer goes off. Change the mixer to second speed and set timer for 4 minutes.

4:35 A.M.: Baguette mix done. Check dough temperature with a probe thermometer—it should be about 75°F. Transfer to the oiled dough tubs, 14 kilos of dough per tub. Put tubs of dough in the retarder for the afternoon baguette bake, in accordance with the day's mix sheet. Record the mix temperature and the time the mix was completed on the mix sheet. Plan on cutting the dough set aside for the morning bake around 6:15 a.m.

4:45 A.M.: Feed the levain, which was last mixed the previous afternoon and is now bubbly, acidic, leathery smelling, and generally nasty. First, throw all but a small amount from the levain into the trash. We handle the levain at this stage wearing food safety gloves because the acidity of the levain can wear out the skin in sensitive spots (I used to get small lesions and splits on my fingertips). The remaining fistful of levain hardly looks like it could initiate the leavening of several hundred loaves of bread, but it does—yeast puts rabbits to shame. Add a few kilos of flour and very warm water to the tub and mix the levain by hand.

4:55 A.M.: Autolyse the ciabatta dough. Once again waddle with tubs of cold water from the fridge to the mixer and carry chilled 50-pound bags of flour from the retarder. Pretend to listen to Rollie, the dairy guy who always shows up about now and starts telling me stories when I'm tired and want to stay focused on my work. Think, *Rollie's a great guy. I wish he'd shut up.* Scale out amounts of flour and water in accordance with formula sheets prepared the day before. Mix on first speed until the water and flour are incorporated.

5:00 A.M.: Begin baking levain breads (Country Blonde, Country Brown, the big *boules*, and walnut bread), which were shaped the previous afternoon and spent the night slowly proofing in the retarder. For the next 20 minutes, load 144 regular-size levain loaves into the oven.

5:25 A.M.: Begin the ciabatta mix. To the flour and water that was mixed in the autolyse, add several tubs of biga—pre-fermented dough that gives the ciabatta its great flavor—plus the dry yeast and salt, and start the mix on first speed. Set a timer.

(We use fresh baker's yeast for the baguette dough and SAF Red Instant yeast for our ciabatta dough, in part because it keeps the morning baker from getting confused about which pair of yeast and salt bowls, scaled out earlier, goes into each mix. Never underestimate the ability of a foggy early morning brain to make a mistake. There isn't a lot of time for reflection.)

Check the breads in the oven. Turn the oven temperature down to 480°F.

Remove the raisin-pecan dough from the retarder and divide it into about two dozen pieces, each scaled to 475 grams. Shape them into little torpedoes. Place the pieces on proof boards and put them in a covered rack.

Check the ciabatta dough, switch the mixer to second speed, and reset the timer. Generously oil seven or eight tubs for the ciabatta dough, which is wet and sticky and requires a few folds during fermentation to build up strength. Not enough oil in the tubs before they

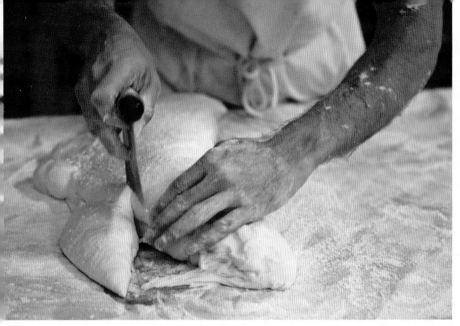

receive the dough dooms the baker to a challenge of dough sticking to the tubs when there's just not much time to deal with it.

Remove the baked bread from the first and second decks of the oven.

5:45 A.M.: Shape the raisin-pecan dough into loaves.

6:00 A.M.: Check the remaining bread in the oven. Finish the ciabatta mix and check the dough temperature.

If the loaves in the third and fourth decks of the oven aren't quite ready, remove the ciabatta dough from the big mixer bowl and cut and weigh it into the oiled tubs. Although this 10-minute task is best done from start to finish without stopping, the timing doesn't always allow that. If there is a 5-minute window before I need to go back to the oven, I'll take it. To remove this dough from the mixer, I wet my left arm completely (the sink's right there), reach inside the mixing bowl to lift a big hunk of dough, and with the other hand wielding the bread knife, cut the dough cleanly where it is still attached to the rest—all the while being careful not to let the dough tear. Put about 7 kilos of dough in each tub (more than that will overflow the bin because it expands over three times when it rises). Stack the tubs on a rolling cart next to the baker's bench. I would usually end up running back and forth: from the mixer, removing the dough, interrupted by the sound of the timer; to the oven to check the bread, and if ready, pull it out.

Having left enough ciabatta dough in the mixer for our multigrain bread, add the grain mixture and incorporate. Remove this dough to a separate oiled dough tub. Scrape out the mixing bowl completely, leaving no bits of dough behind.

Reload the entire oven. Since the baguette dough needs me to hit it when it's ready at 6:15 a.m., not when I'm ready for it, sometimes the second load of the oven just needs to be done fast and that's when the overdrive gear kicks in. When it's time to move fast, well, fast it is.

6:15 A.M.: Begin dividing the baguettes. We do this by hand. Flour the baker's bench, invert a tub of dough over it, and use a scraper to gently ease the dough out of the tub and onto the bench. Next to the dough is a scale. Tamp off any excess oil from the dough using a bar towel, toss some flour on top of the dough, cut with a bench knife, and manually scale each piece of dough. Many bakeries use a piece of equipment called a divider to automate this process, often with excellent results, but I have always preferred to divide and shape our doughs the old fashioned way, by hand.

6:45 A.M.: Put a fold in each tub of ciabatta dough. Put a fold in the tub of levain.

Check the oven and remove the finished levain breads. The levain bake should be finished at this point: big 3-kilo *boules* of Country Blonde, 2-kilo *boules* of Country Brown (reminiscent of *pain Poilâne*), *bâtard* loaves of Country Brown and Country Blonde, demi baguettes of Country Blonde for one of our restaurants, walnut bread, and small loaves of walnut, Country Blonde, and Country Brown.

6:55 A.M.: Start shaping the baguettes. A good baker can divide, rest, and shape at least one hundred baguettes in an hour. While this requires a steady and fast pair of hands and continuous effort without pause, it also gives me my first chance to relax a bit. All of the morning mixes are done, the doughs are rising in their tubs, the levain bread is baked and out of the oven, and hopefully everything is right on schedule. It feels good to be able to shape baguettes and do nothing else for a while, without having to stop to engage in another coincident activity. Of course, there are over one hundred baguettes to shape.

7:45 A.M.: Feed the levain again. Check the production schedule to see how much levain needs to be mixed today. Measure out the amount needed from the first levain mix, throw the rest away, and mix this feeding of the levain in the bread mixer.

Put a second fold in each tub of ciabatta dough.

7:55 A.M.: Begin baking the baguettes, preferably a little earlier. We need baguettes for our early-morning customers and for a *jambon* sandwich we make that is very popular (buttered *ficelle* with a small amount of sliced ham and a slice of good cheese—especially satisfying because the flavors of all the ingredients are in balance and the bread has a sparkling kind of flavor if eaten early enough, while it's still very fresh). My biggest stress point is having the baguettes come out of the oven in time to cool before we have to bag them and get out the door with the first round of morning deliveries. We can't bag hot bread because it ruins it, causing the crust to go limp from the bread's own steam.

8:45 A.M.: Finish baking the baguettes. Clean up around the oven and rack the *couches* to dry. (*Couches* are pieces of linen fabric that we use to support the shaped loaves—baguettes, *boules*, and *bâtards*—while they rise. They absorb some of the dampness of the bread dough, and it's best to dry them out before using them again.)

9:00 A.M.: Cut the ciabatta (my favorite dough to handle and bake) into loaves and buns. Now that the 7 kilos of ciabatta dough in each tub has tripled in size, the dough is sticking to the lids. Invert a tub onto the heavily floured baker's bench and, because I oiled the tubs so generously back at about 5:40 a.m., the dough pops right out. The dough holds the shape of the tub, thanks to the folds I gave it during its rise. Cut the dough, which has the texture of bubbly, gassy Jell-O, into 6-inch-wide loaves 14 to 16 inches long for retail and about 2½ feet long for restaurants. Put the shaped loaves on moderately floured *couches* to proof.

9:30 A.M.: Sweep up around the bread bench. Mix the brioche dough.

10:15 A.M.: Begin baking the ciabatta, loading them into a very hot oven, at nearly 500°F. The unscored loaves naturally crack open along fissures, giving them a nice organic appearance.

11:15 A.M.: Out of the oven and on the cooling rack, the baked ciabatta loaves crackle in a loud staccato, sounding like drummer boys in the woodwork.

Clean up around the oven and say hello to the rest of the day.

THE PHYSICAL PLANT

Ken's Artisan Bakery has an open kitchen that takes up about 1,200 square feet, a counter, a 750-square-foot café space with ten small tables and one big family table, and a 6 by 8-foot room that serves as office, locker room, storage, and home to the sound system. In the office there is a desk, one chair, the safe, about forty pairs of shoes, knapsacks, jackets, hats, scarves, my bookshelf, a big bottle of ibuprofen, a first aid kit, lots of Band-Aids, office drawers, the computer and monitor, the printer, the iPod dock and amplifier, printer paper, spare lightbulbs, a trash can, and our wine inventory, usually consisting of about five cases of wine—oh, and the water heater.

The primary bread station houses the baker's bench, the bread mixer, a hand sink, stacks of flour bags, and a plastic folder holder on the wall with the levain feeding details, daily mix sheets, and formula sheets for croissant and brioche doughs. The mixer at work is a beautiful thing to watch. I can mix up to 135 kilos (almost 300 pounds) of dough at a time. Next to the mixer is a cart that holds a scale, a long serrated knife used to cut dough coming out of the mixer, and a couple of flexible bench knives, one with a straight edge for cutting dough, and the other with a curved edge for scraping out the mixer bowl.

The oven is on the other side of the bakery, about fifteen paces away. In the morning sometimes we run back and forth, tending to bread in the oven and dough in the mixer, feeding the levain, putting folds in the dough, and accepting deliveries from the dairy guy or the eggs lady, tracking footprints of flour with each dash.

PART 3
LEVAIN BREAD RECIPES

CHAPTER 7
UNDERSTANDING LEVAIN

Natural yeast, in its many varieties, is pretty much everywhere—in the air, in the soil, in vegetation—and especially in carbohydrate-rich environments like the skins of fruits and the surface of grains. Natural yeasts lie dormant in flour. Commercial baker's yeast, *Saccharomyces cerevisiae*, is a monoculture—a single strain of yeast cultivated commercially and sold in dried form or in moist cakes.

Prior to the use of commercial monoculture yeasts in the modern era, all leavened bread got its rise from naturally occurring yeast. These types of breads are now known as sourdough in the United States. This is how bread was leavened throughout most of its five thousand years of history.

The French word *levain* is derived from the Latin *levare*, meaning "to rise." The words *mother*, *chef*, and *levain* all describe the same thing: a natural culture the baker uses as a leavening source. Some bakers and texts use different names for the culture at different stages; or they may use more than one culture. *Chef* often refers to a master culture that is fed separately, whereas *starter* refers to a portion of the chef that is fed in one or more stages and added to the final dough mix. I have always worked with a single culture that is fed and kept separately, taking some of that culture at a particular point of ripeness to leaven my final bread dough. I use the word *levain* to describe my culture at all of its stages, and that's the word I use throughout this book. I use the English word *leaven* as a verb.

I avoid referring to my naturally leavened breads as sourdough because too many people associate sourdough with breads that are indeed sour in flavor and sometimes leave a sharp, vinegary aftertaste. In France, sour bread is probably considered a fermentation mistake, while in San Francisco, it's a well-appreciated taste—although that may be changing. My preference is for complex flavors from the grain and fermentation that are subtle, in balance, and not sour.

A levain can support multiple strains of wild yeast, giving the baker an opportunity to create bread and other leavened baked goods with complex aromas and flavors. Such breads also have a more extended shelf life than breads made from commercial baker's yeast. The yeast community in a levain culture consists of billions of rapidly reproducing, gas-belching, single-celled organisms. I like knowing that I can make them do what I want them to do.

Bakers feed their levain cultures anywhere from once a day to every few hours. In the following pages, I'll show you how easy it is to start a new levain culture from scratch using just flour and water and following a once-a-day feeding schedule. Then I'll explain how to feed an established levain, how to store it in the refrigerator if you won't be baking with it every day, and how to restore it for its next use.

MANIPULATING FLAVOR

Baking with a levain culture is a fermentation craft similar in some ways to making wine from grapes and their naturally occurring yeasts: each manipulates fermentation to create an end product that meets a desired flavor profile and degree of complexity.

The character of a naturally leavened bread depends on a number of variables: how much water is in the culture, the temperature of the water used each time the culture is fed, the type of flour, the ratio of levain to new flour each time the culture is fed or refreshed, the feeding schedule, the temperature at which the levain is kept, how ripe the levain is, and how much of the levain is used in the final dough. The aroma, flavor, and appearance of levain breads and the consistency of the product from one day to the next are all expressions of the baker's craft—his or her signature, in a sense. A true artisan baker is someone who understands how to manipulate the relatively small number of variables (which can yield an infinite number of possible results) to produce exactly the bread desired. In this book, I'll give you specific instructions for making and using a natural levain culture my way, and then I'll explain how to adjust the variables to suit your own tastes. Levain breads have the potential to be the most personal breads a baker makes.

The complexity of tastes in a levain bread arise from the community of wild yeasts and bacteria in the culture, fermentation gases, lactic and acetic acids, and, of course, time for these things to accumulate. My revelation "less yeast and more time" definitely applies here. Lengthening the fermentation time of levain doughs by retarding them at cooler temperatures greatly improves flavor. So does using smaller amounts of levain and allowing doughs to ferment for a very long time at room temperature. Bacterial fermentation and acidity add desirable tastes and aromas, but only if enough time is allowed for these very complex biochemical reactions to take place.

Acids are responsible for the sourness in sourdough. The vinegary taste comes largely from acetic acid. Lactic acids are common in milk, and indeed contribute a milky or buttery taste to breads. Both acids are often more evident as an aftertaste, unless the sour character is strong and pronounced. Many naturally leavened breads have a flavor profile that leans more toward one end of the acetic-lactic spectrum than the other. San Francisco sourdough is an excellent example of bread with strong acetic character—think "vinegary." Levain cultures kept in cooler temperatures also lean toward the acetic end of the taste spectrum, as do stiffer levains. Bread made from a liquid levain, with equal parts flour and water (it has a soupy texture), has a distinctive flavor profile that leans toward the lactic acid end of the taste spectrum. Warmer levain cultures encourage lactic acid production, and just like the top-fermented ales that brewers ferment at warmer temperatures, these can produce fermented fruit flavors, especially when they get particularly ripe.

Want a little more detail? Here goes, with a shout-out to Teri Wadsworth and John Paul of Cameron Winery in Dundee, Oregon. The levain is a symbiotic culture of lactic acid bacteria and yeast. Lactic acid bacteria are a diverse group of bacteria that produce lactic acid, carbon dioxide, a small amount of ethanol, and other volatile flavor components as the end product of carbohydrate fermentation. Under the right conditions, lactic acid bacteria can also produce acetic acid. In a levain, the lactic acid bacteria feed mostly on the yeast's metabolic by-products. As with natural yeast fermentation, time is required for the bacteria to grow and produce acids and other flavor components. Lactic acid bacteria are important in a plethora of fermented foods, including yogurt, beer, pickles, sauerkraut, and cheese, and the acidity they produce inhibits the growth of organisms that can cause spoilage.

I could go on about how alcohol can convert to acetic acid when there is an excess of fermentation, but I don't want to distract from the main goal, which is to know how to manipulate the variables at play in the kitchen to make good levain bread. At the end of this chapter is a table, Variations in Levain Cultures, summarizing the variables and their impact on taste.

CULTURE GROWTH

As a new levain culture is being established over the course of several days, it evolves in ways you can see, feel, and smell. At the beginning, right after you start it from scratch by mixing just flour and water, it resembles either bread dough or a batter, depending on how much water is used. Within 48 hours, after two daily feedings, the culture gets gassy, it increases to as much as four times the starting volume, you can see bubbles, and it has a weblike structure from its gluten. As the levain matures it develops a fragrant, sometimes pungent and alcoholic, acidic nose. We use some whole wheat flour in the levain at my bakery, and I call for doing the same in this book's recipes. This results in a funky, leathery ethanol smell in the mature culture. That smell takes my mind to some undefined place, a place that makes me pause and where my eyes are open and not looking at anything at all.

A single hardworking yeast cell can divide, or bud, more than a dozen times. In the right environment, this replication, and that of all of the offspring, produces billions of yeast cells, each producing the gas that leavens and flavors the dough. Every time the levain is fed with flour and water, a new cycle of yeast replication and fermentation begins, and ultimately the entire dough mass is bubbling, lively with potential, and ready to be used to make more bread.

SEPARATING MYTH FROM REALITY

Much is sometimes made of specific sourdough cultures from a particular place or even preserved from a time past. For example, many people say you can only make a bread that tastes like San Francisco sourdough in San Francisco. Likewise, some people believe their levain is special because it's been maintained for decades or it was derived from a special culture that someone gave them or that they ordered by mail. While there are minor populations of yeast and bacteria that are indigenous to specific geographic areas, the primary flora are the same in sourdoughs everywhere. It's not a where-it's-from game: it's how it's made, and with what ingredients, that makes the bread taste the way it does.

Adding Fruit to a Levain

Many people believe their levain has a particular character due to how it was established; for example, with a bunch of grapes added to a mash of flour and water. I disagree. Grape yeasts live on grapes because that's the environment that suits them. Grape yeasts don't flourish in a flour environment. Again, it isn't how a levain is started that determines its performance and flavor profile; what's crucial is how it's maintained. Natural selection will rule in the flour environment. The addition of grapes, apples, or other such ingredients to the starter provides sugars for fermentation and short-term aromatics. Malt would do the same thing: provide food to the yeast. Many of the microorganisms involved in starting a culture can't tolerate the environment as the culture develops; only those that thrive in the environment that is developed and maintained will survive. As Raymond Calvel wrote in *Le Goût du Pain*, "Recipes for this purpose are often quite amusing, including cultures based on grape juice, potatoes, raisins, yogurt, honey, and so on. . . . I simply use the proper type of bread flour."

Having said that, I have nothing against tossing some quality fruit into a mature levain culture for immediate use, and I know of one baker who uses honey in a special levain. My point here is to dispel the myth that a levain carries the elements of its genesis forward in its character. In fact, I've made some very interesting breads by adding fruit to the levain. At my bakery, we once made apple bread with a levain hydrated with apple cider. Best ever was when I grabbed a bucket of apple mash from Steve McCarthy at Clear Creek Distillery and added it to some of the bakery's levain, which then went into a *baba* dough. That *baba au pomme* was one of the best things I've ever eaten.

BALANCE AND THE BAKER'S REWARD

In my naturally leavened breads, I aim for the middle of the lactic-acetic spectrum to produce bread with a mellow aroma and flavor that is satisfying by itself or can complement a variety of foods and wines. This kind of bread flatters whatever it is served with. It tastes great, it's crusty and flavorful, and it's the kind of bread I don't tire of. I want to eat it every day.

The levain recipes in this book use 80 percent hydration for the levain culture. That means the water in the culture amounts to 80 percent of the flour, by weight. Levains can be more stiff, with hydration as low as 60 to 65 percent, in which case they will easily form into a ball. They can also be wetter—as much as 100 percent hydration. Really, a levain can be at any hydration, but the common range is between 60 and 100 percent hydration.

At my bakery, we use a levain with hydration close to that of the final dough it will be used in. I find this approach more balanced, as opposed to mixing in a levain with a substantially different hydration than the dough. The result is bread in which you can taste the wheat, the fermentation, and a subtle chorus of lingering background notes that are all in harmony, without any element of taste outweighing any other.

LEVAIN INGREDIENTS

We use a blend of whole wheat and white flours in the levain at Ken's Artisan Bakery, and I call for doing the same in this book. This is intended to approximate the excellent stone-ground flours produced by a small number of artisan mills in France. It all started for me with the desire to reproduce a brownish country bread like my baker heroes in Paris were baking, or a bread close to it, anyway, here in the United States.

TAKING PURITY TO EXTREMES

For a couple years after I started the bakery, we used coarse sel de Guérande, which I purchased in 20-kilo (44.1-pound) bags that had small puddles of seawater in the bottom. We had to sift through that salt by hand every morning to remove occasional little bits of dirt or seaweed (hopefully nothing from the boots of the guy who had raked the salt). Hey, I took the word *artisan* seriously! But I got tired of cleaning the salt every morning, thinking, *Is this really necessary?* I once had a customer return a loaf of bread because he found a small chunk of dirt in it. *But it's French, Coast-of-Brittany dirt!* We now use clean, pure, beautiful coarse sea salt from Sicily in our levain breads.

Bakers often supplement their natural levain culture by adding baker's yeast to the final dough (not the levain culture). Many of the levain bread recipes in this book call for adding store-bought yeast. This may seem contrary to the purist spirit of levain baking. At first, I felt the same way. When I started my bakery, I set out to create an idealized levain bread made only from a natural culture, without commercial yeast and using *sel de mer* from the coast of Brittany.

The bread was good. I wish I could taste one of those loaves from the early years right now. But with time I found I wanted loaves with a slightly lighter crumb, a bit more volume, and a more delicate harmony of flavors. And adding commercial yeast was the way to achieve that. It results in greater gas production (and thus more volume), and mellows the dough's acidity. An alternative way of adding yeast is to mix a poolish at the same time you feed the levain in the morning, and then combine both types of leavening when mixing the final dough. In the summer of 2003, I started doing this at the bakery—mixing a poolish five hours before mixing the levain doughs (Country Brown and Country Blonde), and adding the poolish to the final dough to help it rise. This worked, but the truth is, it's hard to tell the difference between breads produced using that method and those that have a small amount of baker's yeast added, and the latter is a practice that has been common in France for over one hundred years. The recipes in chapter 9, Hybrid Leavening Doughs, are leavened with levain supplemented with a bit of commercial yeast, whereas those in chapter 10, Pure Levain Doughs, are leavened solely with levain.

LEVAIN SCHEDULE

At Ken's Artisan Bakery, we feed the levain three times a day. There are two reasons why I didn't go that route in this book. First, my bakery is a lot warmer than the typical home kitchen, so the levain matures much more quickly and needs more feedings to keep it from getting sour. Second, I have bakers present most of the hours of the day. I want to offer you ways of making great levain breads without making you a slave to a schedule that would deter most from repeating the effort. This is a book intended to be used over and over.

Therefore, the schedule for feeding levain in this book requires just a single feeding in the morning, about six to nine hours before mixing the final dough. You can maintain the levain with a single feeding each morning, or you can use it to make dough and then store a chunk of the unused levain in the refrigerator, to be refreshed the next time you want to bake with it. All of those details are discussed in depth in chapter 8.

VARIABLES INFLUENCING LEVAIN CULTURES

Hydration

More liquid in the culture leads to greater production of lactic acid. Stiffer cultures have a flavor profile more dominated by acetic acid.

Temperature

Warmer temperatures, meaning 78°F to 90°F (26°C to 32°C), favor lactic acid production. Cooler temperatures, meaning 55°F to 65°F (13°C to 18°C), favor acetic acid production. Warmer cultures develop faster.

Flour

High-extraction flours (milled from a larger portion of the wheat berry than pure white flour), whole grain wheat or rye flours, and high-ash flours (which have a high mineral content) all contribute to more vigorous fermentation. They can also create a volatile culture that requires more frequent feedings to prevent problems. Every type of flour—white, whole wheat, rye, and so on—has its own personality, as will different blends of flours.

Salt

Salt delays the fermentation process, and while some good bakers use salt in their levain culture, I prefer not to, as I'm looking for active development. (Still, certain environments or schedules necessitate the use of small amounts of salt.)

Yeast

Commercial yeast is more vigorous than wild yeasts, so adding even a small amount of packaged yeast to start or boost a levain culture will ultimately result in the commercial yeast dominating and eventually starving out the wild yeasts. Bottom line: Don't use packaged or commercial yeast in a levain culture, either to start it or to maintain it. However, it is okay to use a small amount of baker's yeast in the final bread dough to supplement the fermentation from the levain culture—so long as the unadulterated levain culture remains separate from the bread dough.

CHAPTER 8
LEVAIN METHOD

started the levain we use at my bakery in 1999, in a class I attended at the San Francisco Baking Institute, and I have kept it alive ever since. In that class, we developed levain cultures using only whole rye flour and water. The first several feedings consisted of adding equal amounts of very warm water (85°F to 95°F, or 29°C to 35°C) and whole rye flour to produce a mash of messy, very sticky dough, the most remarkable quality of which was how difficult it was to wash off my hands after mixing. Twice a day we threw away most of the levain, added more flour and warm water, mixed by hand, then covered the levain and returned it to the proofing cabinet. Then we spent the next five minutes washing our hands. At first, nothing much seemed to be happening, but by the fourth feeding we could smell a nice funk, and by the third day the culture was finally expanding and announced itself with a strong-smelling, funky, alcoholic, and acidic perfume. Progress! You too can enjoy the pleasure that begins with a leap of faith and ends with figuring out what to do with the culture once it's active.

There are two stages to concern yourself with. First, it takes several days to establish a good, active levain culture. Second, you need to have a maintenance program for feeding your levain and keeping it active and ready for baking. At a bakery where bread is made every day, it's simple to follow the same schedule every day. For the home baker who wants to bake from a levain once a week, you need a different sort of routine to store your active levain (in the refrigerator works) and to restore it on a schedule that makes it available when you're ready to use it.

The best way to start a levain is to use whole grain flour: whole rye, whole wheat, or a combination of the two. Rye flour doughs are sticky and way more difficult to rinse off your hands than wheat flour doughs, so you'll find it easier to start a levain with whole wheat flour than with whole rye flour. But if whole rye is what you have or what you want to use, that's fine. Whole grain flour is preferable because there's more yeast and mineral content in the bran and outer layers of the wheat or rye berry than in the endosperm.

STEP-BY-STEP GUIDE TO STARTING YOUR LEVAIN

If you're interested in keeping a levain around at all times, then in addition to the 6-quart clear, round tub you use for your poolish and biga, you'll want to have a second one (with a lid) to use as your permanent levain bucket. This tub will be plenty big enough to hold the culture as it begins to develop gas and expand. Reuse the same container for each successive mix without cleaning it. The flora building up inside the container is safe and will be valuable in making the culture active. Before you begin, weigh the empty tub and write the weight down. You'll need this information on Day 4 (and for the rest of the levain's life), when you use 100 grams of the levain as the basis for regular feeding. Knowing the weight of the tub will allow you to simply remove the excess levain and leave the portion to be fed in the tub.

For the first several days of building up your culture, exact measurements aren't necessary, so if I say to use 500 grams of flour and 500 grams of water, it's okay if amounts of either are slightly more or less. If, for example, you accidentally pour in 550 grams of water, there's no need to compensate by adding more flour. However, once your culture is established and you switch to a maintenance routine, using the exact amounts of flour and water and the right water temperatures is necessary if you want to achieve consistent results. Establishing your levain will take five days, as outlined below.

Day 1

ANY TIME BEFORE NOON: Put 500 grams (3¾ cups + 2 tablespoons) of whole wheat flour with 500 grams (2¼ cups) of water at about 90°F (32°C) in a 6-quart round tub and mix by hand just until incorporated. Leave the slurry-like mixture uncovered for 1 to 2 hours, then cover it and let it rest in a warm place. A temperature of 75°F to 90°F (24°C to 32°C) would be ideal, but if you don't have a spot that warm in your house, don't sweat it.

Opposite page: **Starting Your Levain.** First row: Day 1, just after mixing; 24 hours later; tossing all but an eyeballed quarter on Day 2. Second row: Day 3, morning (48 hours since beginning); Day 3, morning, top view; texture of levain on Day 3. Third row: Day 4, morning (more bubbles!); Day 4, morning, side view; texture of levain on Day 4, morning.

Day 2

ANY TIME BEFORE NOON: Throw away about three-quarters of your initial mix (it's fine to estimate the volume). Leave the remainder in the tub. Add 500 grams (3¾ cups + 2 tablespoons) of whole wheat flour and 500 grams (2¼ cups) of 90°F (32°C) water to the goop in the tub and mix by hand just until incorporated. Leave the mixture uncovered for 1 to 2 hours, then cover and let rest in a warm place.

By the end of Day 2 the levain should have expanded to almost the 2-quart line of a 6-quart dough tub, with some small bubbles visible.

Day 3

ANY TIME BEFORE NOON: Progress! The levain should be 2 times the volume it was when you mixed it the previous day, with bubbles throughout and a leathery alcohol smell. Again, throw away about three-quarters of the mixture, leaving the remainder in the tub. Add 500 grams (3¾ cups + 2 tablespoons) of whole wheat flour and 500 grams (2¼ cups) of 90°F (32°C) water and mix by hand just until incorporated. Leave the mixture uncovered for 1 to 2 hours, then cover it and let it rest in a warm place. Later in the day the levain should have a distinctly pungent, "sour porridge" odor. Give it a whiff.

Day 4

ANY TIME BEFORE NOON: The levain should again be back up to the 2-quart line of your 6-quart dough tub, with bubbles throughout. On Day 4, you'll reserve a smaller amount of levain—throw away all but 200 grams (¾ cup) of the mixture. You will want to be accurate with this measurement, so *use your scale* and scoop out levain until the overall weight reading is 200 grams greater than the starting weight of the tub. Add 500 grams (3¾ cups + 2 tablespoons) of whole wheat flour and 500 grams (2¼ cups) of 90°F (32°C) water and mix by hand just until incorporated. Cover and let rest in a warm place.

WEIGH YOUR EMPTY LEVAIN TUB!

Measure the empty weight of the container that will hold your levain culture and record that information somewhere. You can even write it on a piece of painter's tape and affix it to the outside of the container. This way, when it's time to feed or refresh the levain, you can easily determine the weight of the levain by putting the tub on your scale and subtracting the weight of the tub. My levain bucket weighs 410 grams, so I have 100 grams of levain in my bucket when I put it on a zeroed scale and the total weight is 510 grams.

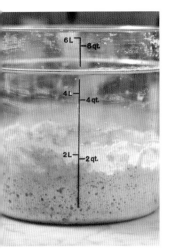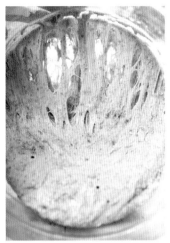

Left to right: Mature levain, in the morning before feeding; preparing to remove all but 100 grams of mature levain; 100 grams of levain in the tub, ready for its next feeding; mature levain after the morning feed.

Day 5

The levain culture should now be vigorous enough to use in any of the levain bread and pizza dough recipes in this book. The best cue that a levain is mature is when, 7 to 8 hours after the morning mix, it has a medium-ripe pungency and, if you wet your hand and pull out a chunk of it, you should feel its gassiness and be able to sense its weblike internal structure. It will be very goopy, with somewhat viscous texture. In any case, on Day 5 you'll switch from building your levain to a regular feeding schedule, using 80 percent hydration, a blend of white and whole wheat flour, and slightly cooler water.

SOMETIME BETWEEN 7 AND 9 A.M.: Throw away all but 150 grams (½ cup + 1 tablespoon) of the mixture. Use your scale and scoop out levain until the weight is 150 grams greater than the starting weight of the empty tub. Add 400 grams (3 cups + 2 tablespoons) of white flour, 100 grams (¾ cup + ½ tablespoon) of whole wheat flour, and 400 grams (1¾ cups) of 85°F (29°C) water to the tub and mix by hand just until incorporated. Cover and let rest in a warm place.

By the afternoon, the levain should be ready for use in dough, so you'll want to go ahead and read the next section, "Using Your Levain," which explains how to maintain the levain culture, what to look for in a mature levain, and how to store and refresh the culture if you won't be using it daily.

USING YOUR LEVAIN

Every time I feed the levain in the morning, I enjoy the gassiness of the culture, which has expanded to three to four times its volume if I haven't used any of it since the previous morning's feeding. When the lid comes off, there's a hot rush of alcoholic perfume. Let that pass, then stick your nose in the levain bucket and take in a big whiff. Get familiar with the fragrance of the levain at this stage and at the point when you're measuring it out for use later in the day. These points of reference—volume and smell—are cues that will be your guide to the final result. With time, experience, and exposure to the process, you'll come to trust your judgment.

With each recipe in chapters 9 through 11, if you follow my instructions on timing and water temperatures and use the precise measurements in this book, you can proceed with confidence. The biggest variable is going to be the ambient temperature. If your kitchen is significantly warmer or colder than mine, which typically hovers around 70°F (21°C) and gets down to about 65°F (18°C) at night, you may need to make adjustments. I suggest getting familiar with the way your levain smells when you take it out of its bucket to use in dough. That smell will directly translate to the flavor of the bread. See how you like the way the bread tastes. If it's too tart or sour, you can adjust next time by using slightly cooler water when feeding the levain in the morning or by mixing the final dough a little earlier in the afternoon, when the levain isn't as ripe. Likewise, if your kitchen is humid and a lot warmer than mine, say 80°F (27°C), then you may want to mix your final dough an hour or two earlier

SEASONAL VARIATIONS

I developed all of the recipes for this book in my home kitchen and tested them during each season. Here in Portland, winters are fairly cold, although not as below-freezing cold as, say, Minnesota or Manitoba. I've found that although my kitchen temperatures are roughly the same year-round, it's still colder in there in winter. As a result my levain culture isn't as active in winter and my levain doughs develop a bit more slowly than in the summer. Your own experience will vary depending on the climate you live in. In winter, I compensate by putting more levain in the final dough than I do in summer—somewhere around 50 grams (3 tablespoons) more. I've put notes regarding this option in the pure levain dough recipes in this book because those are the doughs most affected.

Another wintertime adjustment if the levain is developing slowly is to increase the amount of levain retained in the morning feed by about 30 to 50 grams (2 to 3 tablespoons), keeping the fresh flour and water amounts the same. In summertime, if the bread is too sour, I sometimes reduce the amount of levain retained in the morning feeding. Commercial yeast is much more vigorous than the wild culture in a levain, so hybrid leavening doughs with added baker's yeast (as in chapter 9) will have less seasonal variation than pure levain doughs.

than the recipes prescribe. On the other hand, if you have a hot kitchen, you could follow the schedule I outline and discover that you like the taste of the bread from an extra-ripe levain, which is a little more pungent and sour. If your kitchen is a lot colder than mine, put on a sweater! And compensate by using water at about 95°F (35°C) when feeding the levain in the morning. When feeding the levain, the target temperature is 78°F to 80°F (26°C to 27°C) right after mixing.

This book has levain bread recipes that operate on different schedules. The recipes in chapter 9, Hybrid Leavening Doughs, all follow the same schedule. You feed the levain in the morning, mix the final bread dough in the afternoon, divide and shape into loaves five hours later, and let the loaves rise slowly overnight in the refrigerator before baking them the next morning. The recipes in chapter 9 also use a small amount of baker's yeast (added to the dough, not the levain) to give the bread a lighter crumb and a little extra lift, but their flavor and character are primarily influenced by the levain. The recipes in chapter 10, on the other hand, arc pure levain doughs, without added baker's yeast, and follow a different schedule. You feed the levain in the morning, mix the final dough early in the evening, let the dough undergo overnight bulk fermentation, divide and shape into loaves the next morning, and bake four hours later. Both methods use the same schedule for feeding, storing, and refreshing the levain. So you can let your schedule and taste preferences dictate which approach you use.

All of these breads are well worth the effort, and once you become accustomed to the process, it truly isn't much effort. Time does most of the work.

The breads that result from these two methods—with added baker's yeast and without—are not identical. Hybrid leavening breads have a lighter texture, more volume, and a thinner crust, whereas pure levain breads are pleasingly rustic, being a little less domed and slightly smaller and denser and having bigger holes and more chew to the crust (in a good way). If pure levain breads are baked completely to dark umber in spots, the crust flavors will permeate into the crumb of the bread assertively. Pure levain breads also have more zip on the palate—a bit of a tang, but hopefully not too much—whereas breads with hybrid leavening have a more delicate balance of flavors. I encourage you to try both kinds of recipes so you can learn about the pleasures of each style of levain baking and discover your own preferences.

FEEDING YOUR LEVAIN

The levain recipes in this book assume you have a mature levain culture. If you're going to bake with your levain several days each week, you'll want to have a daily routine for feeding the levain. You can do it each morning, ideally at about the same time, but it can vary by an hour or two in either direction without causing problems. When it's time to feed the levain, use the following formula:

- 100 grams (⅓ cup + 1½ tablespoons) of levain (or a little more in winter; see "Seasonal Variations," page 134)
- 100 grams (¾ cup + ½ tablespoon) of whole wheat flour

- 400 grams (3 cups + 2 tablespoons) of white flour
- 400 grams (1¾ cups) of water, 85°F to 90°F (29°C to 32°C), depending on the season (warmer in winter, cooler in summer)

The target temperature for the levain right after mixing is between 78°F and 80°F (26°C and 27°C). If you aren't sure what temperature of water to use, measure the temperature of the levain after you've mixed it and adjust accordingly next time. Between feedings, cover the levain and let it rest at room temperature.

You can pare down the amount of levain, fresh flour, and fresh water used with each feeding as long as you maintain the same ratios. Here's the formula for maintaining half the amount of levain:

- 50 grams (3 tablespoons) of levain
- 50 grams (⅓ cup + 1 tablespoon) of whole wheat flour
- 200 grams (1½ cups + 1 tablespoon) of white flour
- 200 grams (⅞ cup) of water, 85°F to 90°F (29°C to 32°C), depending on the season

When you remove all but 50 grams (3 tablespoons) of levain from your levain tub, it will look like there's not much left other than an amount you would wash out. It's not much, but it holds a lot of potential!

When you have thrown away all but 100 grams (⅓ cup + 1½ tablespoons) of the levain (think of it as spent fuel), zero the scale. Add the amount of fresh flour needed, then add the amount of water needed, at the specified temperature, and mix by hand just until incorporated. One note on hand mixing levain: These cultures are quite acidic. If you mix levain frequently and have sensitive skin, you might want to use vinyl disposable gloves. They're handy to keep around anyway. I keep a box in my kitchen for various uses, like hand tossing salads.

After using your levain in a recipe, keep the remainder in its tub at room temperature. The next morning—when you regularly feed your levain—refresh the remainder as usual.

STORING AND RESTORING YOUR LEVAIN

If you will not be making dough with your levain culture every day or don't feel like feeding it every day, you need to have a plan for storing your levain on those off days and restoring it as needed. It's best to store it in the refrigerator. After using it in a final dough mix, take about 300 grams (1 cup + 3 tablespoons) of the remaining levain, coat it with a film of water, and put it in a nonperforated plastic bag, then refrigerate for up to 1 month.

When you're ready to use it again, you'll need to plan ahead in order to bring it back and use it at full strength. Here's the procedure I recommend:

STEP 1: TWO DAYS BEFORE YOU PLAN TO BAKE: Remove the levain from the refrigerator and put 200 grams (¾ cup) of it into your empty levain bucket. Discard the remainder. If possible, let the levain sit out at room temperature for 30 to 60 minutes to warm up. Then add 100 grams (¾ cup + ½ tablespoon) of whole wheat flour, 400 grams (3 cups + 2 tablespoons) of white flour, and 400 grams (1¾ cups) of 95°F (35°C) water and mix by hand until just incorporated. Cover and let rest in a warm spot overnight.

STEP 2: THE MORNING OF THE DAY BEFORE YOU PLAN TO BAKE: Feed the levain again, using the same feeding you use for daily levain: Discard all but 100 grams (⅓ cup + 1½ tablespoons) of the levain. Add 100 grams (¾ cup + ½ tablespoon) of whole wheat flour, 400 grams (3 cups + 2 tablespoons) of white flour, and 400 grams (1¾ cups) of water at 85°F to 90°F (29°C to 32°C), depending on the season. Mix by hand until just incorporated.

You have now completed the first step of each of the levain recipes. Cover the levain and let it rest in a warm spot until you mix your dough later that day. After overnight bulk fermentation or proof, depending on the recipe, you will be ready to bake the next day.

SAMPLE SCHEDULE

If you're starting a new levain and want to have it ready for baking bread on, say, a Sunday morning, then start with Day 1 of the section "Step-by-Step Guide to Starting Your Levain" (page 130) the Tuesday before. Although starting a new levain takes five days, each day the process takes just a few minutes.

If you have a levain stored in the refrigerator, here's a schedule for refreshing and feeding it so it will be ready for baking on Sunday morning:

1. On Friday morning, refresh your refrigerated levain following step 1 of the procedure in the section "Storing and Refreshing Your Levain," above.
2. On Saturday morning, toss all but 100 grams (⅓ cup + 1½ tablespoons) of the levain and follow step 2 of the procedure for refreshing.
3. On Saturday afternoon, mix the dough following the recipe of your choice.
4. For hybrid leavening recipes (chapter 9), on Saturday evening divide and shape the loaves and refrigerate overnight for slow proofing. For pure levain recipes (chapters 10 and 11), bulk fermentation extends overnight, and the loaves are divided and shaped the next morning.
5. For hybrid leavening breads, bake on Sunday morning; for pure levain breads, bake at around noon.

CHAPTER 9
HYBRID LEAVENING DOUGHS

PAIN DE CAMPAGNE 140

75% WHOLE WHEAT LEVAIN BREAD 144

BRAN-ENCRUSTED LEVAIN BREAD 147

WALNUT LEVAIN BREAD 151

FIELD BLEND #1 155

FIELD BLEND #2 158

Walnut Levain Bread (page 151).

PAIN DE CAMPAGNE

Pain de campagne is a rustic country bread that has a golden color to its crumb, subtle round flavors from fermentation, and a chewy and delicious crust. It improves with age for a couple of days after baking and can last nearly a week. This version has just a bit of whole wheat flour in both the final dough ingredients and the levain culture. The whole wheat flour boosts the energy of the fermentation and gives the final bread greater depth of flavor and just a touch of acidity on the palate. The long overnight proofing of the loaves in the refrigerator allows a nice complexity of flavors to build. Once you have a mature levain culture, this bread isn't much work and really delivers on taste and texture—and good looks.

Many French bakers use a small amount of rye flour in bread they call *pain de campagne* to give the crumb a slight grayish tint and a hint of rye flavor, whereas I use whole wheat here. Feel free to play with the flour blend. Another mixture that I really like in this recipe is 70 percent white flour, 20 percent whole wheat flour, and 10 percent whole rye flour. For guidance on playing around with

flour blends, see page 190, "Making a Bread (or Pizza) Dough You Can Call Your Own." Just make sure that the total amount of flour in your final dough mix is the same as in this recipe—800 grams (200 grams of flour are in the levain).

One of my common uses for this bread is tearing a couple of slices into croutons, lightly toasting them until slightly crisp, then tossing them in a mustardy vinaigrette, so the vinaigrette really soaks into the croutons, and then with fresh lettuces and a chopped hard-boiled egg. This bread is ideal for onion soup *gratiné* or *ribollita*. It's also excellent spread with pâté or for sopping up sauce, not to mention for sandwiches or morning toast with butter and jam. I sometimes use this bread, very lightly toasted, as an alternative to burger buns.

THIS RECIPE MAKES 2 LOAVES, EACH ABOUT 1½ POUNDS.

BULK FERMENTATION: About 5 hours

PROOF TIME: 12 to 14 hours

SAMPLE SCHEDULE: Feed the levain at 8 a.m., mix the final dough at 3 p.m., shape into loaves at 8 p.m., proof the loaves in the refrigerator overnight, and bake around 8 to 10 a.m. the next morning.

Levain

INGREDIENT	QUANTITY	
Mature, active levain	100 g	⅓ cup + 1½ tbsp
White flour	400 g	3 cups + 2 tbsp
Whole wheat flour	100 g	¾ cup + ½ tbsp
Water	400 g , 85°F to 90°F (29°C to 32°C)	1¾ cups

Final Dough / Baker's Formula

INGREDIENT	FINAL DOUGH MIX QUANTITY		QUANTITY IN LEVAIN	TOTAL RECIPE QUANTITY	BAKER'S PERCENTAGE
White flour	740 g	5¾ cups	160 g	900 g	90%
Whole wheat flour	60 g	½ cup + ½ tbsp	40 g	100 g	10%
Water	620 g, 90°F to 95°F (32°C to 35°C)	2¾ cups	160 g	780 g	78%
Fine sea salt	21 g	1 tbsp + 1 scant tsp	0	21 g	2.1%
Instant dried yeast	2 g	½ tsp	0	2 g	0.2%
Levain	360 g	1⅓ cups			20%*

* The baker's percentage for levain is the amount of flour in the levain expressed as a percentage of the total flour in the recipe.

CONTINUED>>

1a. Feed the levain About 24 hours after your previous feeding of the levain, discard all but 100 grams of the levain, leaving the remainder in your 6-quart tub. Add 400 grams of white flour, 100 grams of whole wheat flour, and 400 grams of water at 85°F to 90°F (29°C to 32°C) and mix by hand just until incorporated. Cover and let rest at room temperature for 6 to 8 hours before mixing the final dough.

1b. Autolyse After 6 to 8 hours, mix the 740 grams of white flour and the 60 grams of whole wheat flour by hand in a 12-quart round tub. Add the 620 grams of 90°F to 95°F (32°C to 35°C) water and mix by hand just until incorporated. Cover and let rest for 20 to 30 minutes.

2. Mix the final dough Sprinkle the 21 grams of salt and the 2 grams (½ teaspoon) of yeast evenly over the top of the dough.

Put a container with about a finger's depth of warm water on your scale so you can easily remove the levain after it's weighed. With wet hands, transfer 360 grams of levain into the container.

Transfer the weighed levain to the 12-quart dough tub, minimizing the amount of water transferred with it. Mix by hand, wetting your working hand before mixing so the dough doesn't stick to you. Use the pincer method (see page 67) alternating with folding the dough to fully integrate the ingredients. The target dough temperature at the end of the mix is 77°F to 78°F (25°C to 26°C).

3. Fold This dough needs three or four folds (see pages 69–70). It's easiest to apply the folds during the first 1½ to 2 hours after mixing the dough.

When the dough is about 2½ times its original volume, about 5 hours after mixing, it's ready to be divided.

4. Divide With floured hands, gently ease the dough out of the tub and onto a lightly floured work surface. With your hands still floured, pick up the dough and ease it back down onto the work surface in a somewhat even shape. Use a bit of flour to dust the area in the middle where you'll cut the dough, then cut it

WHAT IF THE DOUGH ISN'T AT THE TARGET TEMPERATURE?

If the final mix temperature is cooler than 77°F (25°C), don't worry—it may just take longer to increase to 2½ times its original volume. Put the dough in a warm spot, and use warmer water next time you make the recipe. If the dough temperature is above 78°F (26°C), the dough will probably expand faster, depending on the temperature of your kitchen. Use cooler water next time you make the recipe.

into 2 equal-size pieces with a dough knife or plastic dough scraper.

5. Shape Dust 2 proofing baskets with flour. Shape each piece of dough into a medium-tight ball following the instructions on pages 71–73. Place each seam side down in its proofing basket.

6. Proof Place each basket in a nonperforated plastic bag and refrigerate overnight.

The next morning, 12 to 14 hours after the loaves went into the refrigerator, they should be ready to bake, straight from the refrigerator. They don't need to come to room temperature first.

7. Preheat At least 45 minutes prior to baking, put a rack in the middle of the oven and put 2 Dutch ovens on the rack with their lids on. Preheat the oven to 475°F (245°C).

If you only have 1 Dutch oven, keep the other loaf in the refrigerator while the first loaf is baking, and bake the loaves sequentially, giving the Dutch oven a 5-minute reheat after removing the first loaf.

8. Bake For the next step, please be careful not to let your hands, fingers, or forearms touch the extremely hot Dutch oven.

Invert the proofed loaf onto a lightly floured countertop, keeping in mind that the top of the loaf will be the side that was facing down while it was rising—the seam side.

Remove the preheated Dutch oven from your kitchen oven, remove the lid, and carefully place the loaf in the Dutch oven seam side up. Cover and bake for 30 minutes, then uncover and bake for about 20 minutes, until dark brown all around the loaf. Check after 15 minutes of baking uncovered in case your oven runs hot.

Remove the Dutch oven and carefully tilt it to turn the loaf out. Let cool on a rack or set the loaf on its side so air can circulate around it. Let the loaf rest for at least 20 minutes before slicing.

75% WHOLE WHEAT LEVAIN BREAD

This delicious high-fiber levain bread improves in flavor for a couple of days after it is baked. I get flavors of nut butter and Wheatena in this bread and love it with good dairy butter or simply toasted. It's also wonderful with a nice soft Robiola cheese, apricot jam, or potted duck liver.

You may notice that this bread has slightly less yeast than the other breads in this chapter that are made on the same schedule. This is because whole wheat flour has more nutrients for yeast and therefore ferments faster than white flour. The bran in whole wheat flour cuts through the gluten strands in the dough, resulting in a somewhat smaller, denser loaf. Who cares? It's not a brick. The texture and volume of this loaf are very impressive for the amount of whole grain it carries. I love this bread.

THIS RECIPE MAKES 2 LOAVES, EACH ABOUT 1½ POUNDS.

BULK FERMENTATION: About 5 hours

PROOF TIME: 12 to 13 hours

SAMPLE SCHEDULE: Feed the levain at 8 a.m., mix the final dough at 3 p.m., shape into loaves at 8 p.m., proof the loaves in the refrigerator overnight, and bake between 8 and 9 a.m. the next morning.

Levain

INGREDIENT	QUANTITY	
Mature, active levain	100 g	⅓ cup + 1½ tbsp
White flour	400 g	3 cups + 2 tbsp
Whole wheat flour	100 g	¾ cup + ½ tbsp
Water	400 g , 85°F to 90°F (29°C to 32°C)	1¾ cups

Final Dough / Baker's Formula

INGREDIENT	FINAL DOUGH MIX QUANTITY		QUANTITY IN LEVAIN	TOTAL RECIPE QUANTITY	BAKER'S PERCENTAGE
White flour	90 g	½ cup + 3 tbsp	160 g	250 g	25%
Whole wheat flour	710 g	5½ cups + ½ tbsp	40 g	750 g	75%
Water	660 g, 90°F to 95°F (32°C to 35°C)	2⅞ cups	160 g	820 g	82%
Fine sea salt	21 g	1 tbsp + 1 scant tsp	0	21 g	2.1%
Instant dried yeast	1.75 g	Scant ½ tsp	0	1.75 g	0.175%
Levain	360 g	1⅓ cups			20%*

* The baker's percentage for levain is the amount of flour in the levain expressed as a percentage of the total flour in the recipe.

1a. Feed the levain About 24 hours after your previous feeding of the levain, discard all but 100 grams of levain, leaving the remainder in your 6-quart tub. Add 400 grams of white flour, 100 grams of whole wheat flour, and 400 grams of water at 85°F to 90°F (29°C to 32°C) and mix by hand just until incorporated. Cover and let rest at room temperature for 6 to 8 hours before mixing the final dough.

1b. Autolyse After 6 to 8 hours, mix the 90 grams of white flour and the 710 grams of whole wheat flour by hand in a 12-quart round tub. Add the 660 grams of 90°F to 95°F (32°C to 35°C) water and mix by hand just until incorporated. Cover and let rest for 20 to 30 minutes.

2. Mix the final dough Sprinkle the 21 grams of salt and the 1.75 grams (scant ½ teaspoon) of yeast evenly over the top of the dough.

Put a container with about a finger's depth of warm water on your scale so you can easily remove the levain after it's weighed. With wet hands, transfer 360 grams of levain into the container.

Transfer the weighed levain to the 12-quart dough tub, minimizing the amount of water transferred with it. Mix by hand, wetting your working hand before mixing so the dough doesn't stick to you. Use the pincer method (see page 67) alternating with folding the dough to fully integrate the ingredients. The target dough temperature at the end of the mix is 77°F to 78°F (25°C to 26°C).

3. Fold This dough needs two or three folds (see pages 69–70). It's easiest to apply the folds during the first 1½ to 2 hours after mixing the dough.

When the dough is about 2½ times its original volume, about 5 hours after mixing, it's ready to be divided.

4. Divide With floured hands, gently ease the dough out of the tub and onto a lightly floured work surface. With your hands still floured, pick up the dough and ease it back down onto the work surface in a somewhat even shape. Use a bit of flour to dust the area in the middle where you'll cut the dough, then cut it into 2 equal-size pieces with a dough knife or plastic dough scraper.

5. Shape Dust 2 proofing baskets with flour. Shape each piece of dough into a medium-tight ball following the instructions on pages 71–73. Place each seam side down in its proofing basket.

6. Proof Place each basket in a nonperforated plastic bag and refrigerate overnight.

The next morning, 12 to 13 hours after the loaves went into the refrigerator, they should be ready to bake, straight from the refrigerator. They don't need to come to room temperature first.

CONTINUED>>

7. Preheat At least 45 minutes prior to baking, put a rack in the middle of the oven and put 2 Dutch ovens on the rack with their lids on. Preheat the oven to 475°F (245°C).

If you only have 1 Dutch oven, keep the other loaf in the refrigerator while the first loaf is baking, and bake the loaves sequentially, giving the Dutch oven a 5-minute reheat after removing the first loaf.

8. Bake For the next step, please be careful not to let your hands, fingers, or forearms touch the extremely hot Dutch oven.

Invert the proofed loaf onto a lightly floured countertop, keeping in mind that the top of the loaf will be the side that was facing down while it was rising—the seam side.

Remove the preheated Dutch oven from your kitchen oven, remove the lid, and carefully place the loaf in the Dutch oven seam side up. Cover and bake for 30 minutes, then uncover and bake for about 20 minutes, until medium dark brown all around the loaf. Check after 15 minutes of baking uncovered in case your oven runs hot.

Remove the Dutch oven and carefully tilt it to turn the loaf out. Let cool on a rack or set the loaf on its side so air can circulate around it. Let the loaf rest for at least 20 minutes before slicing.

BRAN-ENCRUSTED LEVAIN BREAD

Wheat germ and bran are expelled from the wheat kernel in the modern milling process, leaving just the endosperm, which is milled to make white flour. Bran takes up about 14 percent of the kernel's weight, and germ accounts for 2.5 to 3 percent of the weight. This recipe folds the germ back in and coats the loaf with a small amount of bran. If you want to use more germ in the dough, go for it; up to about 100 grams should be fine. Although I have seen some recipes go higher, I think too much germ in the dough weighs down the crumb. The bran coating, which can tolerate a long baking time, gives the crust a nice crisp crunch and a roasted nut flavor. The bran does have a habit of scattering when you slice the bread—c'est la vie. A handful of bran goes into the proofing baskets and will adhere to the loaves when you remove them for baking.

THIS RECIPE MAKES 2 LOAVES, EACH ABOUT 1½ POUNDS.

BULK FERMENTATION: About 5 hours

PROOF TIME: 12 to 14 hours

SAMPLE SCHEDULE: Feed the levain at 8 a.m., mix the final dough at 3 p.m., shape into loaves at 8 p.m., proof the loaves in the refrigerator overnight, and bake around 8 to 10 a.m. the next morning.

Levain

INGREDIENT	QUANTITY	
Mature, active levain	100 g	⅓ cup + 1½ tbsp
White flour	400 g	3 cups + 2 tbsp
Whole wheat flour	100 g	¾ cup + ½ tbsp
Water	400 g , 85°F to 90°F (29°C to 32°C)	1¾ cups

CONTINUED>>

Final Dough			Baker's Formula		
INGREDIENT	FINAL DOUGH MIX QUANTITY		QUANTITY IN LEVAIN	TOTAL RECIPE QUANTITY	BAKER'S PERCENTAGE
White flour	800 g	6¼ cups	160 g	960 g	96%
Whole wheat flour	0	0	40 g	40 g	4%
Water	620 g, 90°F to 95°F (32°C to 35°C)	2¾ cups	160 g	780 g	78%
Fine sea salt	21 g	1 tbsp + 1 scant tsp	0	21 g	2.1%
Instant dried yeast	2 g	½ tsp	0	2 g	0.2%
Wheat germ	30 g	⅓ cup + 1 tbsp	0	30 g	3%
Wheat bran	0	0	0	20 g (⅓ cup + 1 tbsp)	2%
Levain	360 g	1⅓ cups			20%*

* The baker's percentage for levain is the amount of flour in the levain expressed as a percentage of the total flour in the recipe.

1a. Feed the levain About 24 hours after your previous feeding of the levain, discard all but 100 grams of levain, leaving the remainder in your 6-quart tub. Add 400 grams of white flour, 100 grams of whole wheat flour, and 400 grams of water at 85°F to 90°F (29°C to 32°C) and mix by hand just until incorporated. Cover and let rest for 6 to 8 hours before mixing the final dough.

1b. Autolyse After 6 to 8 hours, mix the 800 grams of white flour and the 30 grams of wheat germ by hand in a 12-quart round tub. Add the 620 grams of 90°F to 95°F (32°C to 35°C) water and mix by hand just until incorporated. Cover and let rest for 20 to 30 minutes.

2. Mix the final dough Sprinkle the 21 grams of salt and the 2 grams (½ teaspoon) of yeast evenly over the top of the dough.

Put a container with about a finger's depth of warm water on your scale so you can easily remove the levain after it's weighed. With wet hands, transfer 360 grams of levain into the container.

Transfer the weighed levain to the 12-quart dough tub, minimizing the amount of water transferred with it. Mix by hand, wetting your working hand before mixing so the dough doesn't stick to you. Use the pincer method (see page 67) alternating with folding the dough to fully integrate the ingredients. The target dough temperature at the end of the mix is 77°F to 78°F (25°C to 26°C).

3. Fold This dough needs three or four folds (see pages 69–70). It's easiest to apply the folds during the first 1½ to 2 hours after mixing the dough.

CONTINUED>>

When the dough is about 2½ times its original volume, about 5 hours after mixing, it's ready to be divided.

4. Divide Lightly dust 2 proofing baskets with flour, then sprinkle 10 grams of wheat bran evenly in each basket.

With floured hands, gently ease the dough out of the tub and onto a lightly floured work surface. With your hands still floured, pick up the dough and ease it back down onto the work surface in a somewhat even shape. Use a bit of flour to dust the area in the middle where you'll cut the dough, then cut it into 2 equal-size pieces with a dough knife or plastic dough scraper.

5. Shape Shape each piece of dough into a medium-tight ball following the instructions on pages 71–73. Place each seam side down in its proofing basket.

6. Proof Place each basket in a nonperforated plastic bag and refrigerate overnight.

The next morning, 12 to 14 hours after the loaves went into the refrigerator, they should be ready to bake, straight from the refrigerator. They don't need to come to room temperature first.

7. Preheat At least 45 minutes prior to baking, put a rack in the middle of the oven and put 2 Dutch ovens on the rack with their lids on. Preheat the oven to 475°F (245°C).

If you only have 1 Dutch oven, keep the other loaf in the refrigerator while the first loaf is baking, and bake the loaves sequentially, giving the Dutch oven a 5-minute reheat after removing the first loaf.

8. Bake For the next step, please be careful not to let your hands, fingers, or forearms touch the extremely hot Dutch oven.

Invert the proofed loaf onto a lightly floured countertop, keeping in mind that the top of the loaf will be the side that was facing down while it was rising—the seam side.

Remove the preheated Dutch oven from your kitchen oven, remove the lid, and carefully place the loaf in the Dutch oven seam side up. Cover and bake for 30 minutes, then uncover and bake for about 20 minutes, until medium dark brown all around the loaf. Check after 15 minutes of baking uncovered in case your oven runs hot.

Remove the Dutch oven and carefully tilt it to turn the loaf out. Let cool on a rack or set the loaf on its side so air can circulate around it. Let the loaf rest for at least 20 minutes before slicing.

WALNUT LEVAIN BREAD

At Ken's Artisan Bakery, we've been making walnut bread in various shapes and sizes since the bakery opened, from loaves to big rounds to crusty, hearty walnut rolls that people mostly buy for breakfast. We lightly roast the walnuts before adding them to the dough. The bread is delicious on its own and is sublime when toasted and slathered with butter and honey. We deliver torpedoes of our walnut bread to some restaurants who then slice it, grill it, and pair it with cheese. At my bakery, we use walnut bread for a sandwich with *fromage blanc* and fresh Bosc pears from Hood River. My friend Steve Jones, who owns Cheese Bar here in Portland, loves this bread paired with Oregon Blue or Caveman Blue cheese, both from Oregon's Rogue Creamery. It's also excellent with a smear of fresh goat cheese. This bread is always best toasted.

THIS RECIPE MAKES 2 LOAVES, EACH ABOUT 1¾ POUNDS.

BULK FERMENTATION: About 5 hours

PROOF TIME: 12 to 14 hours

SAMPLE SCHEDULE: Feed the levain at 8 a.m., mix the final dough at 3 p.m., shape into loaves at 8 p.m., proof the loaves in the refrigerator overnight, and bake around 8 to 10 a.m. the next morning.

Levain

INGREDIENT	QUANTITY	
Mature, active levain	100 g	⅓ cup + 1½ tbsp
White flour	400 g	3 cups + 2 tbsp
Whole wheat flour	100 g	¾ cup + ½ tbsp
Water	400 g , 85°F to 90°F (29°C to 32°C)	1¾ cups

Final Dough / Baker's Formula

INGREDIENT	FINAL DOUGH MIX QUANTITY		QUANTITY IN LEVAIN	TOTAL RECIPE QUANTITY	BAKER'S PERCENTAGE
White flour	740 g	5¾ cups	160 g	900 g	90%
Whole wheat flour	60 g	½ cup + 1 tbsp	40 g	100 g	10%
Water	620 g, 90°F to 95°F (32°C to 35°C)	2¾ cups	160 g	780 g	78%
Fine sea salt	22 g	1 tbsp + 1 tsp	0	22 g	2.2%
Instant dried yeast	2 g	½ tsp	0	2 g	0.2%
Walnut halves or pieces	225 g	About 2 cups	0	225 g	22.5%
Levain	360 g	1⅓ cups			20%*

* The baker's percentage for levain is the amount of flour in the levain expressed as a percentage of the total flour in the recipe.

CONTINUED>>

1a. Feed the levain About 24 hours after your previous feeding of the levain, discard all but 100 grams of levain, leaving the remainder in your 6-quart tub. Add 400 grams of white flour, 100 grams of whole wheat flour, and 400 grams of water at 85°F to 90°F (29°C to 32°C) and mix by hand just until incorporated. Cover and let rest at room temperature for 6 to 8 hours before mixing the final dough.

1b. Roast the nuts At least 1 hour before autolysing, preheat the oven to 400°F (205°C). Put the walnuts in an ovenproof skillet or baking pan and roast for about 12 minutes, until medium dark brown. Let cool to room temperature.

1c. Autolyse Between 6 and 8 hours after feeding the levain, mix the 740 grams of white flour and the 60 grams of whole wheat flour by hand in a 12-quart round tub. Add the 620 grams of 90°F to 95°F (32°C to 35°C) water and mix by hand just until incorporated. Cover and let rest for 20 to 30 minutes.

2. Mix the final dough Sprinkle the 22 grams of salt and the 2 grams (½ teaspoon) of yeast evenly over the top of the dough.

Put a container with about a finger's depth of warm water on your scale so you can easily remove the levain after it's weighed. With wet hands, transfer 360 grams of levain into the container.

Transfer the weighed levain to the 12-quart dough tub, minimizing the amount of water transferred with it. Mix by hand, wetting your working hand before mixing so

the dough doesn't stick to you. Use the pincer method (see page 67) alternating with folding the dough to fully integrate the ingredients. The target dough temperature at the end of the mix is 77°F to 78°F (25°C to 26°C).

Let the dough rest for 10 minutes, then spread the cooled walnuts over the top. Incorporate them into the dough, again using the pincer method alternating with folding until the walnuts are evenly distributed.

3. Fold This dough needs three folds (see pages 69–70). It's easiest to apply the folds during the first 1½ to 2 hours after mixing the dough.

When the dough is about 2½ times its original volume, about 5 hours after mixing, it's ready to be divided.

4. Divide With floured hands, gently ease the dough out of the tub and onto a lightly floured work surface. With your hands still floured, pick up the dough and ease it back down onto the work surface in a somewhat even shape. Use a bit of flour to dust the area in the middle where you'll cut the dough, then cut it into 2 equal-size pieces with a dough knife or plastic dough scraper.

5. Shape Dust 2 proofing baskets with flour. Shape each piece of dough into a medium-tight ball following the instructions on pages 71–73. Place each seam side down in its proofing basket.

6. Proof Place each basket in a nonperforated plastic bag and refrigerate overnight.

CONTINUED>>

The next morning, 12 to 14 hours after the loaves went into the refrigerator, they should be ready to bake, straight from the refrigerator. They don't need to come to room temperature first.

7. Preheat At least 45 minutes prior to baking, put a rack in the middle of the oven and put 2 Dutch ovens on the rack with their lids on. Preheat the oven to 475°F (245°C).

If you only have 1 Dutch oven, keep the other loaf in the refrigerator while the first loaf is baking, and bake the loaves sequentially, giving the Dutch oven a 5-minute reheat after removing the first loaf.

8. Bake For the next step, please be careful not to let your hands, fingers, or forearms touch the extremely hot Dutch oven.

Invert the proofed loaf onto a lightly floured countertop, keeping in mind that the top of the loaf will be the side that was facing down while it was rising—the seam side.

Remove the preheated Dutch oven from your kitchen oven, remove the lid, and carefully place the loaf in the Dutch oven seam side up. Cover and bake for 30 minutes, then uncover and bake for about 20 minutes, until medium dark brown all around the loaf. Check after 15 minutes of baking uncovered in case your oven runs hot.

Remove the Dutch oven and carefully tilt it to turn the loaf out. Let cool on a rack or set the loaf on its side so air can circulate around it. Let the loaf rest for at least 20 minutes before slicing.

FIELD BLEND #1

I'm borrowing a term from the wine world, where *field blend* implies multiple varieties of grapes grown at the same vineyard, combined to produce a single wine. This practice has long been part of the winemaking tradition in Alsace, among other regions. Here I use the term to refer to a bread made with white and whole wheat flours plus white rye flour, which is sometimes labeled "light rye flour," and is just rye flour without the bran or germ (just like white wheat flour). This bread offers a complexity of flavor distinctly its own: influenced happily and not too heavily by the rye, without losing the lightness of a bread made primarily from wheat flour. The next recipe, Field Blend Levain #2 (page 158) is a darker, earthier loaf that uses a bit more whole wheat flour, and either whole rye or pumpernickel rye flour rather than white rye.

This is an excellent sandwich bread. You might also think of it as an accent flavor anywhere you use anything smoked, from smoked salt to smoked fish to smoked meats. If I were to try to build a New York pastrami-on-rye sandwich empire, this first Field Blend recipe is the bread I would use, tossing some caraway seeds into the dough.

THIS RECIPE MAKES 2 LOAVES, EACH ABOUT 1½ POUNDS.

BULK FERMENTATION: About 5 hours

PROOF TIME: About 12 hours

SAMPLE SCHEDULE: Feed the levain at 8 a.m., mix the final dough at 3 p.m., shape into loaves at 8 p.m., proof the loaves in the refrigerator overnight, and bake at around 8 a.m. the next morning.

Levain

INGREDIENT	QUANTITY	
Mature, active levain	100 g	⅓ cup + 1½ tbsp
White flour	400 g	3 cups + 2 tbsp
Whole wheat flour	100 g	¾ cup + ½ tbsp
Water	400 g, 85°F to 90°F (29°C to 32°C)	1¾ cups

CONTINUED>>

Final Dough

INGREDIENT	FINAL DOUGH MIX QUANTITY	
White flour	590 g	4½ cups + 2 tbsp
Whole wheat flour	60 g	½ cup + ½ tbsp
White rye flour	150 g	1½ cups
Water	590 g, 90°F to 95°F (32°C to 35°C)	2⅔ cups
Fine sea salt	21 g	1 tbsp + 1 scant tsp
Instant dried yeast	2 g	½ tsp
Levain	360 g	1⅓ cups

Baker's Formula

QUANTITY IN LEVAIN	TOTAL RECIPE QUANTITY	BAKER'S PERCENTAGE
160 g	750 g	75%
40 g	100 g	10%
0	150 g	15%
160 g	750 g	75%
0	21 g	2.1%
0	2 g	0.2%
		20%*

The baker's percentage for levain is the amount of flour in the levain expressed as a percentage of the total flour in the recipe.

1a. Feed the levain About 24 hours after your previous feeding of the levain, discard all but 100 grams of levain, leaving the remainder in your 6-quart tub. Add 400 grams of white flour, 100 grams of whole wheat flour, and 400 grams of water at 85°F to 90°F (29°C to 32°C) and mix by hand just until incorporated. Cover and let rest at room temperature for 6 to 8 hours before mixing the final dough.

1b. Autolyse After 6 to 8 hours, mix the 590 grams of white flour, the 60 grams of whole wheat flour, and the 150 grams of white rye flour by hand in a 12-quart round tub. Add the 590 grams of 90°F to 95°F (32°C to 35°C) water and mix by hand just until incorporated. Cover and let rest for 20 to 30 minutes.

The rye flour will make this dough a little stickier than bread dough made without rye.

2. Mix the final dough Sprinkle the 21 grams of salt and the 2 grams (½ teaspoon) of yeast evenly over the top of the dough.

Put a container with about a finger's depth of warm water on your scale so you can easily remove the levain after it's weighed. With wet hands, transfer 360 grams of levain into the container.

Transfer the weighed levain to the 12-quart dough tub, minimizing the amount of water transferred with it. Mix by hand, wetting your working hand before mixing so the dough doesn't stick to you. Use the pincer method (see page 67) alternating with folding the dough to fully integrate the ingredients. The target dough temperature at the end of the mix is 77°F to 78°F (25°C to 26°C).

3. Fold This dough needs three or four folds (see pages 69–70). It's easiest to apply the folds during the first 1½ to 2 hours after mixing the dough.

When the dough is about 2½ times its original volume, about 5 hours after mixing, it's ready to be divided.

4. Divide With floured hands, gently ease the dough out of the tub and onto a lightly floured work surface. With your hands still floured, pick up the dough and ease it back down onto the work surface in a somewhat even shape. Use a bit of flour to dust the area in the middle where you'll cut the dough, then cut it into 2 equal-size pieces with a dough knife or plastic dough scraper.

5. Shape Doughs made with rye flour are stickier and need a bit more strengthening than doughs made without. To compensate, "preshape" your dough first: Sprinkle a little flour over the top of each piece, then flip them over, flour side down, and fold the dough by reaching under the mass and pulling floured sections of the dough over and across, eventually enclosing the sticky inner surface of the dough. Then, shape each piece of dough into a tight ball following the instructions on pages 71–73. Place them on the counter seam side down and let rest for about 15 minutes.

After the preshape step, dust 2 proofing baskets with flour. Once again shape each piece of dough into a tight ball. Place each seam side down in its proofing basket.

6. Proof Place each basket in a nonperforated plastic bag and refrigerate overnight.

The next morning, about 12 hours after the loaves went into the refrigerator, they should be ready to bake, straight from the refrigerator. They don't need to come to room temperature first.

7. Preheat At least 45 minutes prior to baking, put a rack in the middle of the oven and put 2 Dutch ovens on the rack with their lids on. Preheat the oven to 475°F (245°C).

If you only have 1 Dutch oven, keep the other loaf in the refrigerator while the first loaf is baking, and bake the loaves sequentially, giving the Dutch oven a 5-minute reheat after removing the first loaf.

8. Bake For the next step, please be careful not to let your hands, fingers, or forearms touch the extremely hot Dutch oven.

Invert the proofed loaf onto a lightly floured countertop, keeping in mind that the top of the loaf will be the side that was facing down while it was rising—the seam side.

Remove the preheated Dutch oven from your kitchen oven, remove the lid, and carefully place the loaf in the Dutch oven seam side up. Cover and bake for 30 minutes, then uncover and bake for about 20 minutes, until dark brown all around the loaf. Check after 15 minutes of baking uncovered in case your oven runs hot.

Remove the Dutch oven and carefully tilt it to turn the loaf out. Let cool on a rack or set the loaf on its side so air can circulate around it. Let the loaf rest for at least 20 minutes before slicing.

FIELD BLEND #2

This second Field Blend of wheat and rye flours is in this book for two reasons: it has a different personality thanks to the use of whole rye or pumpernickel rye flour instead of the white rye flour used in Field Blend #1; and it helps show how you can adjust the flour in these recipes to make a Field Blend with whatever ratio of flours you want to use.

When you are shopping for flour, whole rye flour is often labeled "dark rye flour." Pumpernickel rye flour is whole rye, coarsely ground.

The result is bread that's a bit darker and slightly earthier in flavor than the Field Blend #1 (page 155). Both of these recipes use the same total amount of flour as every other recipe in this

book: 1,000 grams. The levain contributes 200 grams of flour; the remaining 800 grams, used in the final dough, are a "dealer's choice" blend that can be customized as you wish.

I particularly like the blend of flours in this recipe. It includes about as much rye flour as you can work into the dough without losing all the texture and volume of a wheat bread.

THIS RECIPE MAKES 2 LOAVES, EACH ABOUT 1½ POUNDS, AND IS SUITABLE FOR FOCACCIA.

BULK FERMENTATION: About 5 hours

PROOF TIME: 11 to 12 hours

SAMPLE SCHEDULE: Feed the levain at 8 a.m., mix the final dough at 3 p.m., shape into loaves at 8 p.m., proof the loaves in the refrigerator overnight, and bake around 7 or 8 a.m. the next morning.

Levain

INGREDIENT	QUANTITY	
Mature, active levain	100 g	⅓ cup + 1½ tbsp
White flour	400 g	3 cups + 2 tbsp
Whole wheat flour	100 g	¾ cup + ½ tbsp
Water	400 g, 85°F to 90°F (29°C to 32°C)	1¾ cups

Final Dough / Baker's Formula

INGREDIENT	FINAL DOUGH MIX QUANTITY		QUANTITY IN LEVAIN	TOTAL RECIPE QUANTITY	BAKER'S PERCENTAGE
White flour	540 g	4 cups + 3 tbsp	160 g	700 g	70%
Whole rye flour	175 g	1¾ cups	0	175 g	17.5%
Whole wheat flour	85 g	⅔ cup	40 g	125 g	12.5%
Water	620 g, 90°F to 95°F (32°C to 35°C)	2¾ cups	160 g	780 g	78%
Fine sea salt	21 g	1 tbsp + 1 scant tsp	0	21 g	2.1%
Instant dried yeast	2 g	½ tsp	0	2 g	0.2%
Levain	360 g	1⅓ cups			20%*

* The baker's percentage for levain is the amount of flour in the levain expressed as a percentage of the total flour in the recipe.

CONTINUED>>

1a. Feed the levain About 24 hours after your previous feeding of the levain, discard all but 100 grams of levain, leaving the remainder in your 6-quart tub. Add 400 grams of white flour, 100 grams of whole wheat flour, and 400 grams of water at 85°F to 90°F (29°C to 32°C) and mix by hand just until incorporated. Cover and let rest at room temperature for 6 to 8 hours before mixing the final dough.

1b. Autolyse After 6 to 8 hours, mix the 540 grams of white flour, the 85 grams of whole wheat flour, and the 175 grams of whole rye flour by hand in a 12-quart round tub. Add the 620 grams of 90°F to 95°F (32°C to 35°C) water and mix by hand just until incorporated. Cover and let rest for 20 to 30 minutes.

The rye flour will make this dough a little stickier than bread dough made without rye.

2. Mix the final dough Sprinkle the 21 grams of salt and the 2 grams (½ teaspoon) of yeast evenly over the top of the dough.

Put a container with about a finger's depth of warm water on your scale so you can easily remove the levain after it's weighed. With wet hands, transfer 360 grams of levain into the container.

Transfer the weighed levain to the 12-quart dough tub, minimizing the amount of water transferred with it. Mix by hand, wetting your working hand before mixing so the dough doesn't stick to you. Use the pincer method (see page 67) alternating with folding the dough to fully integrate the ingredients. The target dough temperature at the end of the mix is 77°F to 78°F (25°C to 26°C).

3. Fold This dough needs three or four folds (see pages 69–70). It's easiest to apply the folds during the first 1½ to 2 hours after mixing the dough.

When the dough is about 2½ times its original volume, about 5 hours after mixing, it's ready to be divided.

4. Divide With floured hands, gently ease the dough out of the tub and onto a lightly floured work surface. With your hands still floured, pick up the dough and ease it back down onto the work surface in a somewhat even shape. Use a bit of flour to dust the area in the middle where you'll cut the dough, then cut it into 2 equal-size pieces with a dough knife or plastic dough scraper.

5. Shape Doughs made with rye flour are stickier and need a bit more strengthening than doughs made without. To compensate, "preshape" your dough first: Sprinkle a little flour over the top of each piece, then flip them over, flour side down, and fold the dough by reaching under the mass and pulling floured sections of the dough over and across, eventually enclosing the sticky inner surface of the dough. Then, shape each piece of dough into a tight ball following the instructions on pages 71–73. Place them on the counter seam side down and let rest for about 15 minutes.

After the preshape step, dust 2 proofing baskets with flour. Once again shape each piece of dough into a tight ball. Place each seam side down in its proofing basket.

6. Proof Place each basket in a nonperforated plastic bag and refrigerate overnight.

The next morning, 11 to 12 hours after the loaves went into the refrigerator, they should be ready to bake, straight from the refrigerator. They don't need to come to room temperature first.

7. Preheat At least 45 minutes prior to baking, put a rack in the middle of the oven and put 2 Dutch ovens on the rack with their lids on. Preheat the oven to 475°F (245°C).

If you only have 1 Dutch oven, keep the other loaf in the refrigerator while the first loaf is baking, and bake the loaves sequentially, giving the Dutch oven a 5-minute reheat after removing the first loaf.

8. Bake For the next step, please be careful not to let your hands, fingers, or forearms touch the extremely hot Dutch oven.

Invert the proofed loaf onto a lightly floured countertop, keeping in mind that the top of the loaf will be the side that was facing down while it was rising—the seam side.

Remove the preheated Dutch oven from your kitchen oven, remove the lid, and carefully place the loaf in the Dutch oven seam side up. Cover and bake for 30 minutes, then uncover and bake for about 20 minutes, until

dark brown all around the loaf. Check after 15 minutes of baking uncovered in case your oven runs hot.

Remove the Dutch oven and carefully tilt it to turn the loaf out. Let cool on a rack or set the loaf on its side so air can circulate around it. Let the loaf rest for at least 20 minutes before slicing.

The 3-Kilo Boule

It's Wednesday, and this big, round *boule* of levain bread baked Monday morning—about 16 inches in diameter and weighing in at more than 6 pounds—may be at its best right now. Like all of my big levain loaves, the 3-kilo *boule* improves with age for several days after it's been baked. There's something unique about the way flavors develop in big loaves. The flavors integrate and mellow with time, the crumb remains soft, and the crust stays firm yet pliable. I love the variety of textures in this monster. The rich, earthy, sometimes slightly bitter flavor of the crust fascinates me when I think of the field of wheat it came from. The ingredients? Flour, water, salt, and yeast. Bet you saw that coming.

Breads of this size probably date back to times when people only had access to fresh bread one or two days each week and needed loaves large enough to last until the next baking day. There's a connection to European village life, back to when bread was a dietary staple. Many villages weren't big enough to support a bakery that was open every day of the week. Some villages had a communal oven that was fired once a week. Bread had to last until the next bake day, so the loaves were big—I mean really big. I have books with old photos of loaves that appear to be at least 3 feet in diameter. Prior to the twentieth century, bread made up a significant percentage of the calories in the average European diet. Back then, bread and baking were important in a way that's hard to imagine today.

There remain many bakeries, mine included, that still bake large loaves for people who do not have everyday access to a bakery, or who know from experience that large loaves yield superior bread. In my case, almost all of these big fellas are delivered to a handful of good restaurants here in Portland.

I am fond of these large loaves for their historical link to a baking heritage that inspired my métier, and the 3-kilo (6.6-pound) *boule* of Country Blonde is the one bread I can truly call my own. I came up with the recipe for the bakery's Country Brown bread to try to match loaves baked by the French bakers who inspired me—Poilâne, Poujauran, Kamir, Saibron, and other excellent Parisian bakers—despite the differences between the types of flour available in the United States and France. Country Brown is one of my personal favorites in 1.75-kilo (3.9-pound) *boules*, but the 3-kilo Country Blonde *boule* came more directly from my own inspiration and I therefore feel it is more my own bread, not my version of someone else's bread.

In 2004, I traveled back to Paris for my first vacation since opening Ken's Artisan Bakery. It was an opportunity to revisit the *boulangeries* that made me want to become a baker—and to give some long thought to the work we were doing in Portland. I wanted to make some changes to our Country Blonde bread, and on a long walk along the river Seine, I reflected on two principles: our big loaves almost always taste better than our smaller loaves; and my "less yeast and more time" mantra could be applied to make the Country Blonde more delicate and more complex in flavor. I also wanted to adopt a common practice among good French bakers: using a small percentage of rye flour to add earthiness and additional complexity to the flavor of the bread.

After I got home I tinkered with flour proportions (at the time I used four kinds of flour in the Country Blonde dough), the amount of levain and yeast, the timing, dough temperatures, and dough hydration. Meanwhile, I also experimented with large loaf sizes, going all the way up to 4 kilos of raw dough before finally deciding that the 3-kilo *boule* was ideal for several reasons—one deciding factor being the fact that anything bigger than a 3-kilo loaf wouldn't fit in our delivery bags!

We bake the Country Blonde *boules* to a very deep, dark color, sometimes just shy of being burned, in order to get a very particular hit of flavor in the crust. When fully fermented and completely baked, these loaves take on shades of umber and dark crimson that aren't in the typical American's color palette for bread. But the flavor! Oh yeah. And the contrast in both taste and texture between the crust and the light alveolated crumb is sublime.

I started taking the big loaves of Country Blonde around to some of my friends at restaurants in Portland, and before long we were sending ten to fifteen of these behemoths to restaurants around town every day. Persuading the public to buy such big loaves is another story. Most people just don't eat that much bread, so we sell the 3-kilo *boules* in quarters at the bakery.

In France, a big round loaf is sometimes called a *miche*, sometimes a *boule* (this is where the word *boulangerie* came from). The way this bread is used varies with its age, and some families won't even touch the loaf until its second day. The rhythm of each week's meals is sometimes determined, at least in part, by the age of the bread. Early on, it eats well plain, on its own or accompanying other foods. At any point in its life cycle, it's superb when toasted, giving it an ideal crisp outer layer with tender middle bits. But its uses get more interesting with age: bread puddings both savory and sweet, including one of my favorites, summer pudding, made with fresh berries and topped with crème fraîche or whipped cream; slices or chunks of toasted bread topped with soup or stew; bread crumbs, of course, as a topping, in fillings, or for coating battered foods before frying; or, for the ambitious, in winter, as a topping for cassoulet. Of course there are also croutons and crostini, topped with anything you can imagine. Recently I came across an Italian recipe for bread balls that sounds great: old bread pieces soaked overnight in milk, then squeezed out and mixed with a custard of milk, eggs, grated Parmesan, and chopped sage; finally, the mixture is formed into balls and deep-fried. Yum! Peasant food excels at using old bread to good advantage, letting nothing go to waste.

On a recent vacation in Montana where I rented a ranch house in the Centennial Valley, I brought two *boules* of Country Blonde, one for my hosts and the other to get me through seven days of cooking my own meals. Seven days after it was baked, I was still enjoying the bread for toast, croutons, and any other kind of wheaty ballast. I also soaked some torn pieces in cream and sugar and topped them with berries for a dessert.

If you're lucky enough to get your hands on this kind of large loaf, you'll probably wonder what the best way to store it is. The ideal is to let it sit out for the first day, then quarter it and store it at room temperature in a plastic bag for the remainder of its life: up to eight days.

If you want to try baking the 3-kilo *boule*'s home kitchen cousin, the 1.8-kilo (4-pound) *boule*, see the variation on page 172 for Overnight Country Blonde, which you can also apply to the dough for Overnight Country Brown (page 173).

CHAPTER 10
PURE LEVAIN DOUGHS

OVERNIGHT COUNTRY BLONDE 168

OVERNIGHT COUNTRY BROWN 173

PAIN AU BACON 177

Pain au Bacon (page 177).

OVERNIGHT COUNTRY BLONDE

This is a pure levain dough that gets no help from store-bought yeast. It makes beautiful, natural levain bread with just a bit of tang to it. Using a small amount of levain, the long overnight bulk fermentation allows the dough to become nice and gassy by morning, tripling in volume. The shaped loaves are then proofed for about four hours. The aroma and flavor of this bread will directly reflect the character of your levain, with the flavors improving and the acidity mellowing for a couple of days after baking.

At Ken's Artisan Bakery we make a slightly different version of this dough. It begins with a levain feeding at 3:30 a.m., so I didn't include that version here, for obvious reasons. However, this would be a great dough to use to make a scaled-down version of my 3-kilo *boule*, as described on page 162; at 1.8 kilos (4 pounds) total, the amount of dough in this recipe will just barely fit on a standard baking stone for a home oven.

Be sure to bake this bread completely, letting it remain in the oven until it is as dark as possible shy of burning. If you want an even chewier crust, leave the loaves in the oven with the door partly open for a few minutes after turning off the oven.

Once you've perfected this bread, I encourage you to mix it up and try different blends of flours in your final dough mix; just make sure the total amount of fresh flour is 880 grams to complement the 120 grams of flour in the levain. Another option is to fold in about 225 grams of olives, nuts, or other ingredients, as in the recipe for Pain au Bacon (page 177).

THIS RECIPE MAKES 2 LOAVES, EACH ABOUT 1½ POUNDS, OR 1 BIG LOAF (SEE THE VARIATION ON PAGE 172).

BULK FERMENTATION: 12 to 15 hours

PROOF TIME: About 4 hours

SAMPLE SCHEDULE: Feed the levain at 9 a.m., mix the final dough at 5 p.m., shape into loaves at 8 a.m. the next morning, and bake at noon.

Levain

INGREDIENT	QUANTITY	
Mature, active levain	100 g	⅓ cup + 1½ tbsp
White flour	400 g	3 cups + 2 tbsp
Whole wheat flour	100 g	¾ cup + ½ tbsp
Water	400 g, 85°F to 90°F (29°C to 32°C)	1¾ cups

CONTINUED>>

Final Dough			Baker's Formula		
INGREDIENT	FINAL DOUGH MIX QUANTITY		QUANTITY IN LEVAIN	TOTAL RECIPE QUANTITY	BAKER'S PERCENTAGE
White flour	804 g	6¼ cups	96 g	900 g	90%
Whole wheat flour	26 g	3 tbsp	24 g	50 g	5%
Rye flour	50 g	⅓ cup + 1 tbsp	0	50 g	5%
Water	684 g, 90°F to 95°F (32°C to 35°C)	Scant 3 cups	96 g	780 g	78%
Fine sea salt	22 g	1 tbsp + 1 tsp	0	22 g	2.2%
Levain	216 g**	¾ cup + 1 tbsp			12%*

The baker's percentage for levain is the amount of flour in the levain expressed as a percentage of the total flour in the recipe.
**If your kitchen is cooler than 70°F (21°C), increase the amount of levain, perhaps using 250 to 275 grams.*

1a. Feed the levain About 24 hours after your previous feeding of the levain, discard all but 100 grams of levain, leaving the remainder in your 6-quart tub. Add 400 grams of white flour, 100 grams of whole wheat flour, and 400 grams of water at 85°F to 90°F (29°C to 32°C) and mix by hand just until incorporated. Cover and let rest at room temperature for 7 to 9 hours before mixing the final dough.

1b. Autolyse After 7 to 9 hours, mix the 804 grams of white flour, the 50 grams of rye flour, and the 26 grams of whole wheat flour by hand in a 12-quart round tub. Add the 684 grams of 90°F to 95°F (32°C to 35°C) water and mix by hand just until incorporated. Cover and let rest for 20 to 30 minutes.

2. Mix the final dough Sprinkle the 22 grams of salt evenly over the top of the dough.

Put a container with about a finger's depth of warm water on your scale so you can easily remove the levain after it's weighed. With wet hands, transfer 216 grams (or more if your kitchen is cool; see "Seasonal Variations" on page 134) of levain into the container.

Transfer the weighed levain to the 12-quart dough tub, minimizing the amount of water transferred with it. Mix by hand, wetting your working hand before mixing so the dough doesn't stick to you. Use the pincer method (see page 67) alternating with folding the dough to fully integrate the ingredients. The target dough temperature at the end of the mix is 77°F to 78°F (25°C to 26°C).

3. Fold This dough needs three or four folds (see pages 69–70). Because overnight levain dough expands very slowly, it can be folded anytime that's convenient before you go to bed, perhaps doing two or three folds during the first hour and the final fold whenever convenient that evening.

When the dough is nearly triple its original volume, or possibly a bit less in winter, 12 to 15 hours after mixing, it's ready to be divided.

4. Divide With floured hands, gently ease the dough out of the tub and onto a lightly floured work surface. With your hands still floured, pick up the dough and ease it back down onto the work surface in a somewhat even shape. Use a bit of flour to dust the area in the middle where you'll cut the dough, then cut it into 2 equal-size pieces with a dough knife or plastic dough scraper.

5. Shape the dough Dust 2 proofing baskets with flour. Shape each piece of dough into a medium-tight ball following the instructions on pages 71–73. Place each seam side down in its proofing basket.

6. Proof Set the baskets side by side and cover with a kitchen towel, or place each basket in a nonperforated plastic bag. Proofing time should be about 4 hours, assuming a room temperature of about 70°F (21°C). Use the finger-dent test (see page 74) to determine when they are perfectly proofed and ready to bake.

7. Preheat At least 45 minutes prior to baking, put a rack in the middle of the oven and put

2 Dutch ovens on the rack with their lids on. Preheat the oven to 475°F (245°C).

If you only have 1 Dutch oven, put the second loaf into the refrigerator about 20 minutes before baking the first loaf and bake the loaves sequentially, giving the Dutch oven a 5-minute reheat after removing the first loaf.

8. Bake For the next step, please be careful not to let your hands, fingers, or forearms touch the extremely hot Dutch oven.

CONTINUED>>

PROOFING PURE LEVAIN LOAVES

The finger-dent test (see page 74) may indicate that the loaves are proofed after about 3¼ hours. At my house at 70°F (21°C), the window for compete proofing is between about 3½ and 4¼ hours. Initially, I found that the bread baked nicely after a 3-hour proof, but further test bakes had better flavor with a full 4-hour proof, and the loaves didn't deflate.

Invert the proofed loaf onto a lightly floured countertop, keeping in mind that the top of the loaf will be the side that was facing down while it was rising—the seam side.

Remove the preheated Dutch oven from your kitchen oven, remove the lid, and carefully place the loaf in the Dutch oven seam side up. Cover and bake for 30 minutes, then uncover and bake for 20 to 25 minutes, until medium dark brown to very dark brown all around the loaf. Check after 15 minutes of baking uncovered in case your oven runs hot.

Remove the Dutch oven and carefully tilt it to turn the loaf out. Let cool on a rack or set the loaf on its side so air can circulate around it. Let the loaf rest for at least 20 minutes before slicing.

VARIATION: THE 1.8-KILO BOULE

If you want to try making a smaller version of my 3-kilo *boule*, shape the entire amount of dough in this recipe (about 1.8 kilos) into a single round loaf using the same shaping technique used for the smaller round loaves throughout this book (see pages 71–73). This 1.8-kilo loaf will be about the same size as a Poilâne *miche*.

Moderately flour a lint-free kitchen towel about 14 to 16 inches wide, or a couple of overlapped kitchen towels if needed. Place the dough seam side down on the towels, dust the top with flour, and cover by lifting the edges of the towel over the dough from opposite sides. The towel should completely overlap the dough without wrapping it too tightly; leave about 1 inch of slack on either side to allow the dough to expand. Proof at room temperature for 4½ to 5 hours.

At least 45 minutes prior to baking, put a rack in the middle of the oven and put a second rack below it, near the bottom of the oven. Put a pizza stone on the middle rack and preheat the oven to 500°F (260°C). Immerse a second pizza stone in hot water, also for 45 minutes; if it's lying flat, turn it over after about 20 minutes. About 5 minutes before baking the loaf, put the wet pizza stone on the lowest oven rack to provide steam.

It isn't *necessary* to score the loaf, but it is preferable, so if you have a scoring blade score a square around the perimeter of the loaf, with overlapping strokes. Use a floured pizza peel to load the big loaf onto the dry, preheated pizza stone, seam side up. After 5 minutes, lower the oven temperature to 475°F (245°C). Bake for 35 to 40 minutes, but check at the 30 minute mark in case your oven runs hot. (When you open the oven, be prepared for a blast of steam.) Your loaf is done when the crust is baked to a dark brown. Turn off the oven, open the door a few inches, and let the loaf sit in the oven for a few minutes to help set the crust. As usual, let the loaf cool, either on a rack or propped on its side, before slicing.

PAIN AU BACON

Earlier in the book I pointedly wrote about how the craft of an artisan baker is most evident when the ingredients are just flour, water, salt, and yeast. But man, this is great as an indulgence! I chose an overnight levain dough here because it has more acidity than the other doughs, which complements the fattiness of the bacon. Vitaly Paley, chef and owner of the Portland restaurant Paley's Place, wishes I would make this bread for him every day. And after he suggested it for French toast, he recanted and said, "The bread is too precious to cook with. I just want to eat it!"

This bread is impressive eaten still warm from the oven or grilled. It soars when toasted and served with eggs and chilled cider or a glass of bubbly. It shines when made into warm, crisp croutons for use in a salad vinaigrette. It sings tenor high notes in a BLT sandwich with lemony mayonnaise and fresh ripe tomatoes. Toasted bacon bread squares with steelhead roe, anyone? Or how about served with a traditional Maryland oyster stew? If I was in Hawaii, I'd have it for breakfast with eggs and fresh papaya or passion fruit. Here in Oregon, it goes great with roasted pears. Maybe the ultimate Elvis sandwich would be this bacon bread with peanut butter and bananas. And more bacon.

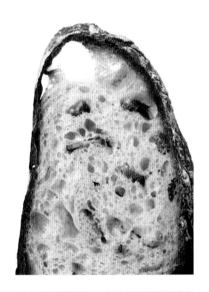

This dough should have a slightly shorter overnight fermentation time than the other pure levain doughs in this book. The bacon fat makes the yeast extra happy, so the dough will develop more quickly.

THIS RECIPE MAKES 2 LOAVES, EACH ABOUT 1½ POUNDS.

BULK FERMENTATION: About 12 hours

PROOF TIME: 3½ to 4 hours

SAMPLE SCHEDULE: Feed the levain at 9 a.m., mix the final dough at 7 p.m., shape into loaves between 7 a.m. and 8 a.m. the next morning, and bake at 11 a.m.

Levain

INGREDIENT	QUANTITY	
Mature, active levain	100 g	⅓ cup + 1½ tbsp
White flour	400 g	3 cups + 2 tbsp
Whole wheat flour	100 g	¾ cup + ½ tbsp
Water	400 g, 85°F to 90°F (29°C to 32°C)	1¾ cups

CONTINUED>>

Final Dough			Baker's Formula		
INGREDIENT	FINAL DOUGH MIX QUANTITY		QUANTITY IN LEVAIN	TOTAL RECIPE QUANTITY	BAKER'S PERCENTAGE
White flour	864 g	6¾ cups	96 g	960 g	96%
Whole wheat flour	16 g	2 tbsp	24 g	40 g	4%
Water	684 g, 90°F to 95°F (32°C to 35°C)	Scant 3 cups	96 g	780 g	78%
Fine sea salt	20 g	1 tbsp + ¾ tsp	0	20 g	2%
Bacon	Cooked crisp bacon (500 g uncooked), with 2 tbsp bacon fat	Yield from 1 lb uncooked, with 2 tbsp bacon fat	0	500 g uncooked	50%
Levain	216 g**	¾ cup + 1 tbsp			12%*

The baker's percentage for levain is the amount of flour in the levain expressed as a percentage of the total flour in the recipe.
** *If your kitchen is cooler than 70°F (21°C), increase the amount of levain, perhaps using 250 to 275 grams.*

1a. Feed the levain About 24 hours after your previous feeding of the levain, discard all but 100 grams of levain, leaving the remainder in your 6-quart tub. Add 400 grams of white flour, 100 grams of whole wheat flour, and 400 grams of water at 85°F to 90°F (29°C to 32°C) and mix by hand just until incorporated. Cover and let rest at room temperature for 9 to 10 hours before mixing the final dough.

1b. Cook the bacon At least 20 minutes before autolysing, sauté the 500 grams of bacon until crisp. Drain on paper towels and reserve 2 tablespoons of the rendered bacon fat. Let cool to room temperature, then crumble.

1c. Autolyse Between 9 and 10 hours after feeding the levain, mix the 864 grams of white flour and the16 grams of whole wheat flour by hand in a 12-quart round tub. Add the 684 grams of 90°F to 95°F (32°C to 35°C) water and mix by

hand just until incorporated. Cover and let rest for 20 to 30 minutes.

2. Mix the final dough Sprinkle the 20 grams of salt evenly over the top of the dough.

Put a container with about a finger's depth of warm water on your scale so you can easily remove the levain after it's weighed. With wet hands, transfer 216 grams (or more if your kitchen is cool; see "Seasonal Variations" on page 134) of levain into the container.

Transfer the weighed levain to the 12-quart dough tub, minimizing the amount of water transferred with it. Mix by hand, wetting your working hand before mixing so the dough doesn't stick to you. Use the pincer method (see page 67) alternating with folding the dough to fully integrate the ingredients. The target dough temperature at the end of the mix is 77°F to 78°F (25°C to 26°C).

Let the dough rest for 10 minutes, then spread the 2 tablespoons of bacon fat over the top and sprinkle the crumbled bacon evenly over the top. Incorporate them into the dough, again using the pincer method alternating with folding until the bacon and fat are evenly distributed.

3. Fold This dough needs three or four folds (see pages 69–70). It's easiest to apply the folds during the first 1½ to 2 hours after mixing the dough.

When the dough is about triple its original volume, or possibly a little less in winter, about 12 hours after mixing, it's ready to be divided.

4. Divide With floured hands, gently ease the dough out of the tub and onto a lightly floured work surface. With your hands still floured, pick up the dough and ease it back down onto the work surface in a somewhat even shape. Use a bit of flour to dust the area in the middle where you'll cut the dough, then cut it into 2 equal-size pieces with a dough knife or plastic dough scraper.

5. Shape Dust 2 proofing baskets with flour. Shape each piece of dough into a medium-tight ball following the instructions on pages 71–73. Place each seam side down in its proofing basket.

6. Proof Set the baskets side by side and cover with a kitchen towel, or place each basket in a nonperforated plastic bag. Proofing time should be 3½ to 4 hours, assuming a room temperature of 70°F (21°C). Use the finger-dent test

(see page 74) to see determine when they are perfectly proofed and ready to bake.

7. Preheat At least 45 minutes prior to baking, put a rack in the middle of the oven and put 2 Dutch ovens on the rack with their lids on. Preheat the oven to 475° (245°C)F.

If you only have 1 Dutch oven, put the second loaf into the refrigerator about 20 minutes before baking the first loaf and bake the loaves sequentially, giving the Dutch oven a 5-minute reheat after removing the first loaf.

8. Bake For the next step, please be careful not to let your hands, fingers, or forearms touch the extremely hot Dutch oven.

Invert the proofed loaf onto a lightly floured countertop, keeping in mind that the top of the loaf will be the side that was facing down while it was rising—the seam side.

Remove the preheated Dutch oven from your kitchen oven, remove the lid, and carefully place the loaf in the Dutch oven seam side up. Cover and bake for 30 minutes, then uncover and bake for 20 minutes, until at least medium dark brown all around the loaf and the bits of bacon studding the crust are completely crisped—maybe even a little charred.

Remove the Dutch oven and carefully tilt it to turn the loaf out. Let cool on a rack or set the loaf on its side so air can circulate around it. Let the loaf rest for at least 20 minutes before slicing, give a nod to Elvis, then enjoy.

CHAPTER 11
ADVANCED LEVAIN DOUGHS

DOUBLE-FED SWEET LEVAIN BREAD 182

WHITE FLOUR WARM-SPOT LEVAIN 185

White Flour Warm-Spot Levain (page 185).

DOUBLE-FED SWEET LEVAIN BREAD

This bread involves feeding the levain two times, just a few hours apart, before mixing the final dough, a technique that I learned from Chad Robertson of Tartine Bakery when I was learning to be a baker. The idea is to build up an active population of yeast in the levain culture with two feedings using very warm water, in a way that limits the buildup of sour flavors. You may notice a larger amount of levain here than in the other bread recipes in this book, the reason being that this levain is less active at the time I introduce it into the dough mix. A long, slow fermentation, followed by retarding the loaves overnight in the refrigerator, creates a bread with an excellent, sweetish levain flavor. The first time I baked this bread in my home kitchen, I thought, "Oh yeah, this is really good." It has a slight musky levain odor to its crumb and a gentle warmth of fermentation flavors that I find very pleasant, especially in the crusty slices.

When you are ready to mix the final dough, I recommend sticking your nose in the levain bucket and taking in a big, deep draft of its odor. It smells great. Almost, but not quite, kind of like beer, with a slight edge of sour wheat. I wish I had the words.

THIS RECIPE MAKES 2 LOAVES, EACH ABOUT 1½ POUNDS.

BULK FERMENTATION: About 5 hours

PROOF TIME: 12 to 14 hours

SAMPLE SCHEDULE: Feed the levain at 7 a.m., feed it again at 10 a.m., mix the final dough between 2 p.m. and 3 p.m., shape into loaves at 8 p.m., proof the loaves in the refrigerator overnight, and bake around 8 to 10 a.m. the next morning.

First Levain Feeding

INGREDIENT	QUANTITY	
Mature, active levain	50 g	Scant ¼ cup
White flour	200 g	1½ cups + 1 tbsp
Whole wheat flour	50 g	⅓ cup + 1 tbsp
Water	200 g, 95°F (35°C)	⅞ cup

Second Levain Feeding

INGREDIENT	QUANTITY	
Levain from the first feeding	250 g	Scant 1 cup
White flour	400 g	3 cups + 2 tbsp
Whole wheat flour	100 g	¾ cup + ½ tbsp
Water	400 g, 85°F to 90°F (29°C to 32°C)	1¾ cups

Final Dough			Baker's Formula		
INGREDIENT	FINAL DOUGH MIX QUANTITY		QUANTITY IN LEVAIN	TOTAL RECIPE QUANTITY	BAKER'S PERCENTAGE
White flour	660 g	5 cups + 2 tbsp	240 g	900 g	90%
Whole wheat flour	40 g	⅓ cup	60 g	100 g	10%
Water	540 g, 90°F to 95°F (32°C to 35°C)	2⅓ cups	240 g	780 g	78%
Fine sea salt	20 g	1 tbsp + ¾ tsp	0	20 g	2%
Instant dried yeast	2 g	½ tsp	0	2 g	0.20%
Levain	540 g	2 cups + 1 tbsp			30%*

* The baker's percentage for levain is the amount of flour in the levain expressed as a percentage of the total flour in the recipe.

1a. Feed the levain About 24 hours after your previous feeding of the levain, discard all but 50 grams of levain, leaving the remainder in your 6-quart tub. (This will look like a very small amount; trust the process.) Add 200 grams of white flour, 50 grams of whole wheat flour, and 200 grams of water at 95°F (35°C) and mix by hand just until incorporated. Cover and let rest at room temperature for 3 hours.

1b. Feed the levain a second time After 3 hours, discard all but 250 grams of levain from the first feeding. Add 400 grams of white flour, 100 grams of whole wheat flour, and 400 grams water at 95°F (35°C) and mix by hand until just incorporated. Cover and let rest for 4 to 5 hours before mixing the final dough.

1c. Autolyse After 3½ to 4½ hours, mix the 660 grams of white flour and the 40 grams of whole wheat flour by hand in a 12-quart round tub. Add the 540 grams of 90°F to 95°F (32°C to 35°C) water and mix by hand just

until incorporated. Cover and let rest for 20 to 30 minutes.

2. Mix the final dough Sprinkle the 20 grams of salt and the 2 grams (½ teaspoon) of yeast evenly over the top of the dough.

Put a container with about a finger's depth of warm water on your scale so you can easily remove the levain after it's weighed. With wet hands, transfer 540 grams of levain into the container.

Transfer the weighed levain to the 12-quart dough tub, minimizing the amount of water transferred with it. Mix by hand, wetting your working hand before mixing so the dough doesn't stick to you. Use the pincer method (see page 67) alternating with folding the dough to fully integrate the ingredients. The target dough temperature at the end of the mix is 77°F to 78°F (25°C to 26°C).

CONTINUED>>

3. Fold This dough needs four folds (see pages 69–70). It's easiest to apply the folds during the first 1½ to 2 hours after mixing the dough.

When the dough is about 2½ times its original volume, about 5 hours after mixing, it's ready to be divided.

4. Divide With floured hands, gently ease the dough out of the tub and onto a lightly floured work surface. With your hands still floured, pick up the dough and ease it back down onto the work surface in a somewhat even shape. Use a bit of flour to dust the area in the middle where you'll cut the dough, then cut it into 2 equal-size pieces with a dough knife or plastic dough scraper.

5. Shape Dust 2 proofing baskets with flour. Shape each piece of dough into a medium-tight ball following the instructions on pages 71–73. Place each seam side down in its proofing basket.

6. Proof Place each basket in a nonperforated plastic bag and refrigerate overnight.

The next morning, 12 to 14 hours after the loaves went into the refrigerator, they should be ready to bake, straight from the refrigerator. They don't need to come up to room temperature first.

7. Preheat At least 45 minutes prior to baking, put a rack in the middle of the oven and put 2 Dutch ovens on the rack with their lids on. Preheat the oven to 475°F (245°C).

If you only have 1 Dutch oven, keep the other loaf in the refrigerator while the first loaf is baking, and bake the loaves sequentially, giving the Dutch oven a 5-minute reheat after removing the first loaf.

8. Bake For the next step, please be careful not to let your hands, fingers, or forearms touch the extremely hot Dutch oven.

Invert the proofed loaf onto a lightly floured countertop, keeping in mind that the top of the loaf will be the side that was facing down while it was rising—the seam side.

Remove the preheated Dutch oven from your kitchen oven, remove the lid, and carefully place the loaf in the Dutch oven seam side up. Cover and bake for 30 minutes, then uncover and bake for 20 to 25 minutes, until medium dark brown all around the loaf. Check after 15 minutes of baking uncovered in case your oven runs hot.

Remove the Dutch oven and carefully tilt it to turn the loaf out. Let cool on a rack or set the loaf on its side so air can circulate around it. Let the loaf rest for at least 20 minutes before slicing.

WHITE FLOUR WARM-SPOT LEVAIN

My inspiration for this bread came from a long-ago visit to a bakery in California that used a stiff white levain held in a very warm part of their bakery. This levain, which the bakery kept on a shelf behind the bread oven, had a beautiful domed top and a medium-ripe, fruity smell that was very attractive. They made delicious sourdough baguettes from this starter, and I wanted to someday try making bread from this kind of levain myself.

In this recipe, you build a levain culture that's completely different from the one in the other levain recipes. You can start with the same base levain, but in this case you'll add only white flour and use less water—only 70 percent hydration—so the consistency will be much stiffer. Then the levain is held in a warm spot—anywhere from about 85°F (29°C) to 90°F (32°C) would be ideal. This bread is impressive, and it's a fun way to show that there are many ways to make up and ferment a levain culture.

The more days this culture is refreshed and allowed to live in its warm environment, the more it will develop its own unique character. If you decide to develop the culture for longer than outlined in this recipe, I recommend feeding it twice a day using the Day 1 schedule outlined below. You may choose to use this culture for other recipes in the book, adjusting the amounts of flour and water in the final dough mix to compensate for this levain having a lower hydration (70 percent) than the book's normal levain. For more details, see Making a Bread (or Pizza) Dough You Can Call Your Own, on page 190.

I think of this as a seasonal summer bread. The challenge is finding the right spot to keep the levain at these warmer temperatures. I used my home oven with the light on and the door slightly open and got a steady 85°F (29°C); with the door closed it hit 100°F (38°C). Don't forget it's in there if you use the oven for baking something else! Alternatively, you may have a spot that's naturally warm, perhaps in the garage or on the porch if it's hot outside, which could be less risky than the oven.

THIS RECIPE MAKES 2 LOAVES, EACH ABOUT 1½ POUNDS.

BULK FERMENTATION: 5 to 6 hours

PROOF TIME: 11 to 12 hours

SAMPLE SCHEDULE: Day 1, feed the new levain at 9 a.m. and again at 6 p.m. Day 2, feed the new levain at 9 a.m., mix the final dough at 3 p.m., shape into loaves at 8 p.m., proof the loaves in the refrigerator overnight, and bake around 7 or 8 a.m. the next morning.

CONTINUED>>

DAY 1

First Levain Feeding

INGREDIENT	QUANTITY	
Mature, active levain	50 g	Scant ¼ cup
White flour	250 g	1¾ cups + 3 tbsp
Water	175 g, 85°F (29°C)	¾ cup

Second Levain Feeding

INGREDIENT	QUANTITY	
Levain from the first feeding	50 g	Scant ¼ cup
White flour	250 g	1¾ cups + 3 tbsp
Water	175 g, 80°F (27°C)	¾ cup

DAY 2

Third Levain Feeding

INGREDIENT	QUANTITY	
Levain from the second feeding	100 g	⅓ cup + 1½ tbsp
White flour	500 g	3¾ cups + 2 tbsp
Water	350 g, 85°F (29°C)	1½ cups

Final Dough

INGREDIENT	FINAL DOUGH MIX QUANTITY	
White flour	750 g	5¾ cups + 1½ tbsp
Water	605 g, 80°F (27°C)	2⅔ cups
Fine sea salt	20 g	1 tbsp + ¾ tsp
Instant dried yeast	1 g	¼ tsp
Levain	425 g	1½ cups + 1 tbsp

Baker's Formula

QUANTITY IN LEVAIN	TOTAL RECIPE QUANTITY	BAKER'S PERCENTAGE
250 g	1,000 g	100%
175 g	780 g	78%
0	20 g	2%
0	1 g	0.1%
		25%*

The baker's percentage for levain is the amount of flour in the levain expressed as a percentage of the total flour in the recipe.

1a. Feed the levain About 24 hours after your previous feeding of the levain, begin to cultivate your new, stiffer culture. Discard all but 50 grams of levain, leaving the remainder in your 6-quart tub. Add 250 grams of white flour and 175 grams of water at 85°F (29°C) and mix by hand just until incorporated. Cover and let rest for 8 hours in a very warm spot at 85°F to 90°F (29°C to 32°C).

1b. Feed the levain a second time After 8 hours, the levain should have grown to three to four times its original volume and you will get a big hit of alcoholic perfume when you remove the lid. It's ripe! The levain should be bubbly, with a nice web structure inside, and in prime condition.

Discard all but 50 grams of the levain from the first feeding. Add 250 grams of white

flour and 175 grams of 80°F (27°C) water and mix by hand, just until incorporated. Cover and let rest in a very warm place overnight.

1c. Feed the levain a third time About 14 to 15 hours later, feed your levain again. It should be similarly developed—about quadruple its original volume. You will get another heady rush of fumes when you remove the lid.

Discard all but 100 grams of the levain from the second feeding. Add 500 grams of white flour and 350 grams of 85°F (29°C) water and mix by hand just until incorporated. Cover and let rest in your warm spot for 6 hours before mixing the final dough. The levain should be up to the 2-quart line on your 6-quart tub.

1d. Autolyse After 5½ hours, combine the 750 grams of white flour and the 605 grams of 80°F (27°C) water in a 12-quart round tub or similar container. Mix by hand just until incorporated. Cover and let rest for 20 to 30 minutes.

2. Mix the final dough Sprinkle the 20 grams of salt and the 1 gram (¼ teaspoon) of yeast evenly over the top of the dough.

Put a container with about a finger's depth of warm water on your scale so you can easily remove the levain after it's weighed. With wet hands, transfer 425 grams of levain into the container.

Transfer the weighed levain to the 12-quart dough tub, minimizing the amount of water transferred with it. Mix by hand, wetting your working hand before mixing so the dough doesn't stick to you. Use the pincer method (see page 67) alternating with folding the dough to fully integrate the ingredients. The target dough temperature at the end of the mix is 77°F to 78°F (25°C to 26°C).

3. Fold This dough needs three or four folds (see pages 69–70). It's easiest to apply the folds during the first 1½ to 2 hours after mixing the dough.

CONTINUED>>

If you want to store your remaining levain culture and do not plan to continue feeding it, then put 300 grams or so in the refrigerator, following the procedures for storing a levain on pages 136–137. This culture will be fine for restoring into this book's normal levain later.

When the dough is about 2½ times its original volume, 5 to 6 hours after mixing, it's ready to be divided.

4. Divide With floured hands, gently ease the dough out of the tub and onto a lightly floured work surface. With your hands still floured, pick up the dough and ease it back down onto the work surface in a somewhat even shape. Use a bit of flour to dust the area in the middle where you'll cut the dough, then cut it into 2 equal-size pieces with a dough knife or plastic dough scraper.

5. Shape Dust 2 proofing baskets with flour. Shape each piece of dough into a medium-tight ball following the instructions on pages 71–73. Place each seam side down in its proofing basket.

6. Proof Place each basket in a nonperforated plastic bag and refrigerate overnight.

The next morning, 11 to 12 hours after the loaves went into the refrigerator, they should be ready to bake, straight from the refrigerator. They don't need to come up to room temperature first.

7. Preheat At least 45 minutes prior to baking, put a rack in the middle of the oven and put 2 Dutch ovens on the rack with their lids on. Preheat the oven to 475°F (245°C).

If you only have 1 Dutch oven, keep the other loaf in the refrigerator while the first loaf is baking, and bake the loaves sequentially, giving the Dutch oven a 5-minute reheat after removing the first loaf.

8. Bake For the next step, please be careful not to let your hands, fingers, or forearms touch the extremely hot Dutch oven.

Invert the proofed loaf onto a lightly floured countertop, keeping in mind that the top of the loaf will be the side that was facing down while it was rising—the seam side.

Remove the preheated Dutch oven from your kitchen oven, remove the lid, and carefully place the loaf in the Dutch oven seam side up. Cover and bake for 30 minutes, then uncover and bake for 20 to 25 minutes, until medium dark brown all around the loaf. Check after 15 minutes of baking uncovered in case your oven runs hot.

Remove the Dutch oven and carefully tilt it to turn the loaf out. Let cool on a rack or set the loaf on its side so air can circulate around it. Let the loaf rest for at least 20 minutes before slicing.

Making a Bread (or Pizza) Dough You Can Call Your Own

You can think of this book's recipes as templates that allow you to adjust flour blends, the leavening, the timing, or the amount of water in a dough, for whatever reason: taste, physical structure (for pizza doughs especially), timeline, convenience, or if you're like me, just for the fun of it, to see what happens.

Have it your way. The recipes in this book are adaptable, and I encourage you to experiment with them to create breads or pizzas that are all your own.

That having been said, I also encourage you to first follow the recipes as written, to build your confidence as a baker and get familiar with my recipes and methods. Then, once you've been successful with these recipes and know what they produce, you can customize to suit your own taste, pantry, or whimsy.

You might want to try making a 50 percent whole wheat bread based on my Saturday 75% Whole Wheat Bread recipe (page 85). Or you might want to change that recipe to include some rye flour, or you might decide to use just 20 percent whole wheat. Perhaps you want to experiment with a liquid levain, using Pain de Campagne (page 140) or any of my other levain breads as a starting point.

And even when you want to follow the recipes exactly, you may have life issues pop out of nowhere that require an on-the-fly schedule adjustment. This happens to most of us. In this essay, I provide tips and tricks that will allow you to adapt, even to unforeseen circumstances. I'll start with adjusting hydration level, then address changing the blend of flours. Next, I'll discuss how you can modify a recipe's schedule. Then, for the advanced baker, I'll discuss some options regarding levain. I have also included some notes on recipe shorthand, which is a useful way to document your work as you go, since the long elapsed timelines are easy to forget (*what time did I mix the dough?*), especially if you want to refer to them for future bakes.

You'll note that volume conversions are omitted from these recipe tables. If you really want to control the variables discussed in the sections that follow, you need to measure your ingredients by weight, for accuracy's sake.

CHANGING HYDRATION

A good candidate for changing dough hydration is the Overnight Pizza Dough with Poolish (page 225). That recipe has 75 percent hydration. But you might want to change the hydration to 70 percent to get a stiffer dough—many will find a stiffer dough easier to shape into a pizza than the softer, stickier 75 percent dough. I get that. And *you* still get the poolish flavor benefit.

Adjusting the hydration is simple. Put less water in the dough! Since the total flour weight is 1,000 grams (as it is in every bread and pizza dough recipe in this book), to change the hydration to 70 percent, simply change total water in the dough from 750 grams to 700 grams (70 percent of the total flour weight). Use the same poolish as in the original recipe and adjust the amount of water added in the final dough mix to 200 grams. That's it. Because this dough is stiffer, it needs only a single fold.

POOLISH PIZZA DOUGH WITH 70 PERCENT HYDRATION

Final Dough		Baker's Formula		
INGREDIENT	FINAL DOUGH MIX QUANTITY	QUANTITY IN POOLISH	TOTAL RECIPE QUANTITY	BAKER'S PERCENTAGE
White flour	500 g	500 g	1,000 g	100%
Water	200 g, 105°F (38°C)	500 g	700 g	70%
Fine sea salt	20 g	0	20 g	2%
Instant dried yeast	0	0.4 g (scant ⅛ tsp)	0.4 g	0.04%
Poolish	1,000 g			50%

Here's another example of how to play around with hydration: Say you wake up in the morning and decide you want to make bread in time for dinner that evening. The Saturday Breads are designed for that schedule. But you want to try using more water in the dough, say 78 percent hydration instead of 72 percent. So you use 780 grams of water instead of the 720 grams called for in the recipe. Because the dough will be wetter and more slack, it needs an additional couple of folds to make up for that. That will give the dough the structural support it needs, helping build up the gluten network, which is relaxed by the extra water.

CHANGING FLOUR BLENDS

I do this all the time. If you want to work with a specific recipe but adjust the flour blend, I think you will find it satisfying to know you have the recipe format down and can make flour changes to suit your taste (or just to use what you have available). The most important thing is to stick with the same total amount of flour in the recipe, since amounts of all the other ingredients are based on ratios to the total flour weight.

Let's change the flour blend in the Overnight White Bread recipe on page 89. The recipe calls for all white flour, but we can change it to a mix of 70 percent white flour, 20 percent whole wheat flour, and 10 percent rye flour. (This will make a bread with a similar blend to what I used in the Field Blend recipes on pages 155 and 158.) Change the white flour to 700 grams, add 200 grams of whole wheat flour and 100 grams of light or dark rye flour—and if you want, you can add a little more water, say 20 grams. But since the rye flour is less absorbent than other flours, for now let's keep the water quantity the same. The yeast and salt quantities also remain the same.

OVERNIGHT "WHITE" BREAD, NOW WITH WHITE, WHOLE WHEAT, RYE FLOUR BLEND

INGREDIENT	QUANTITY	BAKER'S PERCENTAGE
White flour	700 g	70%
Whole wheat flour	200 g	20%
Light or dark rye flour, room temperature	100 g	10%
Water	780 g, 90°F to 95°F (32°C to 35°C)	78%
Instant dried yeast	0.8 g (scant ¼ tsp)	0.08%
Fine sea salt	22 g	2.2%

ADJUSTING THE SCHEDULE

Sometimes you need to adjust timing for the recipe—either because you know in advance that you need more time before working with the dough at the next stage, or because something unexpected comes up and you realize you need to delay the dough. Because bulk fermentation and proofing time are relative to the amount of leavening and the temperature the dough is held at, you can use those variables to give yourself more time. Note that I don't advocate speeding up fermentation or proofing, as this can adversely affect quality.

Here's an example: Say you want to make one of the Saturday Breads, but an eight-hour bulk fermentation works better with your schedule than the five hours in the recipe. In this case, I'd recommend reducing the amount of yeast by about a third and keeping the temperatures the same. Make notes about what you do and how it works out, then adjust the amount of yeast accordingly the next time.

Here's another example, still using the Saturday Breads. Say the day gets on, and by the time you shape the loaves your evening's plans have changed and you won't be around to bake the bread. Immediately after shaping, put the loaves in the refrigerator (in their proofing baskets in nonperforated plastic bags). Then bake them the next morning. Alternatively, say you just need to extend the time between shaping and baking by about an hour. That's fine; just refrigerate the shaped loaves about 50 minutes to an hour after they were shaped; they should hold for a couple of hours. Bake them cold. You won't need to let them come back to room temperature before baking.

Here's another scenario: Perhaps you mixed a final dough at 3 p.m. that would normally be mature and ready to divide and shape into loaves at 8 p.m., but you have a meeting from 7 until 9 p.m. As in the previous example, anytime you need to stretch out the timeline, simply refrigerate the dough. Depending on the outside temperature, you might alternatively put the dough tub or shaped loaves outside—covered if in the dough tub or in plastic bags if shaped and in proofing baskets. There will always be some guesswork in the timing. Keep in mind that it takes awhile for the dough to chill, so it will continue to evolve in the cooler temperatures.

When retarding the dough in this way, beware of any temptation to move on to the next step before the dough is fully evolved. As with adjusting hydration, it's helpful to be familiar with the recipe so you'll be able to recognize when the dough is optimally fermented or proofed. With experience, you'll learn to judge by its appearance.

My overall guidance is that you can elongate the process by refrigerating the dough or holding it at cooler temperatures during bulk fermentation and proofing. With practice you'll learn how to do this and still get excellent (sometimes improved) results. Just be careful not to use dough that isn't fully fermented or proofed when you move on to the next stage, because you'll sacrifice flavor and volume in the baked bread.

On the flip side, there are always going to be times when your dough is moving too slow—this is often a problem in the wintertime. If you have a dough that is supposed to triple in size in five hours but hasn't, or an overnight dough that doubled when it should have increased in volume at least two and a half times, find a warm spot to speed up the dough. The most convenient place I've found is in my oven—with the door ajar and the oven light on, it's just the right temperature. You can use the same approach for a poolish or biga that isn't fully developed. Don't remove the lid of your dough tub because that will dry out the dough. But do pay attention. Warm it up, and you can use your probe thermometer to check the dough temperature; best to not let it get much above 80 degrees. When the dough does get warmer it is fun to see how quickly it evolves. This slow dough situation happens occasionally to every baker. Don't panic, just use your warm spot!

FLOUR ABSORBENCY

As noted, whole wheat flour absorbs more water than white flour. Therefore, if you increase the ratio of white flour in a recipe, you'll need less water to achieve the same dough consistency. Conversely, if you increase the ration of whole wheat flour, you'll need to add more water to achieve the same consistency. Of course, to make a judgment call on the consistency, it's best to be familiar with the recipe using the called-for amounts of ingredients first, so you'll have a baseline to compare to. When increasing the amount of water, it's best to add it in small increments, and to weigh the water rather than eyeballing it. By volume, 30 or 40 grams of water looks like a very small amount, but it can make a big difference.

LEVAIN OPTIONS

This section is mostly for the advanced baker, but you don't need to be a total bread geek to use this guidance. I'll offer two examples here, and from that point you can extrapolate to other "what if?" scenarios.

Adjusting the Flour Blend in Warm-Spot Levain

First, let's look at an example of how to use the all-white flour levain from my White Flour Warm-Spot White Levain Bread recipe (page 185) in other breads. This is a lovely levain culture with special flavor characteristics, so you may want to work with it beyond the all-white flour recipe in this book. This is really as easy as adjusting flour blends, as described earlier in this essay, using some whole wheat or rye flour, or maybe spelt or kamut flour, in the final dough mix. Just be sure to use the same amount of flour in the final dough mix. Instead of using 750 grams of white flour in the final dough mix, use a new combination of flours that adds up to 750 grams. The example below is for a 40 percent whole wheat version; 40 percent of 1,000 grams (the total flour in the recipe, including that in the levain) is 400, so use 400 grams of whole wheat flour and 350 grams of white flour. Likewise, you could use, for example, 100 grams of rye flour, 200 grams of whole wheat flour, and 450 grams of white flour to total 750 grams of flour in the final dough mix.

In the example below, more water is added to compensate for the higher absorbency of the whole wheat flour: 20 grams of water, increasing the hydration from 78 to 80 percent.

WARM-SPOT LEVAIN, 40 PERCENT WHOLE WHEAT

Final Dough		Baker's Formula		
INGREDIENT	FINAL DOUGH MIX QUANTITY	QUANTITY IN LEVAIN	TOTAL RECIPE QUANTITY	BAKER'S PERCENTAGE
White flour	350 g	250 g	600 g	60%
Whole wheat flour	400 g	0	400 g	40%
Water	625 g, 80°F (27°C)	175 g	800 g	80%
Fine sea salt	20 g	0	20 g	2%
Instant dried yeast	1 g (¼ tsp)	0	1 g	0.1%
Levain	425 g			25%*

*The baker's percentage for levain is the amount of flour in the levain expressed as a percentage of the total flour in the recipe.

You may have noticed that the White Flour Warm-Spot Levain Bread recipe on page 185 contains 25 percent of the recipe's flour in the levain culture and uses only 0.1 percent yeast, whereas the hybrid leavening recipes in this book have 20 percent levain and 0.2 percent yeast, and the pure levains have 12 percent levain and no added yeast. I wanted more levain in this recipe to emphasize the specific character of this style of levain. With more levain, I needed less instant yeast. You could take it further and eliminate the baker's yeast altogether, and just give the dough a little longer to rise.

Liquid Levain

Liquid levain is a term any good professional baker knows. As commonly used, it implies a levain culture with equal weights of water and flour and typically all white flour. Liquid levain imparts its own specific character to the bread: I associate it with lactic flavors, which tend to be milky or buttery. If particularly ripe, it might develop a slight overripe fruit taste—this is caused by the volatile esters that form from the combination of alcohol (from extended yeast fermentation) and acids (from bacterial fermentation).

To create a liquid levain, use this book's base levain culture, as described in chapter 8. Then, the day before mixing your final dough, follow the instructions below to transition your levain to a liquid culture. Anytime you change from your base levain culture, the longer you maintain the new conditions and feeding protocol, the more it will take on a new flavor profile, as the wild yeast and bacteria and their acids thrive in the new environment.

As you'll see, the Day 1 feeding is at 100 percent hydration, rather than 80 percent as in the base levain. It also uses only a bit of the mature base levain for the first feeding.

SAMPLE SCHEDULE: Day 1, starting with the base levain from chapter 8, feed the new levain at 9 a.m. and again at 6 p.m. Day 2: feed the new levain at 9 a.m., mix the final dough at 3 p.m., shape into loaves at 8 p.m., proof the loaves in the refrigerator overnight, and bake the next morning.

LIQUID LEVAIN

DAY 1

First Levain Feeding

INGREDIENT	QUANTITY
Mature, active levain	50 g
White flour	250 g
Water	250 g, 95°F (35°C)

Second Levain Feeding

INGREDIENT	QUANTITY
Levain from the first feeding	250 g
White flour	250 g
Water	250 g, 85°F (29°C)

DAY 2

Third Levain Feeding

INGREDIENT	QUANTITY
Levain from the second feeding	100 g
White flour	500 g
Water	500 g, 85°F to 90°F (29°C to 32°C)

A good recipe for experimenting with a liquid levain is the Pain de Campagne on page 140. Substitute your new liquid levain for the standard base levain and use the amounts of ingredients indicated below. Since there's more water in the liquid levain than the book's base levain, there's less water in the ingredients for the final dough than in the original recipe. However, the total hydration remains the same, at 78 percent. The amount of water in the final dough mix is simply decreased by 40 grams to compensate for the additional 40 grams of water in the levain added to the final dough mix.

PAIN DE CAMPAGNE WITH LIQUID LEVAIN

Final Dough		Baker's Formula		
INGREDIENT	FINAL DOUGH MIX QUANTITY	QUANTITY IN LEVAIN	TOTAL RECIPE QUANTITY	BAKER'S PERCENTAGE
White flour	700 g	200 g	900 g	90%
Whole wheat flour	100 g	0	100 g	10%
Water	580 g, 90°F to 95°F (32°C to 35°C)	200 g	780 g	78%
Fine sea salt	21 g	0	21 g	2.1%
Instant dried yeast	2 g (½ tsp)	0	2 g	0.2%
Levain	400 g			20%

RECIPE SHORTHAND

Any time I make an adjustment to a recipe, I record it, even if only temporarily, so I can track what I've done and not depend on my fallible memory to recall if I put, for example, 560 grams or 540 grams of flour in the final dough mix eight hours ago. I keep a pocket-size notebook in my kitchen for just this purpose and I use recipe shorthand. I thought I'd share my system with you, and this seems like a good place, because whenever you tweak a recipe, you should record what you did for reference in process, as well as for later if you want to keep track of what works and what doesn't.

Here's my recipe shorthand for Overnight Pizza Dough with Poolish (page 225):

- *Poolish: 500g flour, 500g water 80°F, 0.4g yeast. 12–14 hrs at room temp 70°F.*
- *No autolyse.*
- *Final dough: 500g flour, 250g water 105°F, 20g salt, poolish. 2 folds. 5–6 hrs to 2½x volume. Divide into 5 (350g each) and shape into balls. 30–60 mins at room temp, then into fridge.*

Then I take notes in process like this:

- *Poolish mix 7 p.m.*
- *Dough mix, water only 95°F, 9 a.m. end mix temp 73°F. Use warmer water next time.*
- *2 folds.*
- *Dough at about 2½x at 3 p.m. Dough balls into fridge at 3:30 p.m.*

Here is my recipe shorthand for Field Blend #1 (page 155):

- *Levain: Feed first thing in the morning. Use 100g mature levain, 400g white, 100g whole wheat, 400g water, 85°F to 90°F. 6 hours at room temp. before final dough mix.*
- *Autolyse: 590g white, 60g whole wheat, 150g white rye, 590g water, 90°F to 95°F. Rest 20–30 mins.*
- *Final dough mix: Add 360g levain, 21g salt, 2g yeast. 3 or 4 folds. 5 hrs to 2½x. Divide, shape, wrap, and into fridge 12 hours.*
- *Bake 475°F, 30 mins lid on, 20 mins lid off.*

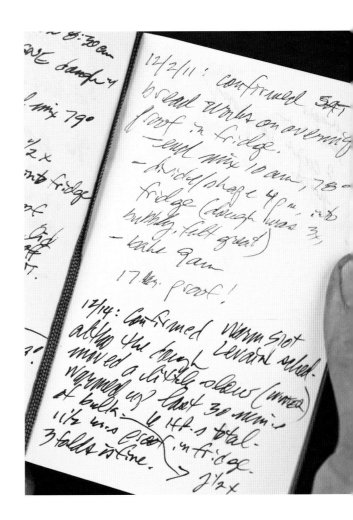

My in-process notes might look something like this:

- *Levain mix, 8 a.m.*
- *Autolyse with 90°F water. Final mix temp 80°F. Use cooler water next time. End mix 2 p.m.*
- *4 folds.*
- *Divide, shape, into fridge at 7 p.m.*
- *Bake 9 a.m. Good result. Yay!*

PART 4
PIZZA RECIPES

CHAPTER 12
PIZZA AND FOCACCIA METHOD

Three and a half years after opening Ken's Artisan Bakery I wanted to work with my staff on a new project, seeing if we could make good pizza in our massive gas-fired bread oven, baking the pies directly on the oven hearth. Pizza is, after all, a kind of bread, so it seemed a natural extension of what we were already good at.

Initial trials went well enough that we decided try it out on the public as a one-night-per-week fun-fest, branding it Monday Night Pizza. At the time, in 2005, Portland was embracing alternatives to the usual dining scene, and creative, nontraditional ventures like Ripe's underground restaurant, Family Supper, and summertime white-tablecloth dinners in farmers' fields produced by Plate & Pitchfork put a kind of Portland-specific, rule-bending fun back into going out for dinner. Turning my bakery into a restaurant one night a week was an evolutionary step from the earlier experiment when we operated as a mini-bistro, and it was a way to take advantage of the talents of some of the people working at the bakery at that time.

The bakery made the *Oregonian*'s top one hundred restaurants that year on the merits of our one-night-per-week pop-up pizza place, and from the first Monday night people were waiting up to an hour for a table, pressed up against the pastry cases and hanging out on the sidewalk with a glass of wine or a beer in hand—the power of pizza! The momentum of Monday Night Pizza birthed Ken's Artisan Pizza, a wood-fired oven pizzeria in Southeast Portland that I opened with our chef, Alan Maniscalco, in 2006. Alan had worked at the bakery for four years, for a while managing the bread and pastry teams, and he also ran the Monday Night Pizza kitchen before helping me open the pizzeria.

At Ken's Artisan Pizza we bake pies inspired by the Neapolitan pizzas that Alan and I had each enjoyed during various trips to Italy. Ours are individual pies, about 12 inches in diameter, with a very thin crust. Our cooks toss the dough in the air in a spiraling fashion to get a perfect distribution of thin dough rather than for effect, but the flying disks make great theater too.

The toppings are on the minimal side, as the intention is for the crust, sauce, and toppings to be in balance. We also aim for a slight char on the bottom and perimeter of the crust. A *slight* char. It isn't easy. Things happen fast at 750°F (399°C). The whole-milk mozzarella

we use is completely melted, a milky ooze with just a touch of brown on top. The tips of the fresh basil leaves that bake on top of the pizza are just a little crisp.

The oven has a big pile of red embers in the back, and you can see its large, dancing flame from the street. We keep thinly split pieces of oak, madrone, and occasionally other hardwoods in a cutout at the base of the oven and constantly feed the oven's fire through each evening's service. In the morning, there's still plenty of heat left for baking croutons and other items before lighting a new flame at noon. The restaurant oven has fire burning in it at least ten hours each day, every day of the week.

This oven, a brick le Panyol model, was built by Timothy Seaton, a third-generation mason who specializes in building wood-burning appliances and serves as chair of the Masonry Heater Caucus for the Hearth, Patio and Barbecue Association, as well as secretary for an international standards organization for wood-burning appliances. Timothy knows his stuff, and he's a fine craftsman. The interior hearth of the oven is nearly six feet in diameter and was built with plenty of mass to hold and radiate intense heat back onto the baking surface. In the morning the oven is still well over 500°F (260°C)—too hot to bake bread. Yet the temperature of the outside of the oven never exceeds 110°F (43°C). It's an impressive beast: a white, igloo-shaped inferno in the middle of the restaurant.

When pizzas bake, they are usually placed in the oven with their backs 1½ to 2 feet from the fire. At this point, the temperature is about 750°F (399°C) near the back of the pizza—it's over 1,000°F (538°C) where the fire is. There is nearly a 100°F (56°C) difference in the temperature of the hearth surface between the front and the back of the pie. Each pizza is rotated as it bakes—and comes out of the oven in about two and a half minutes. The pie is best when the bottom, the top, and the rim of the crust all reach their perfect finished point at exactly the same time. This wood-fired oven is ideal for achieving that type of bake.

A NOTE ON DOUGH HYDRATION

The pizza dough recipes that follow have a hydration of 70 to 75 percent, whereas most traditional pizza dough recipes have a hydration closer to 65 percent. The dough recipes in this book are specifically designed for baking on a pizza stone or on a stone hearth.

For focaccia (which is not baked directly on a hearth, but rather laid out in a pan) you can use wetter doughs than you would for pizza, such as my White Bread with 80% Biga dough (page 106). Since you spread a focaccia dough out in a skillet or on an oiled pan, you can use a slacker dough. By contrast, if you're baking pizza on a stone, you need dough with enough structural character that it can be shaped into a thin disk, dressed with toppings, and then slid onto the preheated baking surface. The wetter the dough, the softer and stickier it will be, making it more difficult to handle at every step except mixing; holes might form during shaping or when sliding the pizza into the oven, and the crust might rupture on the stone if you try to turn it or slide it out before the bottom is fully set.

However, I prefer doughs with higher hydration, even though they're sticky and trickier to work with, because they allow for the full character of fermentation I'm looking for. They also give more poofiness in the rim, provided the fermentation is complete, and have a more delicate texture. Delicate texture also comes from proper high-heat baking and using soft 00 flour or all-purpose flour. The three pizza doughs in this book made with 70 percent hydration are a good middle ground. The recipe for poolish pizza dough, at 75 percent hydration, pushes the boundary and requires a little more finesse. Three key techniques will help deliver success with these higher-hydration, soft pizza doughs. First, folding the dough after mixing it adds needed strength. Second, making pizza from cold dough, straight from the refrigerator, adds further strength. Third, because these doughs are a bit sticky, you need to toss each dough ball, top and bottom, in flour before you begin to shape it so it doesn't stick to your hands. Most people know not to fold raw flour into bread dough during shaping, but the same is not true for pizza dough—in this case, flour is your friend. If you have difficulty working with these doughs, it's okay to decrease the amount of water in the dough by 2 or 3 percent. Note, however, that this will make it more difficult to mix the dough by hand, so you may need to use a mixer instead, and you should be sure to hydrate the yeast first.

How does all of this translate to something you can bake at home? What do I know? First, you can make a great dough. The flavor of the crust will be there. Second, you can use the best-quality ingredients that are not overly expensive. A can of San Marzano tomatoes might be a little pricey, but the cost is less than what you'd pay for an average retail pizza made from mass-market tomatoes, and one 28-ounce can makes enough sauce for five pizzas. Add whole-milk mozzarella packed in brine, a stick of good salami, and fresh basil. And you should already have good olive oil around, along with garlic and chile flakes. If you can get your hands on good-quality dried oregano, that would be great, but if not, don't stress.

PIZZA DOUGH OVERVIEW

Chapter 13 has four recipes for pizza dough, each making enough dough for five pizzas about 12 inches in diameter. All make a fine pizza, and the different recipes offer different schedule options, from a same-day straight dough to overnight doughs using a poolish or levain. Chapter 14 has recipes for two types of red sauce (smooth and chunky), tomato fillets, and then a variety of topped pizzas and focaccia. I recommend you start by making Pizza Margherita (page 233) or The New Yorker (page 235), and from that point, you can have fun making pizzas with a variety of toppings. Pick your dough recipe, pick your sauce recipe, choose your cheese and toppings, and bake your pizza. Plenty of guidance follows here and within the recipes.

> **Italian 00 flour** Pronounced "double-oh" in the United States, this flour comes from near Naples, Italy, and is the standard for Neapolitan pizza. It has a soft quality that you can feel as you handle the dough. It makes dough that is delicate but still has the tensile strength to form into a pizza, and bakes into a delicious and tender pizza crust.

The recipes for pizzas and focaccia in chapter 14 are organized by baking method. Here's a quick overview so you'll know what options you'll have. First, starting on page 233, are recipes for baking pizza on a preheated pizza stone; that's the technique you'll need to use if you want to make a dazzling Neapolitan or New York–style pizza. Then, starting on page 247, you'll find recipes for making deep-dish-style pizza in a cast-iron skillet. This is the ideal if you don't have a pizza stone or simply want to make a homier pizza that involves a little less work (think late night or just home from a long day at work—you want something good but don't want to put a lot of work into it, and there are a couple dough balls in the fridge ready to go). Finally, starting on page 252, you'll find recipes for making focaccia in a skillet or on a baking sheet.

As indicated in the recipe yields in chapters 5, 6, and 9, some of the bread doughs can be used to make focaccia or pizza. Using a cast-iron skillet or a baking sheet is best for many of these doughs. You can make traditional focaccia from the pizza doughs in chapter 13, or a less-traditional focaccia from any bread dough recipe in this book, even if that isn't indicated in the recipe. Depending on the dough you use, the texture of the focaccia will vary, from lighter, with the poolish, biga, and Saturday Bread recipes, to heartier from the levain bread recipes. Each has its own character. Try not to feel too bound by rules. Use what you have on hand and common sense when pairing dough with toppings.

PIZZA DOUGH METHOD

The pizza doughs in this book use the same method as the bread doughs, so you can use the same basic techniques for autolysing, mixing, and folding, as detailed in chapter 4. I'll discuss the remaining steps in detail here to give you a fuller description of the process than is possible in the recipes themselves.

Dividing the Dough

Moderately flour a work surface; you'll need an area about 2 feet wide. With floured hands, carefully ease the dough from the tub onto the floured area. To do this, sprinkle some flour around the edges of the dough tub, tip it slightly, and gently loosen the bottom of the dough if any is sticking to the tub. Don't just pull the dough out; help it out of the tub. After picking it up and easing it back onto the work surface in a somewhat even shape, sprinkle a dusting of flour over the entire top surface of the dough. Then use a dough knife or plastic dough scraper to divide it into five equal-size pieces. You can eyeball it or use a scale. Each piece should weigh about 350 grams. It's best not to add in more than two pieces, or the dough will be hard to shape unless you give it a very long rest period. If you need to add a piece of dough to bring up the weight, fold the additional dough into the middle as you shape the dough into a ball, as described in the next step.

Shaping the Dough Balls

You can use the same method for shaping as used to shape bread dough into rounds, as described in "Step 5: Shape the Loaves" (pages 71–73). Take care not to degas the dough in this step—there's flavor in that gas! Here's a refresher:

1. Stretch one-quarter of the dough at a time up and over the top, pulling each segment out until you get to its maximum stretch, then folding it over the top to the opposite side.

2. Repeat, working your way around the dough and forming it into a round until it holds its shape. Then flip it over and put the seam on the work surface in an area cleared of flour (the clean surface will provide more friction, or grip, so you can add tension to the dough ball in the next step).

3. Cup your hands around the back of the dough ball as you face it. Pull the entire dough ball 6 or 8 inches toward you on the dry, unfloured surface, leading with your pinkies and applying enough pressure so the dough ball grips your work surface and doesn't just slide across it. As you pull, this will tighten up the ball and add tension to it.

4. Give the dough a quarter turn and repeat this tightening step. Proceed in this way until you've gone all the way around the dough ball two or three times. The dough doesn't need to be super tight, but you don't want it to be loose either. The dough ball will need time to relax before it can be shaped into pizza. If you are on a short timeline and will be tossing your pie sooner rather than later, shape the dough balls a little looser, with less tension.

5. Repeat the process with the remaining pieces of dough.

If you used the soft white 00 flour, as you shape it you'll notice how soft and pliable the dough feels. It's a beautiful thing.

Proofing the Dough Balls

Lightly dust a rimmed baking sheet or a couple of dinner plates with flour. Put the dough balls on the pan or plates with some space between them to accommodate their expansion. Use your hand to lightly oil the tops of the dough balls, or simply dust the tops with flour. Cover with plastic wrap and let sit at room temperature for 30 to 60 minutes (or longer for focaccia, as described below), then put into the refrigerator to chill out. I like to let them sit for at least 30 minutes in the refrigerator before turning them into pizza, because I find it easier to shape cold dough without tearing it.

Any leftover dough balls can be kept in the refrigerator a night or two. You may even find that you prefer the next-day dough, as it develops flavor in the refrigerator.

When I'm making focaccia, I sometimes like to let it develop more than I would if I were using it for bread or pizza. With bread dough, structural needs drive the process. After it's been shaped, you bake just before the loaves are overproofed (the proteins break down and stop holding on to the fermentation gases, causing the dough to collapse). This isn't a problem with focaccia, where you aren't looking for maximum expansion. In fact, overproofing allows the focaccia dough to spread out into shape more easily and hold the finger dents where you want them, while still poofing up around the rim enough to achieve the form I'm looking for.

A NOTE ON PIZZA DOUGH YIELDS

You might wonder why or whether you should make enough pizza dough to produce five dough balls if you only want to make one or two pizzas. You can halve these recipes and get the same results. You can also quintuple them! The ingredient ratios remain the same regardless of batch size, but bigger batches are easier to mix in a mixer than by hand.

I like having an extra dough ball or two on hand in case one breaks or tangles while I'm shaping it or in case it doesn't load into the oven well. One time my dog grabbed a pizza just as I was about to put it in the oven, and a hilarious game of tug-of-war ensued. (Why did I set the peel with a fully prepped pizza on the coffee table at dog height?) If I end up with extra dough, I might use it to make a simple focaccia topped with marinara or olive oil, salt, and pepper, which can be eaten fresh or wrapped up and saved for the next day.

And as you might guess, I like the way the flavors evolve when the dough overproofs, developing a slightly more fermented flavor. So, for focaccia, oil the tops of the freshly shaped dough balls, then cover with plastic wrap and let them sit out at room temperature for 2 hours. Then you can either chill them for later use or make focaccia right away.

LET'S TALK SAUCE

Okay, you have your dough balls made up. Now it's time for sauce. What makes a great pizza sauce? The tomatoes. Most store-bought canned tomatoes have too much acidity to make a great pizza sauce, which is why many recipes for pizza sauce include some sugar. When cooked, maybe these tomatoes can make a nice pasta sauce, but we don't cook the tomato sauce for pizza. Rather, it cooks on the pie while it's baking, which allows the sauce to retain a freshness of flavor.

The solution is simple: buy canned San Marzano tomatoes from Italy. These tomatoes are amazing and make the difference between an okay pizza sauce and an excellent one. San Marzano tomatoes are grown and canned near Naples, and they are the only tomatoes allowed on a true Neapolitan pizza. They have a rich, naturally sweet flavor; a high amount of pulp, so they aren't watery; and very low acidity.

You should be able to find canned San Marzano tomatoes at well-stocked supermarkets. If they aren't available in your area, use the best canned plum tomatoes you can find. Alternatively, you can buy them online for just a few dollars per 28-ounce can—a lot cheaper than what you'd pay for a large pizza. Go ahead and buy a case of twelve cans; that way you'll be set for quite a while.

I recommend buying whole San Marzano tomatoes. When you're ready to make sauce, let the tomatoes drain in a colander for about 10 minutes. After draining, what remains is just the whole tomatoes and a thick pulpy residue that you can use to make your pizza sauce. You can capture the juice in a large bowl set underneath the colander and reserve it for another use; for example, I combine the juice with vinegar and spices and use it to marinate chicken or to make Spanish rice.

At this point you can go simple, just adding salt and maybe some olive oil and then pureeing the tomatoes in a blender. I like to add chopped garlic and some chile flakes for a little zip, along with good-quality dried oregano to give the sauce that East Coast pizza flavor I remember from my childhood. (I use oregano on some of my white pizzas too.) Dried oregano is used in the Campania region of Italy and its capital, Naples, and throughout southern Italy and Sicily. I recommend Calabrian oregano, which you can purchase online. However, it's fine to use any good-quality dried oregano that has a nice wild pungency to it—or use none at all. The recipes here are my ideals, and suit my taste. At a minimum you can make a fine pizza sauce with just good tomatoes and a little bit of salt.

A Chicago-style pizza sauce, heaped on generously to match the thickness of the crust, is chunky, not pureed. Since I eat a lot of pizza, I like to mix it up, using chunky or smooth sauce according to whim and regardless of crust thickness.

PIZZA STONE BAKING

As I developed the pizza and focaccia recipes for this book, I was initially challenged, as others before me, in figuring out how to get the best results using a standard home oven with a pizza stone. I landed on the technique of placing the pizza stone in the upper third of the oven and using a combination of baking and broiling. I was fascinated by how good the pizza baked. I hope you get similar results.

Oven Management and Preheating

Set your pizza stone on a rack in the upper portion of the oven so the surface is about 8 inches below the broiler. Preheat the oven to the highest heat setting possible; most home ovens only go up to 500°F or 525°F (260°C or 274°C). If you have a pizza oven that goes higher, I recommend making your first pizzas at 600°F (316°C). Save the super-high-temperature baking until after you've done this a few times. Also, keep in mind that every oven bakes differently, so pay attention and get the best using what you have.

Once the oven has reached the target temperature, continue heating the pizza stone for 20 to 30 minutes, switching to the broil setting for the last 5 or so minutes. This ensures that the pizza stone will be thoroughly saturated with heat before baking. Then turn the setting back to bake, put your pizza in the oven, and bake for 5 minutes at about 525°F (274°C). Change the setting back to broil and then give your pizza about 2 more minutes; the broiler should finish the top of your pie. This technique should produce an excellent thin-crust pizza with a bit of char on the rim and good browning on the bottom of the crust. Keep a pair of tongs handy to pull the pizza from the pizza stone and onto a plate. (If you don't have tongs, use the tines of a fork to pierce the crust and pull the pizza onto the plate.)

I should note that the first time I experimented with using my home oven this way, it freaked out—flashing an error code and beeping until I threw the electrical panel's breaker (unmarked, naturally). I didn't kill—or even injure—the oven, happily. On my second try I went with just 3 minutes on broil before returning to bake mode, and Mr. Oven was okay with that. I mention this because every home pizza baker needs to find a way to tweak their oven to get the highest possible heat without damaging it. I'm sure what happened with my oven was the result of an internal safeguard that shut it off when the temperature reached higher than the highest bake setting.

The point is to use the highest baking temperature your oven allows, and to place the pizza stone about 8 inches below the broiler coil. Switching to broil for a few minutes before baking (if your oven can handle it!), helps to superheat the pizza stone just before you load

THE PIZZA TOSS

The pizza tossing thing—it isn't required, but it is fun. It has a point to it. And it takes plenty of repetition before you get it. If you have a sacrificial dough ball each time you make pizza, try tossing it. If you're right-handed, stretch the dough as described, on your fists, and once it's partly stretched out, use your right fist to spin the dough into the air. If you're left-handed, use your left fist to initiate the spin. The motion here is akin to what your hands go through when you turn the steering wheel in your car to the left. Catch the dough on your fists, then call it good and set it down on the peel—or, repeat the toss if you think the dough can handle it without breaking. I usually toss a dough ball two or three times before setting it down to get an even distribution of thin dough throughout. If you keep at it, each time you make five dough balls with my recipe, try tossing one or two. I bet by the fourth or fifth time you try this, you'll start to get the hang of it. Don't stress; just have fun with it. The point is to achieve a uniform thick-ness—or, rather, thinness. And to show off to your friends as you sing "'O Sole Mio." If achieving the thinnest of crusts is your goal, this is the way to do it. It does take prac-tice. This is one benefit to having extra dough on hand. If you have a ball of dough to spare, try tossing it. If it doesn't work out, you can still shape another piece.

your pie in the oven; this will give you that crisp bottom crust with a bit of color to it, even to the point of being pocked with small black spots like we get from the wood-fired oven at my pizzeria. The reason I call for broiling again at the end of the pizza's baking time is to finish the top of the pizza with very high heat to simulate, as best as possible, a high-temperature commercial pizza oven. Home oven broilers heat up at different speeds, but when they do fire they produce very high heat. Therefore, your pizza can go from perfect to burned pretty quickly, so pay very close attention to this final step of baking. Don't be afraid of getting a touch of char on the rim of the crust, though. It adds visual drama and a crunchy, slightly bitter taste contrast that I totally love.

When you bake your pie, aim for temperature settings and oven position that will allow the toppings, the bottom of the crust, and the rim of the crust to all reach their perfect point simultaneously. This takes a few tries and it's worth it.

Setting Up Your Pizza Station

While the oven is preheating, set up a pizza assembly station. Have the pizza sauce with a large spoon next to where you'll toss or shape your dough, along with extra-virgin olive oil and your other prepared toppings, such as cut up cheese, salami, and basil leaves. Give yourself about 2 feet of width on the countertop to work with the dough, and leave space for the pizza peel right next to you.

There are many ways to handle the dough to make a pizza. Thin crust is typical of a Neapolitan pizza, and while it takes practice, I can offer a few tips to make it work the first time too.

As mentioned, these pizza doughs are very soft, so it's best to start with cold dough, just removed from the refrigerator, when shaping pizzas. This makes it less likely that the dough will rip or be troublesome, and also results in a bit more oven spring for a poofy rim.

Set your pizza peel on the work surface next to where you are working your dough. A wood peel is definitely best. Lightly dust the peel with the same flour you used to make your pizza dough. Don't use cornmeal or other coarse grains.

When working with the pizza doughs in this book, flour is your friend. Generously flour your work surface. Then put a dough ball on the work surface and pat it down onto the flour. Then turn it over and repeat on the other side. Leaving about 1 inch of the outer rim undeflated, punch down the middle, then flip the dough over and repeat.

Using both hands, grab the rim and lift so the crust hangs down vertically, still preserving the outer rim by placing your thumbs about an inch from the perimeter. Let gravity pull the rest of the dough down to stretch it. Run the rim between your hands, working all the way around the circumference of the dough several times. If the dough gets sticky, give both top and bottom another dusting of flour. The easiest way to do this is to keep a floured area on your work surface and just plop the dough down on the flour, then turn it over to dust the other side.

Next, make two fists and position them just inside the rim, with the crust still hanging vertically. Gently stretch and turn the dough repeatedly, still letting the bottom of the dough

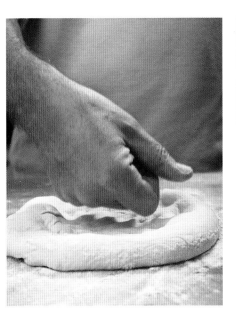

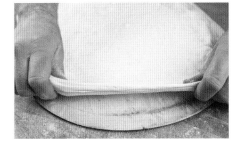

pull down, expanding the surface. Keep a close eye on the thickness of the dough. You want it thin, but you don't want it to tear or develop holes. If you end up with a small tear, don't panic—it's okay to patch it.

Spread the dough onto the lightly floured peel and run your hands around the perimeter to shape it into a round and work out the kinks. Before topping the pie, give the peel a test shake to make sure the dough slides without sticking.

Once you've shaped the dough, spread your sauce over it, not too thickly, using a small ladle or a large serving spoon, and smoothing and spreading the sauce with the back of the spoon. Scatter the toppings over the top, using only moderate amounts so you don't add more weight than the dough can handle. Before sliding the pie into the oven, do another test to confirm that the pizza will slide off the peel—just give the peel a quick shake. If any part of the dough sticks, first try working it out with a few more quick back-and-forth shakes. If that doesn't do the trick, you'll need to gently lift the dough up and toss a bit of flour underneath. Yes, this is difficult, but it's better to find out in advance and deal with it. The first time or two you try this, have an extra ball of dough on hand. Add only minimal toppings to the first pizza and view it as a test pie, so you can get the feel of the peel and how to transfer the pie to the pizza stone, and see what happens after you put it in the oven.

Baking

Once the pizza stone is fully preheated, gently slide the topped pizza onto it. Once you've positioned the pizza, still on the peel, over the baking stone, ease the peel back with a stuttered series of wristy flicks. Once you've done it a bunch of times, you'll have a feel for it and can do it more confidently in a single motion. Be relaxed and it will be fine.

The ideal bake includes mozzarella that's fully melted and slightly browned in spots, a poofy rim with plenty of color, and a crust that's both blond and brown on the bottom, with a few small black spots (it's okay to lift one edge and take a peek). At 525°F (274°C), this should take 7 to 8 minutes altogether, including those last 2 to 3 minutes of broiling, but keep a close

PIZZA BAKING SUMMARY

- Preheat the oven to 525°F for 30 minutes with the pizza stone inside.
- Set up your pizza station.
- Shape and top your pizza.
- Change the oven setting to broil for about 5 minutes.
- Switch the oven back to bake at 525°F.

- Load the pizza into the oven; bake for 5 minutes.
- Switch oven to broil and bake for 2 to 3 more minutes, keeping a close eye on it, until the pizza is done.
- Use tongs to pull the pizza from the stone to a plate.
- Enjoy!

eye on it. At 600°F (316°C) it should take just 4 to 5 minutes altogether, and you may not need to use the broiler to get the best finish on the top. Every oven is different; just know you have the broiler as an option for finishing the pie. At my pizzeria, we bake the pizzas for 2½ to 3 minutes in a wood-fired oven, in the section of the oven that's around 700°F to 750°F (371°C to 399°C). Use your eyes, your nose, and your good judgment.

The baking temperature has a specific effect on the pizza. When baking at 500°F (274°C) for a longer time, you'll get a crisper crust and pizza with less moisture. The hotter the oven and the shorter the baking time, the softer and more moist the pizza. When baked at 700°F (371°C), the result is closer to the real Neapolitan pies, which are baked in a (roughly) 900°F (482°C) oven for just about 90 seconds, and have *a lot* of moisture in them. This ends up being a matter of taste, and of getting the best from whatever setup you have.

Use tongs or a fork to pull the pizza off the stone and onto a plate, then slide the pizza onto a wood surface so you can cut it. At this stage, I like to drizzle a bit (sometimes a lot if it's fresh pressed) of best-quality extra-virgin olive oil over the top. Enjoy the aromas while you slice the pizza, then serve it immediately, with olive oil, chile flakes, and sea salt at the table as garnishes. Some Italian traditionalists prefer to serve the pizza unsliced. That's fine too, but cutting through fresh baked dough on a ceramic plate is more than I want to hassle with. I like to pick up the pieces.

IRON-SKILLET PIZZA

If you don't have a pizza stone, you can bake pizza in a cast-iron skillet. This is also easier than setting up a pizza peel, dusting it with flour, applying the sauce and toppings, and hoping to scooch the uncooked pizza onto the preheated pizza stone. Any of the pizza doughs in this book will work for the crust. Use a 340- or 350-gram dough ball for a thick crust, or a 200-gram dough ball for a thin crust. If you like a lot of sauce and toppings, go for the thick crust, and if you're aiming for a Chicago deep-dish style pizza, use a chunky sauce. (You can also use the iron-skillet method to make a basic focaccia—either thick or thin—by topping the dough simply; for example, with just olive oil and seasonings. This is great as a fresh bread with dinner.)

One of the most important keys for success is that the dough be completely relaxed, with very little tension. If you prepare the Same-Day Straight Pizza Dough (page 218) in the morning for pizza that evening, be sure not to shape the dough balls too tightly, and give the dough balls at least an hour to relax before forming the pizza. Also note that cold dough is easier to shape than dough at room temperature.

About 20 minutes before you want to bake the pizza, position a rack near the bottom of the oven, then preheat the oven to 525°F (274°C). If your oven only goes to 500°F (260°C), that's fine; the pizza will just take a bit longer to bake. When you're ready to shape the crust, remove the dough ball from the refrigerator. Holding the rim, stretch the dough to a circle about 9 inches in diameter, then put it in a dry, room temperature 9-inch cast-iron skillet.

Because the skillet isn't preheated, the pizza will take quite a bit longer to bake than it would on a baking stone; the typical baking time is 15 to 20 minutes. The texture will be different too—this crust will be firmer and generally without floppiness in the middle.

WHAT'S THE DIFFERENCE BETWEEN PIZZA AND FOCACCIA?

I bet there are as many opinions on this topic as there are pizzerias in New York. Some definitions focus on dough thickness, others on whether it's cooked in a pan, and yet others on whether its topped with cheese. At a *focacceria tipica ligure* in Italy, I had focaccia with a crust about ¼ inch thick and topped with tomato sauce and cheese. To me it looked and tasted like pizza. And while some people think of focaccia as being thick, pizza crusts can certainly be thick; pizzas can also be made without cheese and, at least in the United States, you'll find plenty of pizzas baked in pans.

In this book, the focaccias are baked either in a cast-iron skillet or on a sheet pan, whereas the pizzas are (preferably) baked directly on a pizza stone. Except I'm going to cheat and put cast-iron skillet pizza recipes in this book, so if it has cheese I'm calling it "pizza," even if it's baked in a skillet. In terms of ease of execution, pan baking is much simpler than baking on a pizza stone. Spreading the dough out on a pan or in a skillet, covering it with toppings, and putting the pan in the oven may seem less intimidating than pizza baking: tossing the dough, dressing it on the peel, and getting it to slide off easily onto the pizza stone in the oven.

As far as the thickness of focaccia is concerned, I leave it up to you. If you use 200 grams of dough in a 9-inch skillet, the result will be focaccia with thin crust; if you use 350 grams of dough in the same skillet, the result will be a thick crust. Focaccia is great for the variety of toppings you can put on it, which are limited only by your imagination, and for it's versatility. You can serve it alongside a salad and make a meal of it, or cut it into smaller pieces for snacks. And I love how easy it easy to make. Once you've prepared the dough, the only thing you need to dirty is the baking pan, a knife, and a cutting board. You can serve it hot out of the oven, or you can bake it ahead of time as long as there isn't any cheese on it. Reheating previously baked cheese may be fine for the dorm room, but all the joys of the texture of melted cheese disappear the second time around.

To me, a more defining distinction between pizza and focaccia is the texture of the dough. I want specific physical characteristics for pizza dough: structure that can withstand stretching into a round that I can toss and enough strength that it doesn't break when being shaped. But with focaccia I can preshape it into a round as for pizza dough, then finish spreading it in or on the pan. This opens the door to using any dough to make focaccia—even whole wheat or rye, which was great for both dipping into hummus and serving with a delicious pork terrine, flavored with apricots and pistachios, that Greg Higgins (of Higgins Restaurant and Bar) gave me.

MAKING FOCACCIA WITH BREAD DOUGH

The flexibility of being able to use virtually any dough for focaccia is great when it comes to the bread recipes in this book, where I always begin with 1,000 grams of flour and call for dividing the dough into two pieces. If you like, you can bake one loaf as directed for bread and divide the remaining dough into one to three portions to use for making focaccia. Shape those portions into balls when you shape the loaf in the bread recipe, using the method detailed there. Here are some pointers on the size of dough balls for focaccia, depending on how you'll be baking it:

- For thin-crust focaccia baked in a 9-inch skillet, use about 200 grams of dough.
- For thick-crust focaccia baked in a 9-inch skillet, use about 350 grams of dough (the standard size for balls of pizza dough).
- If baking on a sheet pan, use up to 875 grams of dough, which is half the yield of a bread recipe, or whatever fits on your pan, keeping in mind that the thickness will vary depending on the amount of dough and the size of the pan.

As for method, you can basically follow the instructions for either Focaccia Genovese (page 252) or Zucchini Focaccia (page 257), but here's the process in brief.

1. Once the pieces of dough have been shaped into rounds, let them relax, either at room temperature or in the refrigerator, for at least 1 hour beyond what the recipe specifies for proofing time. You can also store the shaped dough balls in the refrigerator for up to 2 days.

2. Coat the dough ball in flour and decompress it on both sides.

3. Preheat the oven to its highest temperature setting.

4. Stretch the dough until it's the size and shape you want: round for a skillet; oblong or rectangular for a baking sheet.

5. Top with whatever you like, depending on the dough, what you have on hand, and your desire.

6. Bake until golden brown on both top and bottom and completely cooked inside.

7. Drizzle extra-virgin olive oil over the top if you like, along with any other seasonings, such as small-flake sea salt.

8. No need to wait—you can go right ahead and slice and serve. However, do note most focaccia is very good served at room temperature, so if you're entertaining, you can bake it up to 1 hour ahead of time.

CHAPTER 13
PIZZA DOUGHS

SAME-DAY STRAIGHT PIZZA DOUGH 218

OVERNIGHT STRAIGHT PIZZA DOUGH 220

OVERNIGHT PIZZA DOUGH WITH LEVAIN 222

OVERNIGHT PIZZA DOUGH WITH POOLISH 225

SAME-DAY STRAIGHT PIZZA DOUGH

This recipe is ideal if you want to make dough in the morning and bake pizza that evening. It's even better if you refrigerate the dough balls overnight and make pizza the next day. What I often do with this recipe is make pizza two days in a row, or pizza one day, and the next day make focaccia, perhaps to serve alongside a meal, as a predinner snack, or for lunch.

Note that the dough doesn't include olive oil, as pizza doughs often do. Therefore it bakes up crisper, with more open holes in the perimeter of the crust, which is how I like it. I do think drizzling olive oil *on* the dough after the pizza is baked is a great idea. The crust will showcase the flavor of the flour, so it's best to use a good flour, preferably soft white 00 flour (see page 204), Caputo brand if you can get it. If 00 flour isn't available, use the best-quality all-purpose white flour you can obtain. The resulting flavors will be delicate, sweet wheat, and ideal for combining with high-quality tomatoes and toppings.

THIS RECIPE MAKES FIVE 340-GRAM DOUGH BALLS, each of which will yield a thin-crust pizza-stone pizza about 12 inches in diameter or a thick-crust iron-skillet pizza. If you use this dough for focaccia, see page 215 for details on amounts of dough for different applications.

BULK FERMENTATION: About 6 hours

PROOF TIME: At least 1½ hours

SAMPLE SCHEDULE: Mix at 10 a.m., shape into dough balls at 4 p.m., and make pizza anytime after 6 p.m. or anytime over the next 2 days.

INGREDIENT	QUANTITY		BAKER'S PERCENTAGE
White flour	1,000 g	7¾ cups	100%
Water	700 g, 90°F to 95°F (32°C to 35°C)	3 cups	70%
Fine sea salt	20 g	1 tbsp + ¾ tsp	2%
Instant dried yeast	2 g	½ tsp	0.2%

1a. Hydrate the yeast Measure 700 grams of water at 90°F to 95°F (32°C to 35°C) into a container. Put 2 grams (½ teaspoon) of yeast in a separate, small container. Add about 3 tablespoons of the 90°F to 95°F (32°C to 35°C) water to the yeast and set aside.

1b. Autolyse Combine the 1,000 grams of flour and the remaining 90°F to 95°F (32°C to 35°C) of water in a 12-quart round tub. Mix by hand just until incorporated. Cover and let rest for 20 to 30 minutes.

2. Mix Sprinkle the 20 grams of salt over the top of the dough. Stir the yeast mixture with your finger, then pour it over the dough. Use a small piece of the autolysed mixture to wipe the remaining yeast goop from its container, then throw it back in the tub.

Mix by hand, wetting your working hand before mixing so the dough doesn't stick to you. (It's fine to rewet your hand three or four times while you mix.)

Reach underneath the dough and grab about one-quarter of it. Gently stretch this section of dough and fold it over the top to the other side of the dough. Repeat three more times with the remaining dough, until the salt and yeast are fully enclosed.

Use the pincer method (see page 67) alternating with folding the dough to fully integrate the ingredients. Cut and fold, cut and fold. The target dough temperature at end the of the mix is 77°F to 78°F (25°C to 26°C).

3. Fold This dough needs one fold (see pages 69–70 for instructions). It's best to apply the fold 30 to 60 minutes after mixing. After folding, lightly coat the dough and the bottom of the tub with olive oil to help prevent sticking.

When the dough is about double its original volume, about 6 hours after mixing, it's ready to be divided.

4. Divide Moderately flour a work surface about 2 feet wide. With floured hands, gently ease the dough out of the tub. With your hands still floured, pick up the dough and ease it back down onto the work surface in a somewhat even shape. Dust the entire top of the dough with flour, then cut it into 5 equal-size pieces with a dough knife or plastic dough scraper. Each piece should weigh about 340 grams; you can eyeball it or use a scale. (If you plan to use any of the dough for thin-crust iron-skillet pizza or focaccia, divide that portion of the dough into 200-gram pieces.)

5. Shape the dough into balls Shape each piece of dough into a medium-tight round following the instructions on pages 71–73, working gently and being careful not to degas the dough.

6. Refrigerate Put the dough balls on a lightly floured baking sheet, leaving space between them to allow for expansion. Lightly oil or flour the tops, cover with plastic wrap, and let rest at room temperature for 30 to 60 minutes. Refrigerate for at least 30 minutes to make the dough easier to shape.

See chapter 14 for instructions for shaping, topping, and baking pizzas. Stored in the refrigerator and tightly covered, any leftover dough will keep for up to 2 days. You may prefer the next-day dough as it develops flavors with more time in the refrigerator.

OVERNIGHT STRAIGHT PIZZA DOUGH

This dough recipe has two advantages: First, the long fermentation allows the dough to develop great flavor. Second, its schedule works for people who have a day job. The timing works like this: mix the dough at 7 p.m.; then, the next morning, give yourself fifteen minutes to divide the dough, shape it into balls, and wrap and refrigerate them. You can use the dough that evening or anytime over the next two days to make pizza or focaccia, using any of the recipes in chapter 14. When you get home from work, all you'll have to do is make a sauce and prepare your toppings as the oven and pizza stone are preheating. As with all of the pizza doughs in this book, use a high-quality all-purpose white flour, preferably 00 flour (see page 204), ideally Caputo brand.

THIS RECIPE MAKES FIVE 340-GRAM DOUGH BALLS, each of which will yield a thin-crust pizza-stone pizza about 12 inches in diameter or a thick-crust iron-skillet pizza. If you use this dough for focaccia, see page 215 for details on amounts of dough for different applications.

BULK FERMENTATION: About 12 hours

PROOF TIME: At least 6 hours

SAMPLE SCHEDULE: Mix at 7 p.m., shape into dough balls at 7 a.m. the next morning, and make pizza that evening or anytime over the next 2 days.

INGREDIENT	QUANTITY		BAKER'S PERCENTAGE
White flour	1,000 g	7¾ cups	100%
Water	700 g, 90°F to 95°F (32°C to 35°C)	3 cups	70%
Fine sea salt	20 g	1 tbsp + ¾ tsp	2%
Instant dried yeast	0.8 g	Scant ¼ tsp	0.08%

1a. Hydrate the yeast Measure 700 grams of water at 90°F to 95°F (32°C to 35°C) into a container. Put 0.8 gram (a scant ¼ teaspoon) of yeast in a separate, small container. Add about 3 tablespoons of the measured 90°F to 95°F (32°C to 35°C) water to the yeast and set aside.

1b. Autolyse Combine the 1,000 grams of flour with the remaining 90°F to 95°F (32°C to 35°C) of water in a 12-quart round tub. Mix by hand just until incorporated. Cover and let rest for 20 to 30 minutes.

2. Mix Sprinkle the 20 grams of salt over the top of the dough. Stir the yeast mixture with your finger, then pour it over the dough. Use a small piece of the autolysed mixture to wipe the remaining yeast goop from its container, then throw it back in the tub.

Mix by hand, wetting your working hand before mixing so the dough doesn't stick to you. (It's fine to rewet your hand three or four times while you mix.)

Reach underneath the dough and grab about one-quarter of it. Gently stretch this section of dough and fold it over the top to the other side of the dough. Repeat three more times with the remaining dough, until the salt and yeast are fully enclosed.

Use the pincer method (see page 67) alternating with folding the dough to fully integrate the ingredients. Cut and fold, cut and fold. The target dough temperature at end the of the mix is 77°F to 78°F (25°C to 26°C).

3. Fold This dough needs one or two folds (see pages 69–70 for instructions). It's best to apply the folds 30 to 60 minutes after mixing. After folding, lightly coat the dough and the bottom of the tub with olive oil to help prevent sticking.

When the dough is 2 to 3 times its original volume, about 12 hours after mixing, it's ready to be divided.

4. Divide Moderately flour a work surface about 2 feet wide. With floured hands, gently ease the dough out of the tub. With your hands still floured, pick up the dough and ease it back down onto the work surface in a somewhat even shape. Dust the entire top of the dough with flour, then cut it into 5 equal-size pieces with a dough knife or plastic dough scraper. Each piece should weigh about 340 grams; you can eyeball it or use a scale. (If you plan to use any of the dough for thin-crust iron-skillet pizza or focaccia, divide that portion of the dough into pieces weighing about 200 grams.)

5. Shape the dough into balls Shape each piece of dough into a medium-tight round following the instructions on pages 71–73, working gently and being careful not to degas the dough.

6. Refrigerate Put the dough balls on a lightly floured baking sheet, leaving space between them to allow for expansion. Lightly oil or flour the tops, cover with plastic wrap, and refrigerate for at least 6 hours.

See chapter 14 for instructions for shaping, topping, and baking pizzas. Stored in the refrigerator and tightly covered, any leftover dough will keep for up to 2 days. You may prefer the next-day dough as it develops flavors with more time in the refrigerator.

OVERNIGHT PIZZA DOUGH WITH LEVAIN

If you've built a levain culture, when you use it to make bread you'll have enough left to make pizza dough too. This pure levain dough recipe, without added baker's yeast, works on a convenient schedule and produces pizza crust with nice poofiness in the rim and a bit more acidity and complexity in taste from the leavening. I don't mean to understate it, this is a great dough. As with all of the pizza doughs in this book, use a high-quality all-purpose white flour, preferably 00 flour (see page 204), ideally Caputo brand.

THIS RECIPE MAKES FIVE 340-GRAM DOUGH BALLS, each of which will yield a thin-crust pizza-stone pizza about 12 inches in diameter or a thick-crust iron-skillet pizza. If you use this dough for focaccia, see page 215 for details on amounts of dough for different applications.

BULK FERMENTATION: 12 to 14 hours

PROOF TIME: At least 6 hours

SAMPLE SCHEDULE: Feed the levain in the morning, mix the dough at 7 p.m., shape into dough balls at 7 a.m. the next morning, and make pizza after 1 p.m. or anytime over the next 2 days.

Levain

INGREDIENT	QUANTITY	
Mature, active levain	50 g	Scant ¼ cup
White flour	200 g	1½ cups + 1 tbsp
Whole wheat flour	50 g	⅓ cup + 1 tbsp
Water	200 g, 85°F to 90°F (29°C to 32°C)	⅞ cup

Final Dough / Baker's Formula

INGREDIENT	FINAL DOUGH MIX QUANTITY		QUANTITY IN LEVAIN	TOTAL RECIPE QUANTITY	BAKER'S PERCENTAGE
White flour	900 g	6¾ cups	80 g	980 g	98%
Whole wheat flour	0	0	20 g	20 g	2%
Water	620 g, 90°F to 95°F (32°C to 35°C)	2¾ cups	80 g	700 g	70%
Fine sea salt	20 g	1 tbsp + ¾ tsp	0	20 g	2%
Levain	180 g**	½ cup + 2 tbsp			10%*

The baker's percentage for levain is the amount of flour in the levain expressed as a percentage of the total flour in the recipe.
**In wintertime, you may need to use a little more levain, up to about 220 grams.*

1a. Feed the levain. About 24 hours after your previous feeding of the levain, discard all but 50 grams of levain, leaving the remainder in your 6-quart tub. Add the 200 grams of white flour, 50 grams of whole wheat flour, and 200 grams of water at 85°F to 90°F (29°C to 32°C) and mix by hand just until incorporated. Cover and let rest for 8 to 10 hours before mixing the final dough.

1b. Autolyse After 8 to 10 hours, combine the 900 grams of white flour with the 620 grams of 90°F to 95°F (32°C to 35°C) water in a 12-quart round tub. Mix by hand just until incorporated. Cover and let rest for 20 to 30 minutes.

2. Mix the final dough Sprinkle the 20 grams of salt over the top of the dough.

Put a container with about a finger's depth of warm water on your scale so you can easily remove the levain after it's weighed. With a wet hand, transfer 180 grams (or more if your kitchen is cool; see "Seasonal Variations" on page 134) of levain into the container.

Transfer the weighed levain to the 12-quart dough tub, minimizing the amount of water transferred with it. Mix by hand, wetting your working hand before mixing so the dough doesn't stick to you. Enclose the salt and levain by gently picking up the dough from underneath and stretching in three or four folds. Use the pincer method (see page 67) alternating with folding the dough to fully integrate the ingredients. Cut and fold, cut and fold. The target dough temperature at the end of the mix is 77°F to 78°F (25°C to 26°C).

3. Fold This dough needs one or two folds (see pages 69–70 for instructions). Make the first fold 30 to 60 minutes after mixing. After the final fold, lightly coat the dough and the bottom of the tub with olive oil to help prevent sticking.

When the dough is 2 to 2½ times its original volume, 12 to 14 hours after mixing, it's ready to be divided.

CONTINUED>>

If you are going to mix a levain bread dough *and* this pizza dough on the same day, you will need to double the levain quantity so you have enough for both mixes: 100 grams levain, 400 grams white flour, 100 grams whole wheat flour, and 400 grams water.

4. Divide Moderately flour a work surface about 2 feet wide. With floured hands, gently ease the dough out of the tub. With your hands still floured, pick up the dough and ease it back down onto the work surface in a somewhat even shape. Dust the entire top of the dough with flour, then cut it into 5 equal-size pieces with a dough knife or plastic dough scraper. Each piece should weigh about 340 grams; you can eyeball it or use a scale. (If you plan to use any of the dough for thin-crust iron-skillet pizza or focaccia, divide that portion of the dough into pieces weighing about 200 grams.)

5. Shape the dough into balls Shape each piece of dough into a medium-tight round following the instructions on pages 71–73, working gently and being careful not to degas the dough.

6. Refrigerate Put the dough balls on a lightly floured baking sheet, leaving space between them to allow for expansion. Lightly oil or flour the tops, cover with plastic wrap, and refrigerate for at least 6 hours (if you want to make pizza sooner, let the dough balls you'll be using sit out at room temperature for 1 hour, then refrigerate for at least 30 minutes before shaping).

See chapter 14 for instructions for shaping, topping, and baking pizzas. Stored in the refrigerator and tightly covered, any leftover dough will keep for 2 or 3 days. You may prefer the next-day dough as it develops flavors with more time in the refrigerator.

OVERNIGHT PIZZA DOUGH WITH POOLISH

This dough has two things going for it: a particular flavor provided by the fermentation of the poolish; and a crisp, poofy-rimmed, delicate crust that has a light texture and open holes. The dough is leavened entirely with the poolish, which incorporates 50 percent of the total amount of flour in the dough.

This dough also has higher hydration than the other pizza dough recipes in the book, using 75 percent water relative to the weight of the flour. This produces a softer dough that requires two folds, preferably during the first hour of fermentation to give it more strength and tenacity. You need to take extra care when shaping pizzas from this soft dough. Although I've learned to toss and twirl this dough it *does* break and tear more easily, so the recommended shaping method for this dough is to use balled-up fists to stretch it into shape (without tossing it), as described on page 211.

Because the dough isn't as strong, it's also important not to load the pizzas down with too much weight from sauce or toppings. A pizza that breaks when you load it into the oven isn't fun to deal with. Another option is to make this dough at a hydration closer to 70 percent. To do so, simply reduce the amount of water in the final dough mix by 40 or 50 grams.

You might think of this as an advanced recipe to try once you're confident with the other pizza doughs in this book. A successful pizza made from this dough is well worth the effort, in taste and texture. It's also a good example of how dough can be leavened solely with a poolish and no added yeast. I love the fact that just 0.4 gram of yeast—a scant ⅛ teaspoon—can leaven a batch of dough that makes five pizzas.

THIS RECIPE MAKES FIVE 350-GRAM DOUGH BALLS, each of which will yield a thin-crust pizza-stone pizza about 12 inches in diameter or a thick-crust iron-skillet pizza. If you use this dough for focaccia, see page 215 for details on amounts of dough for different applications.

POOLISH FERMENTATION: 12 to 14 hours

BULK FERMENTATION: About 6 hours

PROOF TIME: At least 1½ hours

SAMPLE SCHEDULE: Mix the poolish at 8 p.m., mix the final dough at 10 a.m., shape into dough balls at 4 p.m., and make pizza that evening.

CONTINUED>>

Poolish

INGREDIENT	QUANTITY	
White flour	500 g	3¾ cups + 2 tbsp
Water	500 g, 80°F (27°C)	2¼ cups
Instant dried yeast	0.4 g	Scant ⅛ tsp

Final Dough

Baker's Formula

INGREDIENT	FINAL DOUGH MIX QUANTITY		QUANTITY IN POOLISH	TOTAL RECIPE QUANTITY	BAKER'S PERCENTAGE
White flour	500 g	3¾ cups + 2 tbsp	500 g	1,000 g	100%
Water	250 g, 105°F (41°C)	1⅛ cups	500 g	750 g	75%
Fine sea salt	20 g	1 tbsp + ¾ tsp	0	20 g	2%
Instant dried yeast	0	0	0.4 g	0.4 g	0.04%
Poolish	1,000 g	All from recipe above			50%*

* The baker's percentage for poolish is the amount of flour in the poolish expressed as a percentage of the total flour in the recipe.

1. Mix the poolish The evening before you plan to bake your pizza, mix 500 grams of flour and 0.4 gram (a scant ⅛ teaspoon) of yeast by hand in a 6-quart tub. Add 500 grams of water at 80°F (27°C) and mix by hand just until incorporated. Cover and leave out overnight at room temperature. The following time-line assumes overnight room temperature is between 65°F and 70°F (18°C and 21°C).

When fully mature 12 to 14 hours later, the poolish should be about tripled in volume (it comes just below the 2-quart line on my 6-quart Cambro tub), with bubbles popping on the surface at least every few seconds. Pool-ish will stay at this peak level of maturity for about 2 hours, unless your room temperature is warm—say, above 76°F (24°C)—in which case it will be at its peak for just about 1 hour. At this point you can mix the final dough.

2. Mix the final dough Measure 500 grams of flour into a 12-quart round tub, then add the 20 grams of salt and mix by hand.

Pour 250 grams of 105°F (41°C) water around the perimeter of the poolish, loosening it from its tub. Then pour the water and pool-ish into the flour mixture in the 12-quart tub.

Mix by hand, wetting your working hand before mixing so the dough doesn't stick to you. (It's fine to rewet your hand three or four times while you mix.) Use the pincer method (see page 67) alternating with folding the dough to fully integrate the ingredients. The target dough temperature at the end of the mix is 75°F (24°C).

3. Fold This dough needs two folds (sees pages 69–70 for instructions). It's best to apply the folds during the first hour after mixing the dough. After the second fold, lightly coat the dough and the bottom of the tub with olive oil to help prevent sticking.

When the dough is about 2½ times its original volume, about 6 hours after mixing, it's ready to be divided.

4. Divide Moderately flour a work surface about 2 feet wide. With floured hands, gently ease the dough out of the tub. With your hands still floured, pick up the dough and ease it back down onto the work surface in a somewhat even shape. Dust the entire top of the dough with flour, then cut it into 5 equal-size pieces with a dough knife or plastic dough scraper. Each piece should weigh about 350 grams; you can eyeball it or use a scale. (If you plan to use any of the dough for thin-crust iron-skillet pizza or focaccia, divide that portion of the dough into 200-gram pieces.)

5. Shape the dough into balls Shape each piece of dough into a medium-tight round following the instructions on pages 71–73, working gently and being careful not to degas the dough.

6. Refrigerate Put the dough balls on a lightly floured baking sheet, leaving space between them to allow for expansion. Lightly oil or flour the tops, cover with plastic wrap, and let rest at room temperature for 30 to 60 minutes. Refrigerate for at least 30 minutes to make the dough easier to shape.

See chapter 14 for instructions for shaping, topping, and baking pizzas. Stored in the refrigerator and tightly covered, any leftover dough will keep for up to 2 days. You may prefer the next-day dough as it develops flavors with more time in the refrigerator.

CHAPTER 14
PIZZA AND FOCACCIA

SAUCES AND TOPPINGS

SMOOTH RED SAUCE 230

CHUNKY RED SAUCE 230

TOMATO FILLETS 231

PIZZA STONE PIZZAS

PIZZA MARGHERITA 233

THE NEW YORKER 235

SALAMI PIZZA 239

GOLDEN BEET
AND DUCK BREAST
"PROSCIUTTO" PIZZA 241

SWEET POTATO AND
PEAR PIZZA 245

IRON-SKILLET PIZZAS

IRON-SKILLET
MEAT PIE 247

SKILLET PIZZA WITH
TOMATO FILLETS, GARLIC,
AND CHILE 249

FOCACCIA

FOCACCIA GENOVESE 252

FOCACCIA
"PISSALIDIERE" 254

ZUCCHINI FOCACCIA 257

SMOOTH RED SAUCE

This is a smooth tomato sauce flavored with dried oregano, along with optional garlic and chile flakes. Use the best-quality dried oregano you can get; if you can find Calabrian oregano, all the better. Although including chile flakes isn't traditional for Neapolitan pizza sauce, I like the zip. If you can't find San Marzano tomatoes, use the best-quality canned plum tomatoes available.

MAKES ENOUGH SAUCE FOR FIVE 12-INCH ROUND PIZZAS

1 (28-ounce) can whole San Marzano tomatoes
1½ tablespoons extra-virgin olive oil
1 clove garlic (optional)
½ teaspoon fine sea salt
¼ teaspoon dried oregano
¼ teaspoon chile flakes (optional)

1. Place a colander over a large bowl. Drain the tomatoes for 10 to 15 minutes. (Reserve the juice for another use.)

2. Put the olive oil, garlic, salt, oregano and chile flakes in a blender. Add the tomatoes and blend until smooth and thoroughly combined.

CHUNKY RED SAUCE

Sometimes I want a chunkier sauce, and sometimes I like a sauce with a more pure tomato flavor. This recipes satisfies both desires. Again, San Marzano tomatoes are ideal, but if you can't find them, you can substitute the best-quality canned plum tomatoes available.

MAKES ENOUGH SAUCE FOR TWO TO THREE 12-INCH ROUND PIZZAS

1 (28-ounce) can whole San Marzano tomatoes
1½ tablespoons extra-virgin olive oil
Sea salt

1. Place a colander over a large bowl. Drain the tomatoes for 10 to 15 minutes.

2. Tilt the colander and use a wooden spoon to repeatedly push the tomatoes back and forth to break them into a chunky pulp and drain most of the remaining juice. Do this for about 30 seconds, then pour the pulp into a bowl. (Reserve the juice for another use.) Stir in the olive oil and season with salt to taste.

TOMATO FILLETS

Sometimes, it's just the tomatoes you want. Roasting the tomatoes in advance is optional. Uncooked, they'll have a bright flavor. For deeper, more concentrated and complex flavor, roast them slowly with simple seasonings as described here.

MAKES ENOUGH SAUCE FOR THREE 12-INCH ROUND PIZZAS OR THREE TO FOUR IRON-SKILLET PIZZAS

1 (28-ounce) can whole San Marzano tomatoes

Extra-virgin olive oil (optional)

Sea salt (optional)

Thyme sprigs (optional)

1. If roasting the tomatoes, preheat the oven to 325°F (165°C).

2. Place a colander over a large bowl. Drain the tomatoes for 10 to 15 minutes. (Reserve the juice for another use.)

3. Remove the whole tomatoes one at a time and break each into three or four pieces by hand. Put the pieces on a plate to drain. Reserve any remaining pulp for another use.

4. To roast the tomatoes, put them in a shallow baking pan in a single layer. Drizzle olive oil over the top, sprinkle with sea salt, and add a dozen thyme sprigs. Bake for 20 to 30 minutes.

PIZZA MARGHERITA

This is the classic, basic pie that is the standard for Neapolitan-style pizza. It should have a thin crust with some poofiness in the rim, sauce made with San Marzano tomatoes, and fresh mozzarella and basil. The red, white, and green toppings mirror the colors of the Italian flag.

I prefer *fior di latte* mozzarella (literally, "the flower of the milk," and referring to mozzarella made with cow's milk rather than buffalo milk). Grande brand is very good quality, and their Ovoline variety is shaped into 4-ounce balls that are the perfect size for this pizza. Whatever brand you choose, look for fresh mozzarella packaged in liquid brine.

As simple as the Margherita pizza is, defining its ideal incarnation could provoke an hours-long, Chianti-filled evening of lively conversation and not a little arm waving. Should the cheese be just melted, or browned on top? Should the basil leaves be whole or torn? Flat rims or poofy? Should the bottom be spotted with dots of char? Should the rim be lightly browned or have a few charred areas? Should it be finished with olive oil? You get the idea. I'll supply you with the basic formula. You take it from there and bake it the way you like it.

MAKES ONE 12-INCH PIZZA

1 350-gram dough ball from any recipe in chapter 13
White flour for dusting
3 ounces Smooth Red Sauce (page 230)
4 ounces fresh whole-milk mozzarella cheese, cut
    into pieces ½ inch thick at most
6 to 8 whole basil leaves
Extra-virgin olive oil for drizzling (optional)
Fine-flake sea salt, such as fiore di sale (optional)
Chile flakes (optional)

1. Preheat the pizza stone Put your pizza stone on a rack in the upper portion of your oven so the surface is about 8 inches below the broiler. Preheat the oven to 600°F (316°C) if you're lucky enough to have an oven that goes that high; otherwise, simply preheat to the highest possible setting. Once the oven is preheated, continue heating the pizza stone for another 30 minutes, for a total of about 45 minutes.

2. Set up your pizza assembly station Give yourself about 2 feet of width on the countertop. Generously flour the work surface. Position your peel next to the floured area and dust it with flour. Have the sauce, cheese, and basil prepared and at hand, with a ladle or large spoon in the sauce.

3. Shape the pizza Remove the dough ball from the refrigerator, put it on the floured work surface, and gently pat it down a bit to coat the bottom with flour. Leaving about 1 inch of the outer rim undeflated, punch down the middle, then flip the dough over and repeat.

CONTINUED>>

Using both hands, grab the rim and lift so the dough hangs down vertically. Let gravity pull the rest of the dough down and stretch it. Run the rim between your hands, working all the way around the circumference of the dough several times.

Next, make two fists and position them just inside the rim, with the dough still hanging vertically. Gently stretch and turn the dough repeatedly, still letting the bottom of the dough pull down, expanding the surface. Keep a close eye on the thickness of the dough. You want it thin, but you don't want it to tear or develop holes. If you end up with a small tear, don't panic—it's okay to patch it.

Spread the dough on the floured peel and run your hands around the perimeter to shape it into a round and work out the kinks.

4. Superheat the pizza stone About 30 minutes after the oven has reached its set temperature, switch to the broil setting for about 5 minutes to saturate the pizza stone with heat.

5. Top the pizza Spread the tomato sauce over the dough to within an inch of the edge, smoothing and spreading it with the back of the ladle. Distribute the mozzarella and basil leaves evenly around the pie.

6. Bake Turn the oven setting back to bake. Gently slide the pizza onto the pizza stone.

Bake for 5 minutes, then switch to the broil setting and broil for 2 minutes, keeping a close eye on the pizza. Bake until the cheese is completely melted and the crust is golden with spots of brown and a few small spots of char. If the oil separates out of the cheese, it's overbaked. Use tongs or a fork to slide the pizza from the pizza stone onto a large plate.

7. Slice and serve Transfer to a large wooden cutting board. Drizzle extra-virgin olive oil lightly over the top if you like, slice, and serve immediately, passing the salt and chile flakes at the table. Note that a perfectly baked Margherita pizza has a fairly brief window of being optimum for eating. You need to wait long enough that you don't burn your mouth on the molten mozzarella, but it's best to eat it before the cheese cools enough to solidify.

Variation: Top each slice with a handful of arugula.

THE NEW YORKER

This pizza represents my ideal of a classic New York pizza, with a blend of grated cheeses covering a red sauce spiked with dried oregano, optionally topped with pepperoni. Not all of the great New York pizzas are made with shredded cheese, but that's what I prefer for this style of pizza, which is cheesier than the Margherita.

If I were to do this kind of pie in a coal-fired oven like at Lombardi's or Totonno's, it would be bigger than the 12- to 14-inch pizzas we are going to bake on the home kitchen pizza stone. Compensate by cutting the finished pizza into no more than four pieces.

MAKES ONE 12-INCH PIZZA

1 350-gram dough ball from any recipe in chapter 13
White flour for dusting
3 ounces Smooth Red Sauce (page 230)
3 ounces fresh whole-milk mozzarella cheese, grated
2 ounces provolone cheese, grated
4 to 6 whole basil leaves (optional)
12 to 15 slices of pepperoni (optional)
Chile flakes (optional)

1. Preheat the pizza stone Put your pizza stone on a rack in the upper portion of your oven so the surface is about 8 inches below the broiler. Preheat the oven to 600°F (316°C) if you're lucky enough to have an oven that goes that high; otherwise, simply preheat to the highest possible setting. Once the oven is preheated, continue heating the pizza stone for another 30 minutes, for a total of about 45 minutes.

2. Set up your pizza assembly station Give yourself about 2 feet of width on the countertop. Generously flour the work surface. Position your peel next to the floured area and dust it with flour. Have the sauce, cheese, basil, and pepperoni prepared and at hand, with a ladle or large spoon in the sauce.

3. Shape the pizza Remove the dough ball from the refrigerator, put it on the floured work surface, and gently pat it down a bit to coat the bottom with flour. Turn it over and repeat on the other side. Leaving about 1 inch of the outer rim undeflated, punch down the middle, then flip the dough over and repeat.

Using both hands, grab the rim and lift so the dough hangs down vertically. Let gravity pull the rest of the dough down and stretch it. Run the rim between your hands, working all the way around the circumference of the dough several times.

CONTINUED>>

Next, make two fists and position them just inside the rim, with the dough still hanging vertically. Gently stretch and turn the dough repeatedly, still letting the bottom of the dough pull down, expanding the surface. Keep a close eye on the thickness of the dough. You want it thin, but you don't want it to tear or develop holes. If you end up with a small tear, don't panic—it's okay to patch it.

Spread the dough on the floured peel and run your hands around the perimeter to shape it into a round and work out the kinks.

4. Superheat the pizza stone About 30 minutes after the oven has reached its set temperature, switch to the broil setting for about 5 minutes to saturate the pizza stone with heat.

5. Top the pizza Spread the tomato sauce over the dough to within an inch of the edge, smoothing and spreading it with the back of the ladle. Sprinkle the cheeses evenly over the pie and distribute the basil leaves and pepperoni evenly over the top.

6. Bake Turn the oven setting back to bake. Gently slide the pizza onto the pizza stone.

Bake for 5 minutes, then switch to the broil setting and broil for 2 minutes, keeping a close eye on the pizza. Bake until the cheese is completely melted and bubbling, with a few small charred spots, and the crust is golden with spots of brown and a few small charred spots. Use tongs or a fork to slide the pizza from the pizza stone onto a large plate.

7. Slice and serve Transfer to a large wooden cutting board. Drizzle extra-virgin olive oil lightly over the top if you like. Slice and serve immediately, passing the chile flakes at the table.

SALAMI PIZZA

This is the cured meat lover's pizza, essentially a Margherita pizza with the addition of the salami of your choice. At Ken's Artisan Pizza, we have two of these pizzas on our menu: one with a spicy *soppressata* and another with *finocchiona*, made by Olympic Provisions, a local *salumeria* making admirable dry-cured sausages. In each case we peel the salami, then slice it into thin disks—about 1/16 inch thick for the *soppressata* and about 1/8 inch thick for the *finocchiona*. I love the way the meat crisps as it bakes on top of the pizza. The more salami you pile on the pizza, the thinner it should be sliced. My preference is to not overwhelm the other ingredients on the pizza with too much meat; rather, use it as an accent.

Salumi or *salami*? *Salumi* refers to the entire range of cured meat products, typically made from pork (but sometimes from beef), from ham and other salt-cured whole muscles of meat to sausages, including cooked meat emulsions in casings, like mortadella. *Salami* refers to a specific type of *salumi*: dry-cured sausage, usually made from pork, which may be either fresh or aged. Use whatever type of salami you prefer, from pepperoni (an American invention usually made with beef, or with beef and pork) to chorizo, *saucisson sec* to Genovese. When using any variety of salami, I like to cook it on the pizza. Sometimes I make a similar pizza topped with cured meat, such as prosciutto or *coppa*, in which case I like it sliced paper-thin and draped on the pizza immediately after it comes out of the oven.

MAKES ONE 12-INCH PIZZA

1 350-gram dough ball from any recipe in chapter 13

White flour for dusting

3 ounces Smooth Red Sauce (page 230)

4 ounces fresh whole-milk mozzarella cheese, cut into pieces ½ inch thick at most

12 to 18 slices of salami, depending on the size of the salami

4 to 6 whole basil leaves

Fine-flake sea salt, such as fiore di sale (optional)

Chile flakes (optional)

1. Preheat the pizza stone Put your pizza stone on a rack in the upper portion of your oven so the surface is about 8 inches below the broiler. Preheat the oven to 600°F (316°C) if you're lucky enough to have an oven that goes that high; otherwise, simply preheat to the highest possible setting. Once the oven is preheated, continue heating the pizza stone for another 30 minutes, for a total of about 45 minutes.

2. Set up your pizza assembly station Give yourself about 2 feet of width on the countertop. Generously flour the work surface. Position your peel next to the floured area and dust it with flour. Have the sauce, cut-up

CONTINUED>>

cheese, salami, and basil prepared and at hand, with a ladle or large spoon in the sauce.

3. Shape the pizza Remove the dough ball from the refrigerator, put it on the floured work surface, and gently pat it down a bit to coat the bottom with flour. Turn it over and repeat on the other side. Leaving about 1 inch of the outer rim undeflated, punch down the middle, then flip the dough over and repeat.

Using both hands, grab the rim and lift so the dough hangs down vertically. Let gravity pull the rest of the dough down and stretch it. Run the rim between your hands, working all the way around the circumference of the dough several times.

Next, make two fists and position them just inside the rim, with the dough still hanging vertically. Gently stretch and turn the dough repeatedly, still letting the bottom of the dough pull down, expanding the surface. Keep a close eye on the thickness of the dough. You want it thin, but you don't want it to tear or develop holes. If you end up with a small tear, don't panic—it's okay to patch it.

Spread the dough on the floured peel and run your hands around the perimeter to shape it into a round and work out the kinks.

4. Superheat the pizza stone About 30 minutes after the oven has reached its set temperature, switch to the broil setting for about 5 minutes to saturate the pizza stone with heat.

5. Top the pizza Spread the tomato sauce over the dough to within an inch of the edge, smoothing and spreading it with the back of the ladle. Distribute the mozzarella, salami, and basil leaves evenly around the pie.

6. Bake Turn the oven setting back to bake. Gently slide the pizza onto the pizza stone.

Bake for 5 minutes, then switch to the broil setting and broil for 2 minutes, keeping a close eye on the pizza. Bake until the cheese is completely melted, the salami is crisp around the edges, and the crust is golden with spots of brown and a few small charred spots. Use tongs or a fork to slide the pizza from the pizza stone onto a large plate.

7. Slice and serve Transfer to a large wooden cutting board. Slice and serve immediately, passing the salt and chile flakes at the table.

GOLDEN BEET AND DUCK BREAST "PROSCIUTTO" PIZZA

My friends at Chop, a Portland meat counter and charcuterie shop, cure Magret duck breast in the style of prosciutto hams. Feel free to substitute paper-thin slices of Prosciutto di Parma, Serrano ham, or good salt-cured Virginia or Tennessee country ham if duck breast "prosciutto" isn't available. This pizza blends the milky ooze of good mozzarella cheese with the sweetness of golden beets and the salty umami flavors of good cured meat and a little provolone cheese. Be generous with the black pepper and go easy on the chopped rosemary.

MAKES ONE 12-INCH PIZZA

1 350-gram dough ball from any recipe in chapter 13
White flour for dusting
One baseball-sized golden beet
3 to 4 ounces fresh whole-milk mozzarella cheese,
    cut into pieces ½ inch thick
1 ounce grated provolone cheese
1 teaspoon finely chopped fresh rosemary
Ground black pepper to taste
1 to 2 ounces very thinly sliced salt-cured duck
    breast or prosciutto-style ham

1. Preheat the pizza stone Put your pizza stone on a rack in the upper portion of your oven so the surface is about 8 inches below the broiler. Preheat the oven to 600°F (316°C) if you're lucky enough to have an oven that goes that high; otherwise, simply preheat to the highest possible setting. Once the oven is preheated, continue heating the pizza stone for about 30 minutes, for a total of about 45 minutes.

2. Prepare the beet In a medium saucepan, cover the beet with water by 1½ inches and bring to a boil over high heat. Cook for 30 minutes, or until the beet is just soft when tested with the tip of a knife (it should still have a little resistance to the knife).

Drain the beet and let rest for 5 to 10 minutes, until cool enough to handle. Slice off the stem and root, then with a lint-free kitchen towel, rub off the skin. Slice the beet into 3 disks of equal thickness, then quarter the disks to make 12 roughly equal pieces.

3. Set up your pizza assembly station Give yourself about 2 feet of width on the countertop. Generously flour the work surface. Position your peel next to the floured area and dust it with flour. Have the beet, cheeses, and rosemary prepared and at hand, along with the pepper mill.

CONTINUED>>

4. Shape the pizza Remove the dough ball from the refrigerator, put it on the floured work surface, and gently pat it down a bit to coat the bottom with flour. Turn it over and repeat on the other side. Leaving about 1 inch of the outer rim undeflated, punch down the middle, then flip the dough over and repeat.

Using both hands, grab the rim and lift so the dough hangs down vertically. Let gravity pull the rest of the dough down and stretch it. Run the rim between your hands, working all the way around the circumference of the dough several times.

Next, make two fists and position them just inside the rim, with the dough still hanging vertically. Gently stretch and turn the dough repeatedly, still letting the bottom of the dough pull down, expanding the surface. Keep a close eye on the thickness of the dough. You want it thin, but you don't want it to tear or develop holes. If you end up with a small tear, don't panic—it's okay to patch it.

Spread the dough on the floured peel and run your hands around the perimeter to shape it into a round and work out the kinks.

5. Superheat the pizza stone About 30 minutes after the oven has reached its set temperature, switch to the broil setting for about 5 minutes to saturate the pizza stone with heat.

6. Top the pizza Sprinkle the cheeses evenly over the pie, then distribute the beet pieces and rosemary evenly over the top. Grind black pepper to taste.

7. Bake Turn the oven setting back to bake. Gently slide the pizza onto the pizza stone.

Bake for 5 minutes, then switch to the broil setting and broil for 2 minutes, keeping a close eye on the pizza. Bake until the cheese is completely melted and the crust is golden with spots of brown and a few small spots of char. Use tongs or a fork to slide the pizza from the pizza stone onto a large plate.

8. Slice and serve Transfer to a large wooden cutting board and top with the prosciutto. Slice it. Eat it.

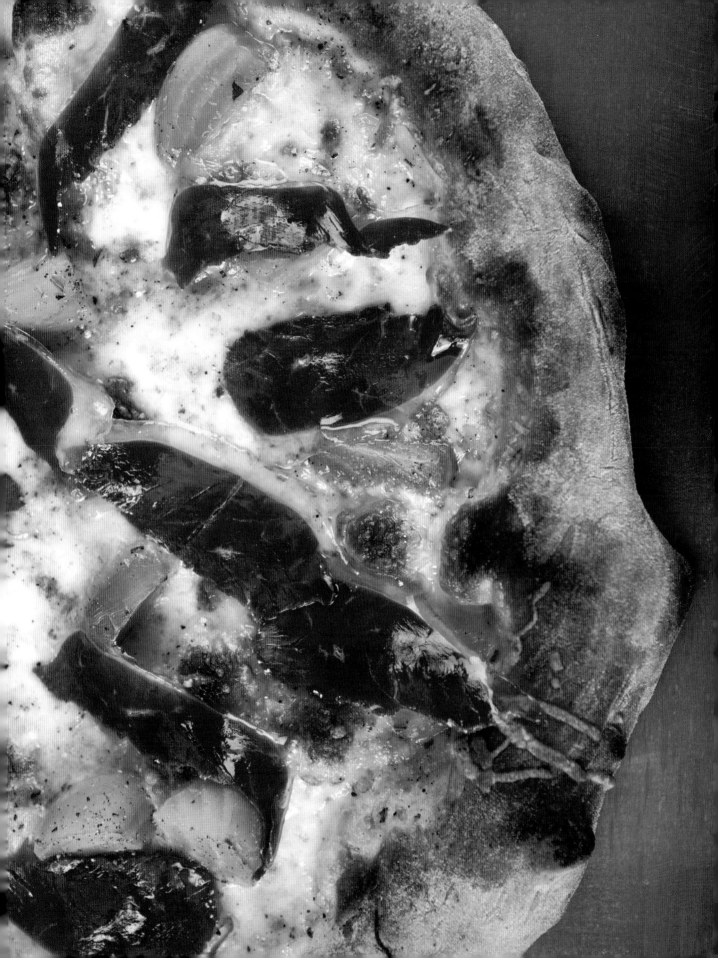

SWEET POTATO AND PEAR PIZZA

Despite the fruit, this is a savory pizza that would go great with a bottle of rosé or bubbles. It's also not bad as an afternoon snack, or for dinner with a roasted bird.

MAKES ONE 12-INCH PIZZA

1 350-gram dough ball from any recipe in chapter 13

White flour for dusting

1 medium sweet potato, cut into ⅙-inch slices

2 tablespoons extra-virgin olive oil

Fine-flake sea salt, such as fiore di sale

1 medium pear, such as Comice or Bosc, cored and cut into ¼-inch slices

1 ounce shaved Pecorino Romano cheese

2 tablespoons chopped cilantro

1 ounce grated fresh ginger

1 ounce oil-packed red chile peppers, chopped (optional)

Ground black pepper to taste

1. Preheat the pizza stone Put your pizza stone on a rack in the upper portion of your oven so the surface is about 8 inches below the broiler. Preheat the oven to 400°F (205°C).

2. Prepare the sweet potato In a medium bowl, toss the sweet potato with 1 tablespoon of olive oil and a pinch of sea salt. Place the sweet potato in an oven-proof skillet and roast for 12 to 15 minutes, or until all the pieces are cooked through but still firm.

3. Continue to preheat the pizza stone Preheat the oven to 600°F (316°C) if you're lucky enough to have an oven that goes that high; otherwise, simply preheat to the highest possible setting. Once the oven is preheated, continue heating the pizza stone for another 30 minutes, for a total of about 45 minutes.

4. Set up your pizza assembly station Give yourself about 2 feet of width on the countertop. Generously flour the work surface. Position your peel next to the floured area and dust it with flour. Have the sweet potato, pear, cheese, cilantro, ginger, and peppers prepared and at hand, along with the remaining tablespoon of olive oil and the pepper mill.

5. Shape the pizza Remove the dough ball from the refrigerator, put it on the floured work surface, and gently pat it down a bit to coat the bottom with flour. Turn it over and repeat on the other side. Leaving about 1 inch of the outer rim undeflated, punch down the middle, then flip the dough over and repeat.

Using both hands, grab the rim and lift so the dough hangs down vertically. Let gravity pull the rest of the dough down and stretch it. Run the rim between your hands, working all the way around the circumference of the dough several times.

CONTINUED>>

Next, make two fists and position them just inside the rim, with the dough still hanging vertically. Gently stretch and turn the dough repeatedly, still letting the bottom of the dough pull down, expanding the surface. Keep a close eye on the thickness of the dough. You want it thin, but you don't want it to tear or develop holes. If you end up with a small tear, don't panic—it's okay to patch it.

Spread the dough on the floured peel and run your hands around the perimeter to shape it into a round and work out the kinks.

6. Superheat the pizza stone About 30 minutes after the oven has reached its set temperature, switch to the broil setting for about 5 minutes to saturate the pizza stone with heat.

7. Top the pizza Drizzle the remaining 1 tablespoon of extra-virgin olive oil over the pie, then distribute the sweet potato and pear slices evenly over the top. Sprinkle the cheese, cilantro, and ginger over the pie, then grind black pepper to taste.

8. Bake Turn the oven setting back to bake. Gently slide the pizza onto the pizza stone.

Bake for 5 minutes, then switch to the broil setting and broil for 2 minutes, keeping a close eye on the pizza. Bake until the cheese is completely melted and the crust is golden with spots of brown and a few small spots of char. Use tongs or a fork to slide the pizza from the pizza stone onto a large plate.

9. Slice and serve Transfer to a large wooden cutting board and slice. Serve immediately.

IRON-SKILLET MEAT PIE

Here's a great way to make pizza in your home oven in a cast-iron skillet, without a pizza stone, and without the fuss that goes with tossing the dough, setting it up on a peel, and successfully transferring it to the preheated pizza stone. As far as the meat is concerned, I'm a traditionalist and very happy with a good salami or sausage that can stand up to the fifteen to twenty minutes of baking time this pizza requires.

You have more flexibility with the skillet pizza to top as heavily as you want. If you'd like to load up Chicago-style with sauce, cheese and toppings, just keep in mind that the more toppings, the longer the bake time.

MAKES ONE 9-INCH IRON-SKILLET PIZZA

1 dough ball from any recipe in chapter 13, 350 grams for a thick crust or 200 grams for a thin crust

3 to 4 ounces of Smooth Red Sauce (page 230) or Chunky Red Sauce (page 230)

3 to 4 ounces fresh whole-milk mozzarella cheese, sliced thin, or a blend of mozzarella and provolone

8 to 10 slices pepperoni or other salami or fresh sausage

1. Preheat the oven Preheat the oven to 525°F (274°C), or as high as it will go if it doesn't reach 525°F (274°C).

2. Shape the pizza Give yourself around 18 to 24 inches of width on the countertop. Generously flour the work surface.

Remove the dough ball from the refrigerator, put it on the floured work surface, and gently pat it down a bit to coat the bottom with flour. Turn it over and repeat on the other side. You can compress the perimeter of this dough. Holding the rim, stretch the dough to the width of your skillet, then put it in a dry 9-inch cast-iron skillet.

3. Top the pizza Spread the tomato sauce over the dough, using more or less sauce depending on your preference. Scatter the cheese evenly over the sauce, then distribute the pepperoni evenly over the cheese.

4. Bake Bake for 15 to 20 minutes, until the dough is baked all the way through, checking the pizza after 10 minutes and keeping a close eye on it during the last few minutes of baking. If you want to slightly char on the crust and brown the toppings, switch the oven to the broil setting for the last few minutes, keeping an especially close eye on it.

5. Slice and serve Remove the skillet from the oven and place it on a heatproof surface. Carefully use tongs or a fork to transfer the pizza to a cutting board. Slice and serve immediately.

SKILLET PIZZA WITH TOMATO FILLETS, GARLIC, AND CHILE

This pizza is one of my favorites for serving as a predinner snack, alongside a salad course, or to accompany a meal. If you want to jazz it up, you could bake it with black olives and add a few strips of anchovy fillet over the pizza after it comes out of the oven. Then you could call it The Sicilian. Since this skillet pizza has no cheese and you don't want to burn the garlic, the baking time is shorter than that of the Iron-Skillet Meat Pie (page 247)—just 12 to 15 minutes. In contrast to my usual preferences, I like this pie baked just until golden brown.

MAKES ONE 9-INCH IRON-SKILLET PIZZA

1 dough ball from any recipe in chapter 13, 350 grams for a thick crust, or 200 grams for a thin crust
8 to 10 Tomato Fillets (page 231)
1 clove garlic, chopped
½ teaspoon dried oregano
¼ teaspoon chile flakes
1 tablespoon extra-virgin olive oil
Fine-flake sea salt, such as fiore di sale (optional)

1. Preheat the oven Preheat the oven to 525°F (274°C), or as high as it will go if it doesn't reach 525°F (274°C).

2. Shape the pizza Give yourself around 18 to 24 inches of width on the countertop. Generously flour the work surface.

Remove the dough ball from the refrigerator, put it on the floured work surface, and gently pat it down a bit to coat the bottom with flour. Turn it over and repeat on the other side. You can compress the perimeter of this dough. Holding the rim, stretch the dough to the width of your skillet, then put it in a dry 9-inch cast-iron skillet.

3. Top the pizza Arrange the tomato fillets evenly over the dough. Sprinkle the garlic, oregano, and chile flakes evenly over the top. Drizzle the olive oil over the top and lightly sprinkle salt over everything, including the rim.

4. Bake Bake for 12 to 15 minutes, until the crust is golden brown and the dough is baked all the way through, checking the pizza after 10 minutes and keeping a close eye on it during the last 5 minutes of baking.

5. Slice and serve Remove the skillet from the oven and place it on a heatproof surface. Carefully use tongs or a fork to transfer the pizza to a cutting board. Slice and serve immediately.

MORE IRON-SKILLET PIZZA IDEAS

Because iron-skillet pizzas get good support from the pan, you can be more liberal with toppings. I've provided a few ideas below, but the possibilities are limited only by your imagination. You want Hawaiian? It's okay by me. Bake these in a 525°F (274°F) oven, or as hot as your oven gets if less than 525°F (274°F).

Iron-Skillet Pizza with Red Grapes, Mozzarella, and Salami

This combination grew out of a suggestion from Chris Cullina of Argyle Winery, to top focaccia with split red grapes and pine nuts. The grapes bake beautifully, their sweetness offset by the cheese and salami that crisps while it bakes. Top the dough with the cheese, salami, oregano, pepper, and grapes, and bake for 15 to 20 minutes.

3 ounces fresh mozzarella cheese, cut into ¼-inch-thick pieces
10 to 12 slices salami
½ teaspoon dried oregano
Cracked black pepper
20 to 24 seedless red grapes, halved

Iron-Skillet Pizza with Cherry Tomatoes and Bacon

For this pizza, the trick is to lightly cook the bacon, rendering some of its fat while leaving it uncooked enough that it will crisp but not burn in the oven while the pizza is baking. Cook the bacon until about halfway to crisp, then let it drain on paper towels before putting it on the pizza. Scatter all of the toppings evenly over the dough and bake for 15 to 20 minutes, until the bacon cooks to a crisp on the pizza and the tomatoes crack and burst under the high heat, oozing their juices into the dough.

12 to 15 whole cherry tomatoes
4 to 6 basil leaves
4 strips of bacon, cut into halves or thirds and lightly cooked
Cracked black pepper

Iron-Skillet Pizza with Cherry Tomatoes, Garlic, and Summer Squash

I like this pan pizza topped with freshly grated Parmigiano-Reggiano cheese right after it comes out of the oven. It tastes like summer. Toss the squash with the olive oil and a bit of salt in a bowl, then scatter the squash, tomatoes, basil, and garlic evenly over the dough. Season with black pepper and additional salt, along with some chile flakes. Bake for 15 to 20 minutes, until the dough is cooked through.

1 small yellow crookneck squash or zucchini, cut into ½-inch cubes

1 tablespoon extra-virgin olive oil

Sea salt

12 to 15 whole cherry tomatoes

4 to 6 basil leaves

1 clove garlic, chopped

Cracked black pepper

Chile flakes (optional)

1 ounce Parmigiano-Reggiano cheese, grated

Deep-Dish Quattro Formaggi Pizza

Marco Frattaroli, chef/owner at Portland's Bastas Trattoria, suggested this combination of cheeses for a classic four-cheese pie. Layer each of the cheeses on the dough in the order listed, then bake for 15 to 20 minutes, until the cheese is bubbly and the crust is golden brown.

2 ounces mozzarella cheese, grated

1 ounce provolone cheese, grated

1 ounce Gruyère cheese, grated

¾ ounce Parmigiano-Reggiano cheese, grated

FOCACCIA GENOVESE

The soulful home of focaccia is along the Ligurian coast of Italy. Genoa is the capital of Liguria, and focaccia Genovese is a staple of the local cuisine. Traditionally, it's made from a very soft dough, spread out in rectangular or round pans and dimpled by the baker's fingers in the process of working olive oil into the dough. After being baked to a golden hue, it's sometimes topped with more olive oil and a sprinkling of salt.

For the basic Focaccia Genovese, use this book's Overnight Pizza Dough with Poolish (page 225), made with either 00 flour or all-purpose white flour. This soft dough can easily be worked to conform to the shape of the baking pan, then you work in the olive oil with your hands, sprinkle on some sea salt, and bake it to a golden color. In this recipe I call for using 800 grams of dough, baked on a 12 by 17-inch baking sheet. However, you could also use two pieces of dough, each between 250 and 350 grams, and bake them in 9-inch cast-iron skillets.

MAKES ONE ROUGHLY 12 BY 5-INCH FOCACCIA

800 grams of dough from any recipe in chapter 13, but preferably Overnight Pizza Dough with Poolish (page 225)
White flour for dusting
½ cup extra-virgin olive oil
Sea salt to taste, fine or small-flake like fiore di sale

1. Bring the dough to room temperature About 2 hours before you plan to bake, remove the dough from the refrigerator and let it warm to room temperature. This step is optional but recommended, as it will make the dough easier to stretch and help it hold the finger dents. In essence, you're slightly overproofing the dough. It will get gassy before you flatten it out, and that's fine.

2. Preheat Preheat the oven to 500°F (260°C). Very lightly coat a 12 by 17-inch rimmed baking sheet with a thin film of oil where your dough will rest while baking.

3. Shape and dimple the dough Put the dough on your floured surface, and turn it over to flour each side. Use your hands to flatten the dough and stretch it to about half the size of the baking sheet.

Using both hands, grab the rim and lift, letting gravity pull the rest of the dough down. Run the rim between your hands, working all around the circumference of the dough for one or two turns. Transfer the dough to the baking sheet. Pour the olive oil over the dough and spread it evenly over the dough with both hands, simultaneously spreading the dough out evenly in the shape of the pan. Enjoy working the oil into the dough with your fingers, pressing down to make dimples, and using the viscosity of the oil to spread the dough out in the pan. If the dough resists, let it rest for 10 minutes, then return to it. You want the dough flattened and dimpled evenly all around. It feels great.

4. Bake Bake for 12 to 15 minutes, until the top is golden brown, the bottom is firm, and the dough is completely baked through. (With experience you can judge the doneness with a quick look, but if you aren't sure, pull it out of the oven and snip through the rim with kitchen scissors to see if there's any raw dough inside.)

5. Slice and serve Sprinkle salt over the top. Cut the focaccia into strips (it's fine to do this while it's still hot), and serve.

FOCACCIA TOPPING IDEAS

As I've mentioned a few times, I think the sky's the limit when it comes to focaccia. Any type of bread dough can be used, and you can really let your imagination run wild with toppings. Here are a few suggestions to get you started. Then enjoy crafting your own, season by season.

- Fresh tomatoes, olives, and rosemary
- Pizza sauce and chopped garlic
- Cheese or a combination of cheeses
- Sliced stone fruit, butter, and sugar
- Chopped herbs

FOCACCIA "PISSALIDIERE"

Pissalidière is a savory pastry from Southern France, usually made with caramelized onions, black olives, and anchovies on puff pastry dough. I like to top focaccia the same way, and add red chiles for both color and kick. We use oil-packed Calabrian chiles for our Arrabiata Pizza at Ken's Artisan Pizza, and I copped some of those for this recipe. The heat naturally compliments the olives and anchovies, and this focaccia tastes to me like summer vacation on the Mediterranean coast. Serve it with chilled rosé and a simple green salad. You can caramelize the onions a day or two in advance.

MAKES ONE ROUGHLY 12 BY 5-INCH FOCACCIA

800 grams of dough from any recipe in chapter 13
White flour for dusting
1 medium yellow onion, sliced thin
½ tablespoon butter
12 to 14 salt-cured black olives
6 anchovy fillets, dredged in their packing oil
1 ounce oil-packed red chile peppers, drained
    and chopped
2 teaspoons olive oil
Sea salt to taste, fine or small-flake like fiore di sale

1. Bring the dough to room temperature About 2 hours before you plan to bake, remove the dough from the refrigerator and let it warm to room temperature. This step is optional but recommended, as it will make the dough easier to stretch and help it hold the finger dents. In essence, you're slightly overproofing the dough. It will get gassy before you flatten it out, and that's fine.

2. Caramelize the onions Place the onions, salt, and butter in a skillet and cook over medium-high heat, stirring often to prevent sticking. After five minutes, reduce the heat to low. Cook for another 20 minutes, stirring occasionally, and make sure to scrape up any dark bits that stick to your pan. Once the onions are soft and completely brown, turn off the heat and set aside.

3. Preheat Preheat the oven to 500°F (260°C). Very lightly coat a 12 by 17-inch rimmed baking sheet with a thin film of oil where your dough will rest while baking.

4. Shape and dimple the dough. Put the dough on your floured surface, and turn it over to flour each side. Use a fist and then your fingers to flatten out the dough and stretch it out gently until it is at the desired thickness (I prefer medium-thin for this).

When the dough is stretched out and before placing it on your baking sheet, spread a very light film of olive oil over one side of the dough, then place the dough oiled-side down on the baking seet. Dimple the dough with your fingers.

5. Top the focaccia Arrange the onions evenly over the top, being careful not to overload the focaccia, then spread the olives and anchovy fillets on top.

6. Bake Bake for 12 to 15 minutes, until the top is golden brown, the bottom is firm, and the dough is completely baked through. (With experience you can judge the doneness with a quick look, but if you aren't sure, pull it out of the oven and snip through the rim with kitchen scissors to see if there's any raw dough inside.)

7. Slice and serve Cut the focaccia into strips (it's fine to do this while it's still hot), and serve.

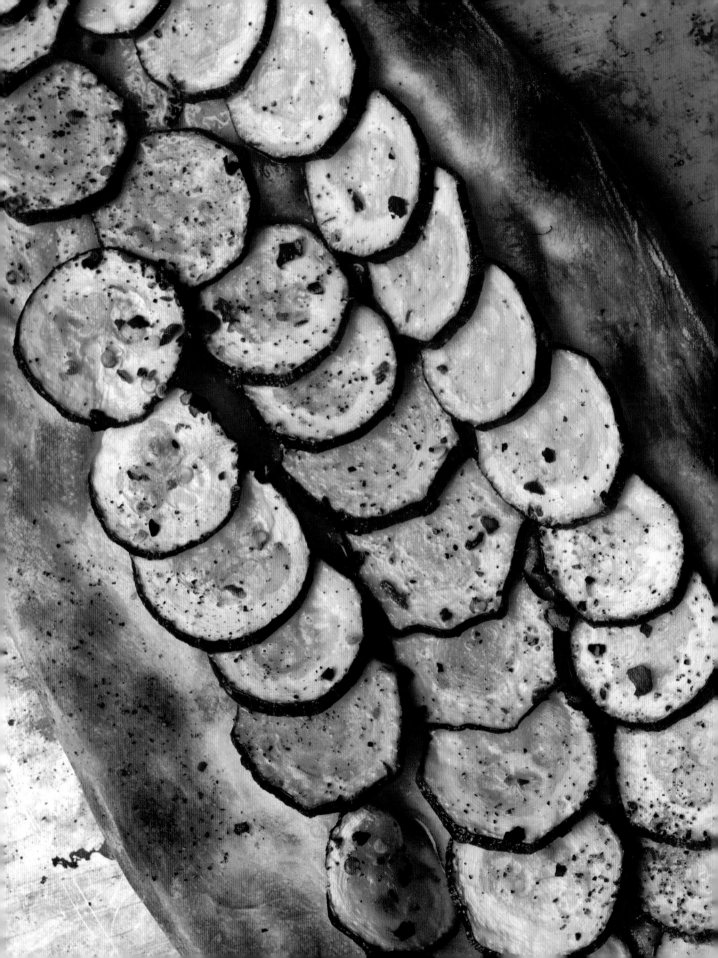

ZUCCHINI FOCACCIA

This recipe is one of my favorites in the summertime and early autumn, when garden-fresh zucchini is abundant. Thinly sliced disks of zucchini are spread out across the dough and resemble fish scales if you stand back and squint. Don't use the softball bat–sized zucchinis from your Aunt Zelda's garden for this; use zucchini that's just a couple of inches in diameter. This focaccia looks cool if the dough is shaped into a freeform oblong on a sheet pan.

MAKES ONE ROUGHLY 12 BY 5-INCH FOCACCIA

800 grams of dough from any recipe in chapter 13
2 zucchini, about 2 inches in diameter, thinly sliced
2 tablespoons extra-virgin olive oil
Sea salt to taste, fine or small-flake like fiore di sale
Ground black pepper
Chile flakes (optional)

1. Bring the dough to room temperature About 2 hours before you plan to bake, remove the dough from the refrigerator and let it warm to room temperature. This step is optional but recommended, as it will make the dough easier to stretch and help it hold the finger dents. In essence, you're slightly overproofing the dough. It will get gassy before you flatten it out, and that's fine.

2. Preheat the oven and prepare the zucchini Preheat the oven to 500°F (260°C). I don't recommend oiling the baking pan, but if you choose to, only oil the part of the pan that will have dough on top of it, otherwise the oil will smoke. Toss the zucchini with 1 tablespoon of olive oil and a sprinkling of salt until evenly coated.

3. Shape the dough Moderately flour the work surface. Put the dough on the flour and turn it over to coat each side with flour. Use your

hands to flatten the dough and stretch it to a size and shape you like. Transfer to a rectangular baking pan and, using floured hands, stretch it out further if necessary and fine-tune the shape. (Alternatively, you can put the dough in a rimmed baking sheet, lightly coat the dough with oil, and stretch it out to fill the pan, pushing it to the sides of the pan in each direction.)

4. Top the focaccia Spread the remaining 1 tablespoon of olive oil over the top and use your hand to evenly distribute it over the surface. Arrange the zucchini over the top, overlapping the slices. Season with freshly ground black pepper.

5. Bake Bake for 12 to 15 minutes, until the crust is golden brown, the bottom is firm, and the dough is completely baked through. (With experience you can judge the doneness with a quick look, but if you aren't sure, pull it out of the oven and snip through the rim with kitchen scissors to see if there's any raw dough inside.)

6. Slice and serve Cut the focaccia into strips (it's fine to do this while it's still hot), and serve, passing the chile flakes at the table.

LAGNIAPPE: OREGON HAZELNUT BUTTER COOKIES

I was once testing a tart dough made with nut meal and was happy to discover that the dough also made excellent cookies, and this apparently remained bookmarked somewhere in my memory. Years later, when we were starting the Monday Night Pizza venture at my bakery, I wanted to offer complimentary fresh-baked cookies to go out to each table with the check as a lagniappe—a little something extra. This is the recipe we used. The lagniappe is something of a baker's tradition (think "baker's dozen"), so this recipe seems a fitting way to end the book.

We still make these cookies, continuing to use hazelnut meal delivered to the bakery directly from Freddy Guys hazelnut orchard in Oregon's Willamette Valley. Hazelnut meal is readily available in markets and online. Alternatively, you could use almond meal, and in either case, you can grind your own from whole, shelled nuts.

MAKES ABOUT 75 COOKIES

500 grams bread flour
250 grams hazelnut meal
125 grams granulated sugar
300 grams cold butter, cut into ½-inch cubes
2 eggs
20 grams cold water
½ cup heavy cream
Granulated white or turbinado sugar, for sprinkling

Using a handheld mixer or a stand mixer fitted with the paddle attachment, mix the flour, hazelnut meal, sugar, and butter until sandy. Add the eggs and water and mix until the mixture comes together around the beaters or the paddle.

Transfer the dough to a lightly floured work surface. Divide it into 4 equal portions and shape each into a firm roll about 2 inches in diameter. Wrap each log in parchment paper or plastic wrap and refrigerate for at least 3 hours, until firm. (For any logs you won't bake within a couple of days, store them in a ziplock bag in the freezer for up to 3 months. Thaw them in the refrigerator overnight before slicing and baking.)

To bake the cookies, preheat the oven to 375°F (190°C). Line a baking sheet with parchment paper.

Cut the chilled dough into ¼-inch-thick slices and place them on the lined pan, leaving about ½ inch of space between them. Brush the cream over the tops of the cookies, then sprinkle each with a bit of sugar.

Bake for 10 to 15 minutes, until golden brown.

METRIC CONVERSION CHARTS

VOLUME

Formulas

1 teaspoon = 4.9 milliliters
1 tablespoon = 3 teaspoons = 14.8 milliliters = 3 teaspoons
1 cup = 16 tablespoons = 237 milliliters = 16 tablespoons
1 liter = 4.25 cups

U.S.	METRIC	IMPERIAL
1 tablespoon	15 ml	½ fl oz
2 tablespoons	30 ml	1 fl oz
¼ cup	60 ml	2 fl oz
⅓ cup	90 ml	2.7 fl oz
½ cup	120 ml	4 fl oz
⅔ cup	150 ml	5.3 fl oz
¾ cup	180 ml	6 fl oz
1 cup	240 ml	8 fl oz
1¼ cups	300 ml	10 fl oz
2 cups (1 pint)	480 ml	16 fl oz
2½ cups	600 ml	20 fl oz
4 cups (1 quart)	950 ml	32 fl oz

WEIGHT

Formulas

1 ounce = 28.3 grams
1 pound = 16 ounces = 453.6 grams
1 kilogram = 2.2 pounds

U.S./IMPERIAL	METRIC
½ oz	15 g
1 oz	30 g
2 oz	60 g
¼ lb	115 g
⅓ lb	150 g
½ lb	225 g
¾ lb	350 g
1 lb	450 g

TEMPERATURE

Formulas

⁹⁄₅ C + 32 = F
(F − 32) x ⁵⁄₉ = C

FAHRENHEIT	CELSIUS	GAS MARK
250°F	120°C	½
275°F	135°C	1
300°F	150°C	2
325°F	165°C	3
350°F	175°C	4
375°F	190°C	5
400°F	200°C	6
425°F	220°C	7
450°F	230°C	8
475°F	245°C	9
500°F	260°C	

LENGTH

Formulas

1 inch = 2.5 cm
1 foot = 12 inches = 30 cm
1 cm = 0.4 inch

ACKNOWLEDGEMENTS

Particular thanks to friends who tested this book's recipes—the original, cumbersome versions and the final, hopefully-not-too-information-packed recipes you see in this book: Molly Wizenberg, Jenna Murray, John McCreary, Suzy Narducci, and Greg Higgins. Additional thanks to special friends who were there for guidance, editorial support, and technical Q & A: Shawna McKeown, Kat Merck, Eve Connell, Teri Wadsworth, and John Paul.

To Alan Weiner, a supremely gifted photojournalist who could make a loaf of bread look like a work of sculpture, and a field of wheat at sunset look like a slice of heaven.

Particular thanks to the editorial and creative staff at Ten Speed Press. My editor, Emily Timberlake, helped turn my web of scattershot ideas into an organized structure and guided me in ways that always had a sense of rightness to them. Designer Katy Brown turned the words and photos into a book with such a clean and beautiful aesthetic that I continue to be dazzled each time I gaze at it. I will be forever appreciative of their outstanding work.

To the gifted bakers and teachers who helped me learn my craft: Jean-Marc Berthomier, Didier Rosada, Philippe Le Corre, and Ian Duffy.

Most importantly, to the mentors who helped open my mind to baking at the highest level: Michel Suas of the San Francisco Baking Institute and TMB Baking, and Chad Robertson and Elisabeth Prueitt of San Francisco's Tartine Bakery. Michel is someone I will always look up to, and he helps in so many ways, always with good humor and good advice, it's impossible to list them all. If we are lucky in life we find the right teacher at the right moment. For me that happened when I met Chad and Liz in 1999. They readily shared with me their approach to baking, and I will always be thankful for their generosity. I learned much about levain and French country–style bread baking from Chad, as well as a way of thinking about food that agreed with me. His sharing of lessons learned unlocked many doors for me. A thousand thank-yous.

Jack London wrote, "I would rather be ashes than dust! I would rather that my spark should burn out in a brilliant blaze than it should be stifled by dry rot. . . . The proper function of man is to live, not to exist. I shall not waste my days in trying to prolong them. I shall use my time."

I had recently become friends with Jimi Brooks, a Willamette Valley winemaker, when he died suddenly in October 2004. Jimi lived large and fully. He wouldn't take his days for granted or let his friends talk pipe dreams without prodding them to act on those dreams. Jimi's memorial service brought friends and family together to appreciate his life and share his loss. Several people spoke, telling mostly funny stories that still made us want to cry. Somebody finished by reading this Jack London quote. It characterized the fire that burned inside Jimi's frame, and these words rung around and around in my head: *I shall use my time.*

INDEX

A

Advanced levain doughs
  Double-Fed Sweet Levain
    Bread, 182–84
  White Flour Warm-Spot
    Levain, 185–88
Amylase, 51
Anchovies
  Focaccia "Pissalidière,"
    254–55
Ascorbic acid, 34
Autolyse step
  benefits of, 33–34
  history of, 33
  incorporating flour and
    water, 65
  instant dried yeast and, 34
  measuring and, 64–65
  skipping, 65
  time for, 64, 66
  water temperature and, 65–66

B

Bacon
  Iron-Skillet Pizza with Cherry
    Tomatoes and Bacon, 250
  Pain au Bacon, 177–79
Baker's percentages, 41–42, 63
Baking
  in Dutch ovens, 4, 38, 40, 47,
    75–77
  oven temperature and, 38,
    40, 75
  pizzas, 208–13
  time for, 75
Bay Village Bakery, 13, 14, 15
Beet, Golden, and Duck Breast
  "Prosciutto" Pizza, 241–42
Berthomier, Jean-Marc, 41–42
Biga
  definition of, 31

50% Whole Wheat Bread with
  Biga, 109–11
poolish vs., 32
taste and, 30
texture of, 32
using, 30–33
White Bread with 80% Biga,
  106–8
Bocuse, Paul, 17
Bouchon Bakery, 13
Boules, 162–64
Bran-Encrusted Levain Bread,
  147–50
Bread (general)
  basic method for, 64–77
  flavor complexity scale for,
    61, 62
  guiding principles for, 41
  large loaves of, 162–64
  shaping loaves, 71–72
  storing baked, 77
  troubleshooting, 40–41
Bread (recipes)
  Bran-Encrusted Levain Bread,
    147–50
  Double-Fed Sweet Levain
    Bread, 182–84
  Field Blend #1, 155–57
  Field Blend #2, 158–61
  50% Whole Wheat Bread with
    Biga, 109–11
  Harvest Bread with Poolish,
    103–5
  Overnight Country Blonde,
    168–72
  Overnight Country Brown,
    173–75
  Overnight 40% Whole Wheat
    Bread, 93–95
  Overnight White Bread, 89–91
  Pain au Bacon, 177–79

Pain de Campagne, 140–43
The Saturday 75% Whole
  Wheat Bread, 85–88
The Saturday White Bread,
  81–84
75% Whole Wheat Levain
  Bread, 144–46
Walnut Levain Bread, 151–54
Weeknight White Bread, 91
White Bread with 80% Biga,
  106–8
White Bread with Poolish,
  98–101
White Flour Warm-Spot
  Levain, 185–88
Bread Bakers Guild of America,
  12, 14
Bulk fermentation
  allowing for complete, 36
  extending time for, 26, 29–30
  in the refrigerator, 37
  testing limits of, 38

C

Calvel, Raymond, 2, 33, 34, 124
Cheese
  Deep-Dish Quattro Formaggi
    Pizza, 251
  as focaccia topping, 253
  Golden Beet and Duck Breast
    "Prosciutto" Pizza, 241–42
  Iron-Skillet Meat Pie, 247
  Iron-Skillet Pizza with Red
    Grapes, Mozzarella, and
    Salami, 250
  The New Yorker, 235–36
  Pizza Margherita, 233–34
  Salami Pizza, 239–40
  Sweet Potato and Pear Pizza,
    245–46
Chef, definition of, 121
Chunky Red Sauce, 230

Cookies, Oregon Hazelnut
  Butter, 258
Country Blonde
  history of, 163–64
  1.8-kilo *boule* variation, 172
  Overnight Country Blonde,
    168–72
Country Brown
  history of, 163
  Overnight Country Brown,
    173–75
Crust
  character of, 38
  color of, 40
  oven temperature and, 38
Cullina, Chris, 250

D

Decollogne-Lecocq mill, 51
Deep-Dish Quattro Formaggi
  Pizza, 251
Della Fattoria, 13, 14–15
Dividing step
  for bread dough, 71
  for pizza dough, 205
Dixon, Jim, 22
Double-Fed Sweet Levain Bread,
  182–84
Dough
  autolyse process and, 33–34,
    64–66
  bulk fermentation for, 26,
    29–30, 36, 38
  dividing, 71
  extensibility of, 33–34
  folding, 35, 69
  gluten network in, 35
  handling gently, 37
  kneading, 37
  mixing, 67–69
  proofing, 37–38
  shaping, 71–72
  strength of, 34
  transferring, from proofing
    basket to Dutch oven, 75–76
  wet vs. stiff, 34, 36

See also Advanced levain
  doughs; Doughs made
  with pre-ferments; Hybrid
  leavening doughs; Pizza
  doughs; Pure levain doughs;
  Straight doughs
Doughs made with pre-ferments
  50% Whole Wheat Bread with
    Biga, 109–11
  Harvest Bread with Poolish,
    103–5
  Overnight Pizza Dough with
    Poolish, 225–27
  White Bread with 80% Biga,
    106–8
  White Bread with Poolish,
    98–101
Dough tubs, 46–47
Duck Breast "Prosciutto" and
  Golden Beet Pizza, 241–42
Duffy, Ian, 14
Dutch ovens
  baking in, 4, 38, 40, 47, 75–77
  brands of, 47
  preheating, 74
  sizes of, 47

E

Enzymes, role of, 51
Equipment, 45–49
Extensibility, definition of, 33–34

F

Farming, 54–55, 57
Field Blend #1, 155–57
Field Blend #2, 158–61
50% Whole Wheat Bread with
  Biga, 109–11
Finger-dent test, 38, 74
Flavor complexity scale, 61, 62
Flour
  absorbency of, 193
  changing blend of, 191–92,
    193, 194
  incorporating water and, 65
  protein content of, 49, 57
  quality of, 49

at room temperature, 49
  traditional production of,
    50–51
  types of, 49–50
  variability of, 41
Focaccias
  Focaccia Genovese, 252–53
  Focaccia "Pissalidière,"
    254–55
  hydration and, 203
  making, with bread dough,
    77, 215
  pizzas vs., 214
  thickness of, 214
  toppings for, 253
  Zucchini Focaccia, 257
Folding, 35, 69
Frattaroli, Marco, 251
Fruit
  as focaccia topping, 253
  in levain cultures, 124–25
  See also individual fruits

G

Gluten
  definition of, 51
  network, 35
  role of, 51
Golden Beet and Duck Breast
  "Prosciutto" Pizza, 241–42
Grapes, Red, Iron-Skillet Pizza
  with Mozzarella, Salami,
  and, 250
Guiding principles, 41

H

Harvest Bread with Poolish,
  103–5
Hazelnut Butter Cookies,
  Oregon, 258
Higgins, Greg, 19, 214
Holt, Tim, 11
Hybrid leavening doughs
  Bran-Encrusted Levain Bread,
    147–50
  Field Blend #1, 155–57
  Field Blend #2, 158–61

Pain de Campagne, 140–43
75% Whole Wheat Levain
    Bread, 144–46
Walnut Levain Bread, 151–54
Hydration, changing, 191

Ingredients, 49–53
Institut Paul Bocuse, 17, 41
Iron-skillet pizzas. *See* Pizzas

Jones, Steve, 151
Jorin, Robert, 15

Kaplan, Steven, 51
Keller, Thomas, 13
Ken's Artisan Bakery
    bread baker's shift at, 112–17
    history of, 1, 16–23
    idea for, 11–12
    location of, 17, 18
    Monday Pizza Night at, 201–2
    opening day of, 18
    physical layout of, 117
Ken's Artisan Pizza, 202,
    239, 254
Kneading, 37
Kunz, Mike, 55

Lactic acid bacteria, 123
Lagniappe (Oregon Hazelnut
    Butter Cookies), 258
Lahey, Jim, 4, 43
Le Corre, Philippe, 15
Levain
    balance and, 125
    container for, 130, 132
    culture growth for, 123–24
    definition of, 31, 121–22
    etymology of, 121
    experimenting with, 194–96
    feeding, 126, 135–36, 137
    flavor and, 122–23
    flour and, 125, 127, 130
    fruit and, 124–25
    hydration of, 125, 127

ingredients for, 127
liquid, 195–96
salt and, 125, 127
schedule for, 126, 137
seasonal variations for, 134
starting, 129–33
storing and restoring, 136–37
temperature and, 127
using, 134–35
yeast and, 53, 122, 124,
    126, 127
See also Advanced levain
    doughs; Hybrid leavening
    doughs; Pure levain doughs
Limits, testing, 38
Liquid levain, 195–96

Maillard reaction, 40
Maniscalco, Alan, 202
McCarthy, Steve, 124
McMahon, Tom, 12–13
Measurements
    baker's percentages, 41–42, 63
    of flour and water, 64–65
    metric, 42, 259
    volume, 27, 42, 63, 259
    weight, 27, 41–42, 63, 259
Miches, 12, 163
Mixing step, 67–69
Mother, definition of, 121

National Baking Center, 14, 15
The New Yorker, 235–36

Olives
    Focaccia "Pissalidière," 254–55
    as focaccia topping, 253
Oregano, 208
Oregon Hazelnut Butter Cookies
    (Lagniappe), 258
Oven
    preheating, 74–75, 208–10
    temperature of, 38, 40, 48,
        75, 83
Oven mitts, 48, 75

Oven thermometers, 48, 75
Overnight Country Blonde,
    168–72
Overnight Country Brown,
    173–75
Overnight 40% Whole Wheat
    Bread, 93–95
Overnight Pizza Dough with
    Levain, 222–24
Overnight Pizza Dough with
    Poolish, 225–27
Overnight Straight Pizza Dough,
    220–21
Overnight White Bread, 89–91

Pain au Bacon, 177–79
Pain de Campagne, 140–43
Paley, Vitaly, 19, 177
Pâte fermentée, 31
Paul, John, 123
Pear and Sweet Potato Pizza,
    245–46
Pépin, Claudine, 22, 23
Pépin, Jacques, 22, 23
Pepperoni. *See* Salami
Perry, Sara, 19
Pincer method, 68–69
Pistolet shape, 98
Pizza doughs
    dividing, 205
    hydration of, 203
    method for, 204–7
    Overnight Pizza Dough with
        Levain, 222–24
    Overnight Pizza Dough with
        Poolish, 225–27
    Overnight Straight Pizza
        Dough, 220–21
    overview of, 204
    proofing, 206–7
    Same-Day Straight Pizza
        Dough, 218–19
    shaping, 205
    tossing, 209
    yields of, 207

Pizzas
  assembly station for, 210–11
  baking, in cast-iron
    skillets, 213
  baking, on pizza stones, 208–12
  Deep-Dish Quattro Formaggi
    Pizza, 251
  equipment for, 48–49
  focaccias vs., 214
  Golden Beet and Duck Breast
    "Prosciutto" Pizza, 241–42
  Iron-Skillet Meat Pie, 247
  Iron-Skillet Pizza with Cherry
    Tomatoes and Bacon, 250
  Iron-Skillet Pizza with Cherry
    Tomatoes, Garlic, and
    Summer Squash, 251
  Iron-Skillet Pizza with Red
    Grapes, Mozzarella, and
    Salami, 250
  making, with bread dough, 77
  The New Yorker, 235–36
  Pizza Margherita, 233–34
  Salami Pizza, 239–40
  Skillet Pizza with Tomato
    Fillets, Garlic, and Chile, 249
  Sweet Potato and Pear Pizza,
    245–46
  See also Pizza doughs; Pizza
    sauces and toppings
Pizza sauces and toppings
  Chunky Red Sauce, 230
  oregano for, 208
  Smooth Red Sauce, 230
  tomatoes for, 207–8
  Tomato Fillets, 231
Poilâne, Lionel, 1, 11–12, 22, 51
Poilâne, Max, 12
Poolish
  biga vs., 32
  definition of, 31
  Harvest Bread with Poolish,
    103–5
  Overnight Pizza Dough with
    Poolish, 225–27
  taste and, 30

  texture of, 32
  using, 30–33
  White Bread with Poolish,
    98–101
Pre-ferments
  definition of, 31
  types of, 30–31
  using, 30–33
  See also Biga; Doughs made
    with pre-ferments; Poolish
Preheating
  for bread baking, 74–75
  for pizza baking, 208–10
Proofing
  definition of, 72
  finger-dent test for, 38, 74
  for pizza dough, 206–7
  for pure levain loaves, 171
  in the refrigerator, 37
  testing limits of, 38
  time for, 37–38, 72, 74
  for yeast, 52, 66, 72
Proofing baskets, 48
Prueitt, Elisabeth, 14, 15
Pure levain doughs
  Overnight Country Blonde,
    168–72
  Overnight Country Brown,
    173–75
  Overnight Pizza Dough with
    Levain, 222–24
  Pain au Bacon, 177–79
  See also Advanced levain
    doughs

Q

Quattro Formaggi Pizza, Deep-
  Dish, 251

R

Recipes
  baker's percentages in, 41–42
  choosing, 61–62
  comparing, 43
  experimenting with, 190–97
  for novice bakers, 62
  reading, 62–63
  shorthand for, 196–97

Retarder, definition of, 29
Richter, Mark, 55
Rise
  final. *See* Proofing
  first. *See* Bulk fermentation
Robertson, Chad, 4, 13, 14, 15,
  51, 182
Rosada, Didier, 15

S

Salami
  Iron-Skillet Meat Pie, 247
  Iron-Skillet Pizza with Red
    Grapes, Mozzarella, and
    Salami, 250
  The New Yorker, 235–36
  Salami Pizza, 239–40
Salt
  -free breads, 52
  incorporating, into dough, 67
  in levain cultures, 127
  quantity of, 52
  sea, 125
  types of, 52
Same-Day Straight Pizza Dough,
  218–19
San Francisco Baking Institute,
  14, 17, 67, 129
The Saturday 75% Whole Wheat
  Bread, 85–88
The Saturday White Bread, 81–84
Sauces. *See* Pizza sauces and
  toppings
Scales, 2, 47–48, 64
Schedule
  adjusting, 192–93
  of a bread baker, 112–17
  management, 4
Schreiber, Cory, 19
Scoring, 76
Scott, Alan, 15
Seaton, Timothy, 202
75% Whole Wheat Levain Bread,
  144–46
Shaping step
  for bread dough, 71–72
  for pizza dough, 205

Shepherd's Grain collective, 55, 57

Skillet pizzas. *See* Pizzas

Smooth Red Sauce, 230

Soltner, André and Simone, 23

Sourdough. *See* Levain

Spitz, Dan, 19

Sponges, 31

Sprints, Alan, 112

Squash
  Iron-Skillet Pizza with Cherry Tomatoes, Garlic, and Summer Squash, 251
  Zucchini Focaccia, 257

Starter, definition of, 121

Straight doughs
  definition of, 31
  Overnight 40% Whole Wheat Bread, 93–95
  Overnight Straight Pizza Dough, 220–21
  Overnight White Bread, 89–91
  Same-Day Straight Pizza Dough, 218–19
  The Saturday 75% Whole Wheat Bread, 85–88
  The Saturday White Bread, 81–84
  Weeknight White Bread, 91

Strength, definition of, 34

Suas, Michel, 2, 17

Sweet Potato and Pear Pizza, 245–46

T

Tartine Bakery, 14, 182

Temperature
  conversion chart for, 259
  for final mix, 28, 29, 65–66, 68–69, 83
  of flour, 49
  of oven, 38, 40, 48, 75, 83
  relationship of time and, 26, 29–30
  of water, 28, 29, 65–66

Thermometers
  instant-read probe, 48
  oven, 48, 75

Time
  adjusting, 192–93
  importance of, 25, 26
  relationship of temperature and, 26, 29–30

TMB Baking, 17

Tomatoes
  canned, 207–8
  Chunky Red Sauce, 230
  as focaccia topping, 253
  Iron-Skillet Meat Pie, 247
  Iron-Skillet Pizza with Cherry Tomatoes and Bacon, 250
  Iron-Skillet Pizza with Cherry Tomatoes, Garlic, and Summer Squash, 251
  The New Yorker, 235–36
  Pizza Margherita, 233–34
  Salami Pizza, 239–40
  Skillet Pizza with Tomato Fillets, Garlic, and Chile, 249
  Smooth Red Sauce, 230
  Tomato Fillets, 231

Troubleshooting, 40–41

Tubs, 46–47

V

Vitamin C, 34

Volume measurements, 27, 42, 63, 259

W

Wadsworth, Teri, 123

Walnut Levain Bread, 151–54

Water
  changing hydration, 191
  incorporating flour and, 65
  measuring, 64–65
  quality of, 52
  temperature of, 28, 29

Weber, Ed, Kathleen, and Aaron, 15

Weeknight White Bread, 91

Weight measurements, 27, 41–42, 63, 259

Wesen, Rollie, 22, 23

Wheat
  farming, 54–55, 57
  kernels, components of, 50
  See also Flour

White breads
  Overnight White Bread, 89–91
  The Saturday White Bread, 81–84
  Weeknight White Bread, 91
  White Bread with 80% Biga, 106–8
  White Bread with Poolish, 98–101
  White Flour Warm-Spot Levain, 185–88

Whole wheat breads
  50% Whole Wheat Bread with Biga, 109–11
  Overnight 40% Whole Wheat Bread, 93–95
  The Saturday 75% Whole Wheat Bread, 85–88
  75% Whole Wheat Levain Bread, 144–46

Y

Yeast
  commercial, 53, 121
  fresh, 52
  incorporating, into dough, 67
  instant dried, 34, 52
  in levain cultures, 53, 122, 124, 126, 127
  natural, 121
  in pre-ferments, 32–33
  proofing (dissolving in water), 52, 66, 72
  storing, 52

Z

Zucchini
  Iron-Skillet Pizza with Cherry Tomatoes, Garlic, and Summer Squash, 251
  Zucchini Focaccia, 257

To my parents, John and Frances Forkish

Published in the United States by Ten Speed Press, an imprint of the Crown Publishing Group,
a division of Random House, Inc., New York.
www.crownpublishing.com
www.tenspeed.com

Ten Speed Press and the Ten Speed Press colophon are registered trademarks of Random House, Inc.

The wheat diagram on page 50 is used with permission from the North American Millers Association.

Library of Congress Cataloging-in-Publication Data
Forkish, Ken.
  Flour water salt yeast : the fundamentals of artisan bread and pizza / Ken Forkish.
    p. cm.
    Includes index.
1. Bread. 2. Pizza. I. Title.
  TX769.F67 2012
  641.81′5—dc23

2012012080

ISBN 978-1-60774-273-9
eISBN 978-1-60774-274-6

Printed in China

Design by Katy Brown

10 9 8 7 6 5 4 3

First Edition